CW00671631

TR for Triumph

Chris Harvey

The Oxford Illustrated Press

Reprinted 1985
Printed in Great Britain by J.H. Haynes & Co Limited

ISBN 0 902280 94 5

The Oxford Illustrated Press, Sparkford, Nr. Yeovil, Somerset
Published in North America by Haynes Publications Inc,
861 Lawrence Drive, Newbury Park, California 91320

Contents

Acknowledgements

It's a difficult task listing the people who helped you write a book because there are always so many and so little space to acknowledge them all. But from the factory point of view, Anders Clausager, of British Leyland Heritage, provided invaluable help, particularly in supplying the archival pictures. From the technical point of view, Bill Piggott and Bob Soden, of the TR Register, were of tremendous help and organised many of the cars that were the subject of special photography; the others were provided by Ian Clarke and the enthusiastic members of the TR Drivers' Club. I must also thank Reg Woodcock and his ever-present 'manager', Graham Peach, for telling me so much about what it has been like to be involved with TRs since the 1950s, not only from the racing but from the practical point of view, as well; Dick Penney of Paradigm Engineering was also very helpful and gave me a never-to-be-forgotten road run in Richard Morrant's production racing TR6. And to all the people who have exchanged TR talk with me at motor races and concours since these cars first appeared . . . and especially to my wife, Mary Harvey, for helping me take the Hilton Press Services pictures, along with Ray Hutton, editor of *Autocar*, for loaning me a precious transparency of the TR3 he enjoyed so much; and to John Dunbar, Maurice Selden, Martin Elford, Stephen Tee, Gary Scott and Kathy Ager of London Art-Technical and my close friend, Paul Skilleter.

My special thanks also to Jane Marshall, of Oxford Illustrated Press, and to John Haynes of Haynes Publishing, for waiting patiently for a book that took a lot longer to prepare than I ever imagined!

Colour Plates

Plate 1 The clean simple lines of the original TR2.

Plate 2 The TR3 acquired a distinctive grille in its radiator intake.

Plate 3 The Swallow Doretti shows off its fine bodywork to advantage.

Plate 4 The TR3A was evidence of Michelotti's first involvement with the TR.

Plate 5 The TR3A still makes a highly-competitive club racer.

Plate 6 The Kastner TRs made a great name for themselves in America.

Plate 7 The TR4 rally cars were really rugged as privateer Harold Hamblin demonstrated in the 1963 Monte Carlo Rally.

Plate 8 The TR4A with its trend-setting Surrey top.

Plate 9 The Dove coupé offered much improved carrying capacity along the lines of an Aston Martin.

Plate 10 An immaculate TR4 engine at a concours.

Plate 11 The front of the Dove remained exactly the same as the TR4 on which is was based.

Plate 12 Tony Pond gives his TR7 a baptism in the 1976 Manx International Rally.

Plate 13 The petrol injection TR5 captured with a most appropriate registration number.

Plate 14 Production sports car racer Nigel Bancroft proves that his TR5 is still fully competitive at Oulton Park in 1983.

Colour Plates continued

Plate 15 The American specification TR6 featured far stronger bumpers late in its run.

Plate 16 The little that can be improved on the TR5 other than perhaps the substitution of TR6 wheels.

Plate 17 Richard Morrant roars to another lap record in production sports car racing with his TR6 at Silverstone in 1982.

Plate 18 Oh to be in England with a TR7, its top open to the world.

Plate 19 The long sweeping lines of the TR7 Drophead.

Plate 20 One of the very rare TR8s that escaped in righthand drive form.

Plate 21 Pond at his best in the TR7 V8 on the Manx International in 1978.

Plate 22 Still the TR7 V8s thunder on ... with Roger Clarke's ex-Sparkrite example preparing for modified sports car racing at Snetterton in 1983.

Plate 23 One man's idea of a TR8, a TR7 with a strong Range Rover influence, in British off-road racing in 1983.

Plate 24 The TR8 in British Rallycross events in 1982.

Plate 25 Club runs are a pleasure for the TR Register...

Plate 26 ... and so are test days for the TR Drivers' Club.

I

From TR1 to TR8

Nostalgia has caught up with the Triumph TR at last, which is more than can be said for most things which tried. From those heady days of the 1950s when it was the first really cheap way to experience the thrills of 100-mph motoring, it became a working-class sports car that lived on a reputation for rugged reliability, until the name TR (for Triumph Roadster) was finally devalued by the unreliable, wedge-shaped TR7. Then Triumph tried again with the TR7 Drophead and the wonderful TR8, and suddenly everybody saw the light: the TR7 should never have had a turret top, it should have been topless like everything else in the 1970s. And as for the TR8, it was the answer to all that the environmental laws of the 1970s had snatched away: it was a rip-roaring, open-topped, sports car of refreshingly simple construction that didn't cost the earth. In other words, a true TR.

But, sadly, it came too late. Triumph, who had struggled desperately for financial survival even as they had made the first TR, could not carry on building sports cars, even under the umbrella of British Leyland. The umbrella, weighed down by the showering debts of trying to sell saloon cars, folded, taking the sports car down with it. Isn't it strange how you never seem to know what you've got till it's gone?

Now all that remain are the survivors of nearly 380,000 Triumph TRs built between 1953 and 1981. And thanks to the astonishingly solid construction of these cars, a surprisingly high number have survived. The older TRs were hardly ever treasured by their owners but they are now being restored to their former glory by people who realise that they will never again be able to buy a new one.

But there will be no restoring the first one, the posthumously named TR1. Originally called the '20TS' (for Triumph Sports), it was inspired by the emotions of one man, Sir John Black, chairman of Standard-Triumph, who introduced it because he was annoyed at his company's failure to take over the tiny Morgan family firm, he was jealous of the success of the cheap MGs, and was determined to get even with William Lyons, of Jaguar, who had outmanoeuvred him to put his firm at the head of the sports car market.

So he demanded of his design team a cheap and simple car that could give

Walter Belgrove's original sketch of the TR1 emphasised his clever combination of lines ancient and modern: the exposed spare wheel, cutaway doors, sweeping front wings, and helmet rear guards belonged to a traditidional sports car, but within the restrictions of a very tight budget, the flat bonnet, blunt front and very wide cockpit were elements of a far more modern concept.

Standard a share of the burgeoning market for sports cars in the United States that had been created by MG and creamed off by Jaguar. He didn't really care what it looked like although he thought it might be best with a 'traditional' square-cut body like the MG TD (then made in large numbers), or the Morgan Plus-4 (made in minute quantities). As a result, he offered only £16,000 for special tools to make the new body—a ludicrously-low sum by motor industry standards. Mechanical parts had to come from whatever saloon cars were being produced by Standard-Triumph. From this brief it was amazing that stylist Walter Belgrove and engineer Harry Webster were able to design such a good car body; a Triumph against adversity you would say!

But within six months they had built a brand-new car from their parts bin that could perform well and, more important to Sir John, be produced very cheaply. Within the restrictions of the body-tooling budget—which mitigated against any panel with a double curvature—the 20TS was as modern as could be imagined. And because it had to be capable of 90 mph (10 mph more than MG's TD), it was powered by one of the most rugged engines ever made, the famous four-cylinder that was found in both the Standard Vanguard saloon and the Ferguson tractor on which so many of the company's fortunes hinged. All the new car needed was to be made roadworthy...

For this purpose, Standard-Triumph hired a racing car engineer, Ken Richardson, who attacked the project with demonic energy. It was a good job that he was a dedicated development man, as the 20TS appeared to be such a bargain when it made its debut at the 1952 London Motor Show that it soon became obvious it could be sold in far larger quantities than Sir John had imagined. That Richardson, with the support of Webster's department, was able to almost completely rework the car under the skin within a few months, without overspending, was another tribute to Triumph. In the process, the performance went over 100 mph to put it on a par with the glamorous new Austin-Healey 100 that had been launched at the same show.

The Healey, based on components made by the rival British Motor Corporation, had a much more curvaceous body ... but it cost an extra £200 to build, a considerable sum in those days. It was a race to see who could get their cars off the production lines first, and both the Triumph and the Austin-Healey were neck and neck as they headed for the goldmine in America already being exploited by MG and Jaguar. Some of the new cars (christened the TR2), stayed at home to be sent to selected dealers who could be relied upon to show them in the best light in competition. This proved to be a wise decision because when a TR2 won Britain's RAC Rally early in 1954 it forged ahead in the sales race.

One of the TR2 prototypes, number two, was registered MVC 575 and prepared with optional performance equipment for a highly-impressive publicity run averaging 124 mph on the Jabbeke motorway in Belgium. It was an almost standard car, with only the bumpers removed and an undershield fitted—the securing screws of which can just be seen at the bottom of the front apron—and rear spats for better streamlining. The windscreen and side curtains were also changed for more aerodynamic versions on the fastest runs. The spats were options that were only rarely ordered by early customers, who preferred to leave the wheels exposed for rapid changes in rallying. This prototype car also had a unique bonnet badge which was replaced by the well-known TR badge for production. The air intake grille was also altered a little and a guide fitted for the starting handle.

For the next three years, rally fields were dominated by the TR2 and the facelifted TR3 that followed in 1955, and it was the demands of international rallying that led Triumph to score a tremendous technological first when the TR3 became the first mass-produced car to use disc brakes. In spite of all this the price stayed amazingly low (the same as MG), because virtually nothing was spent on developing the body, engine, or chassis. Although this meant that the TR3, and the TR3A, with their chassis rails still running under the rear axle, were uncomfortable, it also meant that sales soared because TR owners were willing to put up with a bit of discomfort and hairy handling in return for a bargain basement sports car. And anyway, roads were generally long, smooth and straight, in America, where the vast majority of TRs were sold.

How the styling department worked: one of Belgrove's last tasks before he quit Standard-Triumph was to rework the front of the TR2 at minimum cost. So he took a photograph of a TR2 and painted on what was to be the definitive TR3 grille, with only the number changed on its badge. A cheap and efficient way of making the TR look rather like a Ferrari!

Once the TR3 had been updated mechanically, with disc brakes at the front, it became a really formidable car—and a very popular one in America, with its Michelotti grille, in TR3A form. Californian publicity pictures emphasised the 'getaway from it all' abilities of the TR as a pair of models hit the Hollywood trail with whitewall tyres . . .

The influential American dealers demanded—and got—a re-run of the TR3A (dubbed the TR3B), after a new body was produced at last on the TR4 in 1961, to compete with a new breed of more luxurious sports car such as the Sunbeam Alpine with its wind-up windows. The Triumph designers also invented the brand-new 'Surrey' top on the TR4, which combined all the attributes of an open car and a coupé, but was too far ahead of its time to be appreciated by many people except Porsche, who copied it and, five years later, doubled their market with the 911 Targa. Naturally, the TR4 cost more—that's why the TR3B was built—but it also suffered other disadvantages: now that the car was heavier the fuel consumption figures were not so good, and with developments in the big saloon cars surging ahead, the TR4 was comparatively not so impressively fast, nor so comfortable.

To improve the comfort, Triumph decided to do something about the TR4's back suspension and in 1965, the Triumph (the Standard part had

British publicity pictures of Michelotti's new TR4 emphasised the attractions of an open car by time-honoured means, even if it might have been hard to explain how the beehive hair-do of the late 1950s and early 1960s could stay in place in an open TR.

vanished with a take-over) designers came up trumps with a brilliantly cheap independent system which they inserted in the TR4A. The reactionary American dealers wouldn't accept these cars at first, insisting on a cheaper solid-axle version until their customers forced them to change.

But there were customers to consider in other parts of the world, too, particularly in Europe where many miles of motorway had been opened since the TR first came on the scene, and they were demanding a car that could be hammered all day at more than the standard 110 mph. There was not a way in which more power could be extracted from the old four-cylinder engine, so Triumph had to take another saloon car engine, a turbine-like six-cylinder, and make it more powerful than the sports car four, whilst at the same time meeting the monstrously-restrictive American mission regulations. Out of all this uncertainty, the backroom boys triumphed again: they tamed the wild camshaft with fuel injection intended to meet the new smog laws and produced the six-cylinder TR5 that was the fastest to date.

Unfortunately this great technological advance cost a lot of money—and even more if extra devices were to be added to qualify it for sale in America—so the Europeans got a 120-mph TR5 and the Americans a TR250 with the old carburettors that, ironically, passed the emission tests by careful tuning. Even more ironically, these carburettors had only been developed in the first place as a patent-dodging way of copying the SU carburettors made by BMC, which were costing Triumph too much...

The TR4A featured a new independent rear suspension as an almost-standard option which gave a much-improved ride and handling. This car was also fitted with the Surrey hardtop which at that time was unique, and good for exotic hairdressing. Strangely, and despite the enthusiasm of sales director Lyndon Mills, this removable roof, which retained the rear window when the car was open and predated Porsche's Targa top, was not so popular as might have been expected.

The TR5 had only minor styling changes, including imitation magnesium-style wheeltrims which were popular at the time, but its fuel-injection engine made it the fastest TR ever. The TR250 without fuel injection, marketed at the same time, looked just the same except for 'go-faster' stripes as the best that could be done to restore the power taken away by emission regulations.

Once the Americans realised that their new TR was no faster than the old—after all it had no more power—they demanded a new body. Their demand coincided with the merger of Triumph with their rivals MG, Jaguar and Austin Healey to form British Leyland in 1968. The Italian stylist Michelotti, who had designed some great bodies for Triumph, including the TR4, was too busy with other BMC projects to produce a new TR, but once more the Triumph men fell on their feet: the German coachbuilder Karmann Ghia was looking for work. In little over a year and on a budget almost as tight as that of Belgrove, they restyled the TR5 to create the TR6. Body aside, it was really a TR5, or TR250 and to distinguish one from the other, the U.S. version was called the TR6 Carb (in the fervent hope that customers would drop the 'Carb' and not notice the difference) and the English, just the TR6. Because there was neither the time nor the money to pare away the last few pounds by painstaking development, the TR6 and TR6 Carb weighed a little more than the TR5 and TR4A—making them a little slower—but even so they were the last of the traditional TRs, that is cars with a good old-fashioned chassis, two seats and an open top.

Karmann Ghia did a brilliant job of remodelling the TR into the TR6, giving it a far more modern appearance with few sheet metal changes. In this form—with or without the American regulation overriders—the model soldiered on until 1976 to become the last of the great 'hairy-chested' British sports cars.

The TR6 was a great car, but it couldn't go on forever, and the Triumph men won an internal battle to design British Leyland's new sports car to take over from the TR and the rival MGB. It was based on a careful analysis of the U.S. market because that was by far the biggest sector for British Leyland—and it suffered dreadfully as a result. Contrary to appearances, the Americans did not really know what they wanted at that time. Without a doubt, the people who actually bought sports cars or might be persuaded to do so, wanted an open car with all the comfort of a saloon. But the people in charge, the politicians, had a new bandwagon as their brave new world entered the 1970s: safety. You had to be protected from yourself and for this reason it seemed certain that there would be legislation against the open car.

This meant that the new TR had to have a steel roof, particularly if projected airbag restraints were to be kept in place. By the 1970s, fitting a steel roof to a sports car was not simply a case of tacking on an extra bit of tin. If the car was to be designed properly so that it was as light as possible and did not use an unnecessary amount of precious petrol, the roof had to be a stressed part of the bodyshell. In other words, once you had committed yourself to the enormous tooling costs of building a new car with an integral roof, you couldn't cut it off just like that. How Triumph wished they could have done so, because no sooner than they had put the TR7 into production than a court in Cincinnati, Ohio, concerned with airbags, effectively legislated against the politicians' bids to outlaw the open car.

It wouldn't have been so bad if British Leyland had got the top right—but, as it was, it looked like the turret of a tank and clashed with the wedge-shaped bodyshell to which they had committed themselves in an attempt to meet all known laws or future ones governing every aspect of car design from bumper height to fuel consumption. The only other mistake with the TR7 was to bow to marketing pressure that a two-seater car needed a boot big enough for two sets of golf clubs—which resulted in the back end looking like a battleship. Strong words, but none of this would have mattered too much if the car had been allowed to live on its merits, which easily outweighed the styling deficiences so apparent in retrospect. The TR7 handled like a dream and was a thoroughly comfortable, modern, sports car insofar as the rules at the time allowed.

The dramatic wedge shape of the TR7 is highlighted in this picture. It was a win-or-bust gamble that didn't come off in terms of sales, although people have now learned to live with it quite happily.

But it had the problem of being built at a factory plagued by industrial strife and soon it had a dreadful reputation for unreliability—little of which was due to design. Eventually a four-month strike in an inflation-racked Britain killed complementary models in the TR7 range and led to production being switched to another part of the country. As a result, the TR7 lost what impetus it had gained in the sales race despite ever-increasing success in competition. Against all the odds, production was resumed to far higher quality standards, but, by then, its market was collapsing in a worldwide recession that hit car sales—especially those of luxuries like sports cars—very hard. The topless TR7, called the Drophead, and the fabulous TR8 with its well-proven eight-cylinder engine and all the performance that everybody had been crying out for, came too late. By 1979, British Leyland was struggling under immense financial pressure and the sports cars had to go to the wall as a strong British pound made them loss-makers in the United States when BL bravely tried to keep their price competitive. The last one produced left the line on 5 October, 1981—two days before its place was taken by a saloon car produced under licence from Japan. Ironically, the value of the pound plunged before all remaining stocks of TRs had been sold. If they could have stayed in production, they would have been money-spinners.

The wedge shape suited the open TR7 and the TR8, pictured here, far better.

II

The Classic TRs

Simplicity was the keynote of the TR1. Much of the car's design was influenced by the lack of money available to build new jigs and equipment for production cars to follow. At first it was thought that the pre-war Standard Flying Nine saloon car chassis could be used with a few modifications. It was about the right size and there were several hundred surplus examples of this obsolete frame in stock, which would be enough for the first year's production at the rate originally visualised by Sir John Black. Perhaps a new, improved, chassis could be designed once production was under way and it could be seen how well the car was selling. It would need independent front suspension if it was to be at all competitive with the MG TD, but fortunately Triumph had just such a system available from either the Mayflower or Vanguard saloons. Their wishbone and coil suspension was all the more attractive because it could be grafted on to the Flying Nine's leaf-sprung chassis quite easily. The Mayflower's rear axle was also quite suitable for use with a sports car, and was more attractive than that of the Vanguard because it was lighter. There was no choice over the engine and transmission, however: the 2-litre Vanguard unit would have to be used if a top speed of 90 mph was to be attained. Sir John was not too worried what the body looked like so long as the car could be made cheaply enough. He thought the best idea might be to use a traditional one like that of the MG, although he was ready to consider a more modern body if it could be made as cheaply.

With these parameters in mind, stylist Walter Belgrove set about designing the cheapest possible body for a sports car—an open two-seater. His main concerns were to keep the frontal area as small as possible so that wind resistance was at a minimum, and to design the panels in such a way that no double-action presswork was needed; this would save a lot of money in production. As a result, all the panels were joined on the centre line—the front wings, for instance, having a joint at the top. The headlight nacelles were let into the top of the centre nose panel so that the wings could be kept simple and the tail turned out to be rather stubby because of the restrictions presented by the chassis and a desire to keep overhang to a minimum. The spare wheel was mounted in an exposed position, too, but Sir John who said he didn't mind because that was how MG and Morgan did it. Keeping down the front and rear

The TR1 was even more compact than the TR2 which was to follow, with no grille at all in the air intake, and simple, bolted-on, sidelights.

Standard-Triumph prepared this TR2 chassis for show, with its white enamel and chrome-plated fittings—including a non-standard support for the steering column—in stark contrast to the normal black paint and bare metal. But the layout of the chassis and mechanical components can be seen quite clearly.

overhang saved weight, to the benefit of the car's performance. Cutaway doors (already used by MG and Morgan) were also adopted so that the body could follow the chassis lines more easily—thereby saving weight, drag and, possibly, expensive structures to support the body. The lines of the door cutouts dictated the long flowing forms of the wings. One of the advantages of joining the wings to the body at the tops by the cheapest method possible (nuts and bolts), was that it reduced repair costs, which in turn kept down insurance ratings—two important selling points. Subsequently it has made the TR far easier to restore, although this was certainly not in the minds of the designers early in 1952!

They ran into more problems than they had at first anticipated when they examined the Flying Nine's chassis more closely. It was not stiff enough for a modern sports car and the open-section cruciform between its boxed side members was in the wrong place. Its side rails also ran below the rear axle, which limited its travel on rebound to a total of only 4.25 inches (against a more practical 5.3 inches at the front). Although MG had just got over this problem by sweeping their chassis rails up over the axle, running them underneath was common at that time and the relative lack of suspension movement was not expected to cause trouble with the stiff springs (90 lb at the back, 82 lb at the front), still in vogue for sports cars.

There was little time to build one prototype—let alone the two demanded by Sir John—so the side members and various other bits and pieces of a Flying Nine chassis were used for the TR1. It had pressed steel towers welded to the front with a sturdy large-diameter cross piece to stop them from collapsing inwards. A smaller tube ran across the front of the frame for additional support. The cruciform was then moved backwards and reconnected to the side members by tubes which doubled as body supports. The cruciform attachment points were arranged to co-incide with the suspension mountings and triangulated reinforcing pieces at the front to stiffen it up as much as possible. A tubular cross piece at the back of the chassis provided extra strength and the rear suspension mountings. A small detachable cross member, to support the rear of the engine because the cruciform had been moved so far back, completed the lash-up.

The brief to produce the smallest and lightest practicable car was followed with enthusiasm. A wheelbase of 7 ft 4 ins—just midway between that of the Flying Nine and its close relative, the Flying Ten—was adopted with a track of only 3 ft 9 ins to keep the frontal area and weight to a minimum. The wheelbase had been dictated partly by the minimum space needed to squeeze in the Vanguard power unit and transmission and to leave enough room for the occupants to sit low down between the engine and front suspension and the rear wheel arches. Overall length worked out at only 11 ft 9 ins with a width of 4 ft 7.5 ins, and a height of 4 ft 3 ins with the hood erect.

The Mayflower's front suspension was chosen because it had more modern tubular shock absorbers than the older lever-arm devices of the Vanguard. Worm and nut steering—which gave a turning circle of 32 ft—was used in conjunction with a three-piece track rod. The engine was not mounted ahead of the front axle line because of the desire to keep the frontal area to a minimum (around 15 sq ft in this case) although it would have allowed an even shorter wheelbase or provided room for small seats behind those of the two main occupants. It was mounted right up to the top reinforcing member of the front suspension, though. This meant that the cross-tube had to be made detachable so that maintenance could be carried out. The radiator was fitted ahead of this tube with its top lower than the front of the engine to allow the car's nose to sweep down. As a result, a filling chamber had to be provided on the front of the engine as the highest point in the cooling system. The fuel tank and spare wheel were mounted behind the rear axle line to give a good balance and to help traction.

The rear axle, a slightly narrower version of that used in the Mayflower, was mounted on half-elliptic leaf springs which also provided its location. This was the cheapest form of suspension that the Triumph designers could think of, with the springs angled down at the front to promote understeer. Lever-arm dampers were used at the back to save the cost and weight of the higher mounting towers that would have been needed for tubular shock absorbers. The car's centre of gravity was low despite its ground clearance of 6 ins, so anti-roll bars could be ruled out for the same reason.

Steel disc wheels were fitted to keep down costs. With this over-riding factor in mind, the diameter was as small as was practical in view of what the tyre manufacturers could produce at that time—15 ins with a 4-inch rim to take a 5.50-section tyre. These wheels were pierced to help ventilate the drum brakes. They were Lockheed hydraulic with twin leading shoes at the front and what was then a larger-than-average width of 1.75 ins, which it was calculated was enough to cater for a top speed of 85 mph and a target weight of 1750 lb.

A TR2 chassis as it would have run down the production line, with simple unadorned engineering: no fancy frills for components that would not normally meet the eye. The tall thin tyres were also the normal wear on sports cars at the time this picture was taken in 1953.

The rear end of the TR2 production chassis, showing the rugged simplicity—and limitations—of the rear suspension.

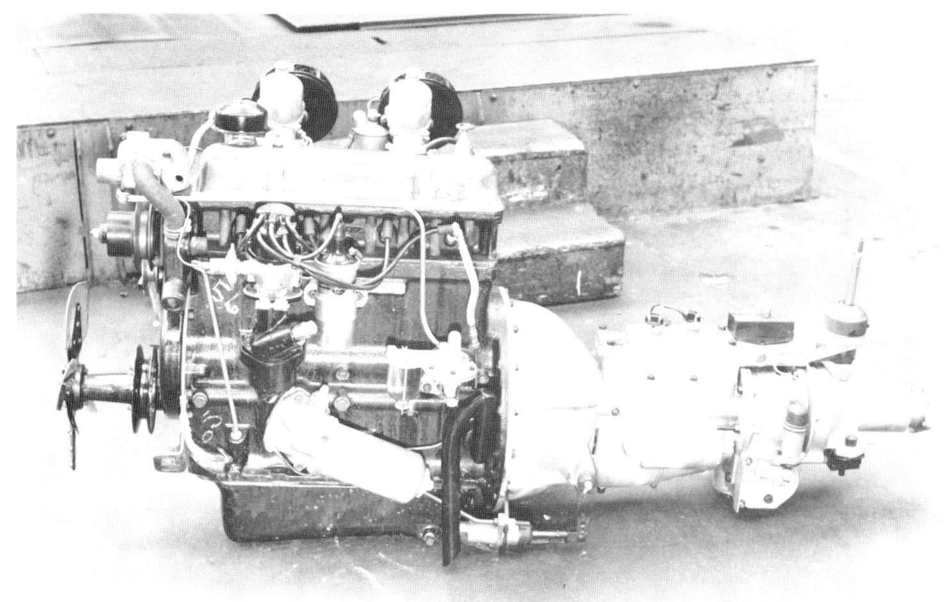

The engine and transmission as it was used in the TR2 with the long, vital, crankshaft damper, the practical high-mounted ignition, the readily-accessible clutch release, and the overdrive wired to work, initially, only on top gear. The remote control linkage for the gear lever was adopted after the TR1 prototype had been shown with a longer crooked lever that would not have offered such a positive change.

The engine in this first car was a slightly modified Standard Vanguard four-cylinder unit, with its capacity reduced from 2,088 cc to 1,991 cc to take it within the 2-litre class for international competition. This engine, which also found a home in more basic form in the Ferguson light tractor, had been built with simplicity in mind for a long life and easy maintenance. That is why it was fitted with easily-removable wet cylinder liners—a practical feature that was to endear it to amateur engineers throughout the world because it made it so simple to rejuvenate this extraordinary tough engine: you just slapped in new pistons and liners, gave it a quick valve and bearing job, and it was often as good as new! The Triumph engineers used these features to good advantage, too, fitting liners with a 83 mm bore, instead of the normal 85 mm, to achieve the required reduction in capacity without extensive work on the cast-iron cylinder block. The robust crankshaft, which had three white metal main bearings of 2.479 ins diameter, was connected to H-section rods which gave a stroke of 92 mm. The big ends were split diagonally to allow the connecting rods and pistons to be withdrawn upwards through the cylinder bores instead of down past the crankshaft area—another plus point for the amateur engine builder who was grateful not to have to remove the crankshaft in order to replace the pistons. The camshaft, on the near side, had four bearings and ran direct in the crankcase with a cast iron sleeve at the front journal. It was operated by a duplex roller chain with the distributor and the oil pump driven from the top and bottom, respectively, of a vertical shaft meshed to the camshaft by a skew gear. Another pair of skew gears under the distributor drove a rev counter. The camshaft's final function—apart from operating the pushrods to the inlet and exhaust valves—was to drive an AC mechanical fuel pump. The cylinder liners were seated at the bottom on special figure-of-eight washers, one to each pair of liners, and at the top, against the gasket of the cast iron cylinder head. The split-skirt flat-topped pistons, which were made of aluminium alloy, had gudgeon pins secured by circlips—all basic and well-tried engineering.

Initially, the cylinder head, with its inverted bathtub combustion chambers, had a relatively low compression ratio of 7:1—which was quite common in those days because of the difficulties in many countries, including Britain, in obtaining good-quality petrol—with eight ports and vertical overhead valves returned by double valve springs. Twin constant-vacuum semi-downdraught SU carburettors were fitted for the first time to a Vanguard engine, although it had already been featured in the Triumph 2000 roadster and the Renown saloon. In conjunction with a special rake-type manifold coupling the inlet ports and a cast exhaust manifold with a single outlet, the engine produced 71 bhp against 68 in its normal form with a single downdraught carburettor. Triumph did not visualise having to extend this engine further at first: they thought 71 bhp would be enough for the required performance.

The Triumph engineers were lucky in that when they mounted the large cooling fan directly to the crankshaft, with a casting to take its drive under the chassis cross-piece, it proved to be an excellent damper than enabled the engine to run much more smoothly at high revs. This had not been the intention; mounting the fan in such a way had been simply to help squeeze in the engine as far forward as possible. The power was harnessed at the other end by the 9-inch single dry plate clutch with nine springs that was used in the saloon cars. It was operated hydraulically by a pendant pedal from the master cylinder unit on the scuttle top, which also supplied the brakes (operated by a similar pedal). The normal gearbox used with the engine had only three forward ratios, all with synchromesh. Triumph managed to redesign this economically with four forward ratios in the same casing, although it was possible to fit synchromesh only to the top three gears. A remote central gearlever completed this neat piece of work, with ratios of, top, 1:1, third 1.32, second 2, first 3.58, and reverse 4.28. A necessarily-short propellor shaft was connected to a hypoid bevel rear axle with a ratio of 3.89 to give overall forward gearing of 3.89, 5.15, 7.81 and 13.15. The reverse gear was even lower at 16.66 leading some wags to suggest that a TR could back up a vertical wall!

The fittings were simple, with a flat windscreen to avoid the expensive tooling costs associated with more complex shapes. The interior was stark, but no more so than that of any other sports car in those days, with a fully detachable hood. Neat touches included a petrol filler cap concealed in the centre of the exposed spare wheel, although the anxiety to save money was evident from the unadorned air intake for the engine. Early styling sketches had suggested a chrome-plated surround for the vent, but Triumph felt that they could get away without anything because the latest Ferraris had just started such a trend on the race track. In any case, they had a similar front in mind for their new Standard Eight saloon, which was on the drawing board.

When the TR's target top speed was raised to 100 mph and it was obvious that its sales would be higher than originally anticipated, the chassis and engine redesign got under way and the exposed tail treatment was revised. The front was left alone with the exception of making the bumpers and overriders simpler to produce and saving money by incorporating the sidelights low in the front panel rather than as expensive free-standing units on top of the wings. The new Austin-Healey 100, which was obviously going to be a rival despite its higher price, had a luggage boot with an external lid, so the TR had to have one. MG were still getting away without one on their TD, but surely they, too, would soon have to move with the times, reasoned Triumph. So room for a spare wheel was found under the boot floor, which meant moving the fuel tank—and filler—to a position above the rear axle. Luggage could then be carried above the wheel and behind the tank in a neat, squared-off, tail, the lid being mounted on money-saving exposed hinges like the bonnet. Ten inches was added to the overall length together with some extra weight—but a lot more power was being extracted from the engine which would more than counter this. Stylist Walter Belgrove also designed an exceptionally good-looking hard top for the car in the revolutionary new glass fibre material, but a decision on whether or not to offer this was deferred until after Triumph could see how the car was selling.

Meanwhile the designers, including Harry Webster and John Turnbull, set to work on strengthening the chassis. It was not worth using any of the old parts, so they designed a new one along the same lines to preserve the existing dimensions, which were adjudged as ideal. Part of the attraction for these measurements, it had to be admitted, was that they economised on the need for new tooling and jigs. This factor also influenced the decision not to follow MG's example and run the side members over the rear axle. Instead, these members were simply made deeper and from stronger steel with extensive boxing. The cruciform was also reworked with gussets and additional stiffening plates to help make the chassis more rigid—which, in turn, reduced the near lethal wobbling that was a feature of the TR1. The cruciform changes were made after testing on Belgium's notorious pave and the rear damper brackets were beefed up at the same time. No trouble was experienced with the exhaust system, however, which ran through the cruciform.

The suspension stood up to the pounding quite well, but it was still considered wise to replace the Mayflower's pressed steel lower wishbones with forgings for extra strength. The inner rubber suspension pivot-bearing bushes were also replaced with nylon ones to give more accurate wheel movement and increased bearing life. The stub axle flanges were stiffened at the same time although no failures were experienced at that point.

As a first stage of engine tuning, Triumph were able to raise the compression ratio to 8.6:1 because better-quality petrol was now becoming more readily available; the engine's power output was then nearly 80 bhp. After this, tuning was chiefly confined to work on the camshaft and valves. First, the valve lift was increased from 0.36 ins to 0.375 ins, then the timing was changed to give more overlap. This took the power up to 84 bhp. Next, the inlet valves were increased from 1.5 ins in diameter to 1.5625 ins, which liberated another 3 bhp. Further development with the 1.5-inch carburettors' needles and the distributor obtained 90 bhp at 4,800 rpm, despite the compression ratio being lowered a fraction to 8.5:1. Maximum torque was a very healthy 117 lb/ft at 3,000 rpm.

Increasing the engine's power from 68 bhp to 90 was not so simple as that, however, because the unit had to remain utterly reliable. The first problem encountered when the compression ratio was raised was that the cylinder head wanted to go with it; cracks developed around some of the securing stud bosses. The trouble was cured by extending the bolts to the bottom of the block to be screwed into the crankcase, which was much thicker and stronger than the lugs which had been provided further up. This also meant that the water jackets surrounding the cylinder liners were held in compression, rather than under tension, which was a good thing. Cylinder head gaskets continued to give trouble, however, as a result of the bottom gaskets collapsing under the increased stud loading. New figure-of-eight steel gaskets coated in resin solved this problem after production tolerances were revised and special care taken with cleanliness on assembly. In other words, a good initial seal was vital.

Sustained running at as much as 5,200 rpm—Triumph were to recommend a red line of 5,000 rpm—in top gear was too much for the big end bearings, so indium-coated lead-bronze ones were substituted. This problem occurred when direct top gear was used in such a test rather than the overdrive which Triumph had decided to offer as an option, and it persisted when the new bearings were subject to even more strain. The next step was to improve the lubrication system, and the problem was only solved when the crankshaft drillings were modified to spread the oil better in the new bearings, which needed greater clearances.

The connecting rods had not given way at that point, but the big end bolts were increased to 0.4375 ins in diameter as a precaution, with a dowel location system that also helped assembly. Mysterious problems with number one exhaust valve burning out intermittently in endurance tests at 6,000 rpm were eventually traced to the camshaft flexing and were cured by the offending end being made thicker than the other! A lot of development time was spent fiddling with the crankcase breather as well, to stop oil being thrown out under fierce cornering, such as during Ken Richardson's, stints on MIRA's banking. The cooling fan also had to be given a rubber mounting on its boss to stop bad vibrations and the radiator modified with a small extension on the back to its filler to allow more room for coolant expansion.

The gearbox and Laycock de Normanville overdrive—on top gear only—gave no problems, but the crown wheel bolts in the rear axle had to be stepped up from 0.3125 ins to 0.375 ins and fitted with locking tabs. Lubrication problems similar to those evident with the crankcase were cured by fitting traps to stop the axle's lubricant washing out the wheel bearing grease. The bearings' taper rollers were increased in number from 16 to 18 and their cups' clearances eased out to prevent failure under load. The extra power from the engine also meant that it was possible to raise the rear axle ratio to 3.7:1 at the same time, giving overall ratios of top 3.7, third 4.9, second 7.4, first 12.5, and reverse 15.8.

Not surprisingly, the brakes needed attention as well, fade eventually being reduced by increasing the front drums in diameter and width to 10 ins by 2.25 ins and fitting them with Mintex M20 linings. They juddered a bit at first, but this was cured by giving them a better finish inside. The steering wheel vibrated a lot, too, so its scuttle mountings received an extra strengthening bracket.

The only other problem encountered during continuous 100-mph testing was with the windscreen; it bowed in at the middle. This was mitigated by bending it out again—gently—by about 0.75 ins and pressing it more firmly into its frame. Then the wind made it straighten out at speed! The hood sealing was improved with a tongue-and-groove surround and the bodywork was pushed out a bit to give more elbow room, with a measurement of 42 ins between the sides. The bucket seats did a good job of locating the occupants, but the driver on right-hand steering cars now received special attention from the handbrake lever, relocated on the side of the transmission tunnel. It didn't matter who sat in the seat, it rubbed their legs.

All this work, particularly on the chassis and the steel body's tail, increased the weight from 1,708 lb to 1,848 lb. But the fuel consumption was still exceptionally good because of the low drag factor of the body, and even more so when the optional overdrive (which gave an overall top gear ratio of 3.03:1) was used.

The first two TR2s (chassis numbers TS1 and TS2), were assembled in July 1953 by Triumph's experimental department to check that everything fitted together properly. The first real production car was made in August after the factory re-opened following its annual holiday. It took several months for all the tooling to be made ready and outside suppliers to slot in the sports car work, so the first 140 chassis were assembled by Triumph, before Sankeys took over, with bodyshells being made by Mulliners in Birmingham. There was simply not enough room at Triumph's factory in Canley to produce all the components for more than a trickle of TRs in addition to their saloons, so only about 250 cars were completed in 1953. Two hundred went for export, mostly to North America, with 50 remaining in Britian. Many of these cars went to dealers who were willing and able to use them in competition and help publicise the new model. A lot of them were registered in Coventry before delivery to the dealers, giving rise to speculation that they were works cars. Although the dealers received preferential treatment over suppliers, they were not, in fact, prepared by the works.

As soon as the TR2 was in proper production at the beginning of 1954, an early example which had been retained by the works was released for road tests. The initial reaction of the motoring press was highly favourable, and, combined with good results in competition, they stimulated demand. As a result, Triumph realised that they could sell a lot of optional extras with the cars, thus increasing their profit margin dramatically. Initially, the TR2 was offered only with simple additions, such as a heater, the overdrive, leather upholstery, and Dunlop Road Speed tyres which were superior in some ways to the standard rubberware. But by May the TR2 was being offered with knock-on wire wheels to improve brake cooling and present a more sporting appearance (apart from saving time when changing tyres in a long-distance race), a cast aluminium sump to stiffen up the

The interior of the TR2 was as simple and practical as the rest of the car, with instruments and glove locker so arranged that the steering column could be swopped from left to right with the minimum of alteration on the production line. The handbrake lever stayed where it was during such changes however, as anybody who ever took the wheel of a right-hand-drive car can testify.

bottom end of the engine and to help disperse better the heat generated by high revs, stiffer front springs and larger rear shock absorbers for competition types who were willing to put up with a rougher ride to combat the notorious rear-wheel lift, aero-screens to reduce the frontal area by about 3 sq ft at the expense of comfort, an undershield that hardly anybody bought because of overheating problems, rear wheel spats for a similar improvement in aerodynamics and to make the car look more fashionable, a metal cockpit cover for racing men, a radio, special tool roll and tools, two-speed screen wipers for hard-pressed rallyfolk, fitted suitcases for the tourists, and a telescopic steering column and dished wheel to give a wider variety of driving positions.

None of these changes caused much disruption on the production lines, but there were two glaring inadequacies that needed rectification. Nothing could be done about the chassis, or lack of suspension movement, economically but something had to be done about the doors, which no salesman could talk his way around. It looked fairly simple to cut a bit—about 2 inches—off the bottom and fill in the resultant gap between the front and rear wings. But it was not as simple as that because the floor had to be modified as well. Whatever Triumph did, it meant spending money on tooling, so to their credit they did the job properly, fitting a new centre section, the substantial sills of which stiffened the body a lot.

Everything the keen driver needed according to the TR legend: this optional tool roll was one of Standard-Triumph's ways of making a better profit from a very competitively-priced car.

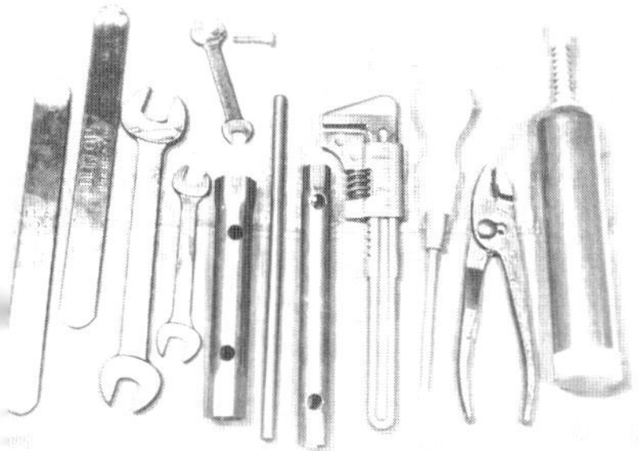

The re-engineered short-door TR2 was also given a snug optional glass fibre hard top, which became a popular fitting for rally folk. It not only made the car more civilised, you could also see far more from its much wider rear window than through the slot in the canvas hood of the early cars.

Early problems with fade and snatch from hard-pressed brakes were alleviated by making the back drums the same size as the front, thus taking the total lining area up to 175 sq ins from 148 sq ins. The glass fibre hard top was also put into production in time for the winter, with new sliding sidescreen windows. One of its most attractive features was a panoramic rear window but it made the canvas top's little slot feel really claustrophobic, so the hood was modified to give its window more wrapround. The screen wipers were also repositioned with their pivot points further apart to improve visibility in bad weather, as a result of suggestions by the rallying dealers. They had been quick to note, too, that the overdrive would provide useful extra ratios if its control was required to allow its use on second and third gears. No trouble was experienced with this modification, so it was introduced from chassis number TS6266, although many of the earlier cars were so modified by the original owners. The ratios thus liberated were: overdrive top 3.03; direct top 3.7; overdrive third 4.01; direct third 4.9; overdrive second 6.06; and direct second 7.4. It was not worth making the overdrive operational on first gear and the extra torque generated would have put its reliability at risk. Before this change was standardised, the rear brakes had been uprated at chassis number TS5443 and the doors changed at TS4002, and wider, 4.5-inch rim, steel wheels phased in, the whole package being completed in time for the London Motor Show in October 1954.

How the TRs were assembled: once the power train had been installed in the chassis, with suspension, the complete trimmed bodyshell was lowered onto it. Today's enthusiasts will note the lack of underseal on the bodyshell ... rock salt was a rare commodity on icy roads in those days.

The Swallow Doretti

Meanwhile the first radical fruits of Sir John's visit to the United States in February 1953 were about to become apparent. Coachbuilder Eric Sanders had also visited California seven months earlier, in July 1952, and decided that there was a ready market for $3,000 sports cars (as was being demonstrated by the Austin-Healey 100, and in higher spheres, with the Jaguar XK 120), by the time Sir John arrived with the TR1. Sanders, whose finances came from the giant Tube Investments firm visualised a car using a tubular frame of rather more advanced design than that employed by the TR's predecessors and which was becoming increasingly popular on sports racing cars at that time. This stiffer new frame would support an Italian-style body which would help keep Sander's Swallow Coachbuilding Company at Walsall in business. All that was needed was a set of proprietary components—engine, transmission and running gear—to make what he considered would be a very profitable car.

Sir John was quite willing to supply the essential mechanical components when approached about this project, because he realised that it would be complementary to the TR2, rather than competitive. It would also enable him to take a tilt at the higher price bracket dominated by Jaguar. As a result of much coming and going across the Atlantic, it was decided to call the car the Swallow Doretti after Triumph's stunning blonde Southern Californian distributor, Dorothy Dean! Doretti sounded right because the lines of the coachwork would be distinctly like one of the current sports-racing Ferraris. With comfort in mind, this luxurious little sports car was given a 7-inch longer wheelbase to make the ride smoother, with a body 5.5 ins wider.

The Swallow Doretti did not look like a TR at all, with its Ferrari-style grille predating that of the TR3.

The standard of trim on the Doretti was superior to that of the TR2, as befitted a car aimed at a higher price bracket.

The lay out of the chassis was similar to that of the normal TR2 frame, however, except that the cruciform was not needed because it had a strong, MG-style, scuttle hoop, outriggers and another, lower, hoop just in front of the final drive. Radius arms were fitted to the rear suspension in an attempt to limit the wheel hop they knew would still be present with the underslung main tube formation. The front suspension, which had strengthened lower links, was mounted on tubular cross members. The standard TR2 power unit was installed further back in the chassis to give a 50/50 weight distribution. Swallow's experience in making aircraft components strongly influenced the construction of the body. It had an inner skin of 22-swg steel welded to the chassis for additional strength with the 16-swg alloy outer panels bolted on. The front of the car, which had a distinctive oval grille, looked very much like a Ferrari, but the back, strangely, resembled that of the TR1, except that the spare wheel was concealed. As a result, the overall length of 12 ft 8 ins was only an inch longer than the TR2, but the Doretti's luggage accommodation was decidedly limited! With hindsight, it appears to have been a curious decision, but perhaps the desinger, F.G. Rainbow, was more influenced by Sir John than Walter Belgrove had been with the TR2. The entire car was finished to a very high standard, as befitted the product of a coachbuilder. The interior was rather old-fashioned, however, in that it allowed only a bolt-upright driving position reminiscent of cars of the 1930s and the rather narrow doors were almost as long as those of the early TR2s. Moving the engine back also meant that the transmission intruded far more into the cockpit than it did with the TR2.

However, the overall impression was of a much more expensive car and there were high hopes for it in the prestige market, particularly on the West coast of America. The Doretti project, which was running to low profit margins, lost a lot of impetus, however, following Sir John's accident, and by the time a single fixed-head coupé had been built in 1955, it was doomed. This car was almost exactly like the open ones, with its roof following the similar lines to those of the TR2's hard top.

The Doretti was certainly good looking ... if only it had had a less confined cockpit and more room for luggage.

The TR3

Standard-Triumph were heavily engaged in launching a new unitary-construction Vanguard in 1955, so no alterations were made to the TR2 until the Motor Show in October. These were relatively few, but the new model was called the TR3 for maximum sales impact, with the TR2 still being listed (but not built, the actual change-over point being at chassis number TS8657), enabling existing stocks to be sold without a discount. The TR3 was slightly more expensive at an extra £25—taking it to £650 before tax—in basic form, but it offered more as well. The most obvious change was the addition of a grille in the air intake, modelled along the lines of yet another Ferrari, with 'egg-box' styling: this took care of the most oft-repeated criticism over appearance. In addition, stainless steel beading was put in the wing joints, chromium plating was used for the exposed hinges, both improvements making virtues out of styling deficiencies. More importantly, larger, 1.75-inch SU carburettors were substituted with suitably enlarged ports to take the power up to 95 bhp. Fuel consumption rose, but not by a great deal, and it was felt that the extra power would be a greater marketing attraction than ultimate economy, particularly in America where petrol was still cheap. The cockpit panels were also modified slightly to give more interior room (the TR3 measured 44 ins across the front seats against

One of the first TR3s, a factory demonstrator that was subsequently fitted with wire wheels and driven by Nancy Mitchell in the 1957 Mille Miglia road race.

There's no doubt about it, you can sit comfortably on the back seat of a TR3 as these models tried so genially to demonstrate. But see how far the front seats had to go forward on this car, fitted with the optional GT kit's door handles.

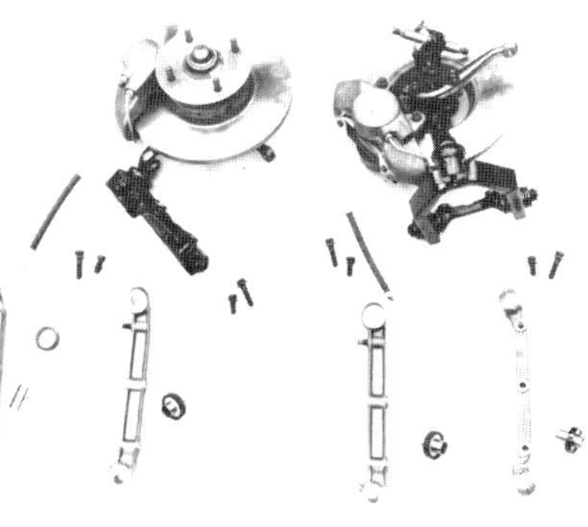

All the parts that were needed to convert a drum-braked TR3 into one with discs

Interior of a TR3 with its lined steel hard top bolted on securely and its sidescreens held in place by sturdy brackets. Rally drivers with fast-moving elbows taped sponge rubber padding over the brackets.

42 ins for the TR2), and to allow a small rear seat to be fitted as an optional extra. Despite the cramped nature of such accommodation—the front seats had to be pushed well forward to give any legroom in the back—many customers ordered it for the times they needed to transport children, or, in a very confined state, an extra adult. A scuttle ventilator with a push-pull knob was also incorporated with the sliding sidescreens that had been available before only with the hard top. The passenger's grab handle was also chromium-plated in keeping with the hinges, and, more practically, the optional tool roll was standardised. A 4.1:1 axle ratio was also offered for competition-minded customers.

Cars raced at Le Mans in 1955 by the works had used a modified cylinder head and inlet manifold with up to 5 bhp more at 5,000 rpm. This unit was phased in from engine number TS9350E towards the end of the year, but not on every car as supplies did not seem able to keep up with production. To add to the confusion, soon after yet another cylinder head and inlet manifold were developed combining the best features of the original and the 'Le Man's equipment. This was called the 'high port' head and was phased in from engine number TS12606E. However, the other heads and manifolds were still fitted to some cars until engine number TS13051E produced in August 1956, when supplies of the earlier equipment finally ran out!

At virtually the same time, from chassis number TS13046 (the first car produced after the 1956 summer holidays), the history-making Girling disc brakes were fitted to the front of the TR3, increasing its track to 3 ft 10.5 ins. Discs were not fitted to the back because they would have forced a price rise and they were not vital. In addition, there was—and still is—a problem with providing an efficient handbrake on discs because they lack the self-servo effect of drum brakes such as those fitted to the TR. At the same time, the latest Vanguard Phase 111-type rear axle was substituted. This unit used the same gears as those of the earlier TRs, but had stronger half-shafts with new Timken taper roller bearing hubs. It was also heavier, and led to the track being increased to 3 ft 10 ins. These substantial improvements—other than for the extra weight of the axle—were of great benefit to Triumph's competition department, of course, as was a change of material to steel for the optional hard top at about the same time. The new hard tops, which looked exactly like the original glass fibre ones, were bolted to the body at no less than eight points, with the result that its rigidity was greatly improved on rough roads—such as those used in rallies. The only drawbacks were that the extra weight made the car a little less stable in extreme conditions because its centre of gravity was raised and the fittings were such that it was difficult to convert an open car to a hard-top one after it had been built. The glass fibre top did not have such elaborate fixings, so it was kept in stock for a while to sell to customers who had already bought open cars. When the factory-fitted steel hard top was specified as part of a 'GT kit', the TR3 was also given external lockable door handles to make access more convenient and unauthorised entry more difficult. There was still a considerable feeling that it was not wise to fit lockable handles to soft top cars because it might invite a thief to slash the hood, which might be worth more than the contents of the car...

The GT kit also extended to a boot lid with conventional key locking and two small handles in place of the earlier coachlocks, retained on the spare wheel compartment cover. The reversing lights were a rally-related extra.

The TR3A was equipped with the GT kit as standard other than for the hard top, which remained an extra. The headlights were also recessed into the new nose pressing.

The TR3A

There was a considerable demand for the new door handles on soft top cars, however, so they were standardised with the introduction of the TR3A from chassis number TS22014 in the autumn of 1957. Similar handles were fitted to the boot lid, and, far more striking, a revised nose panel and new full-width grille were adopted. Initial production was entirely for export because stocks of right-hand-drive TR3s were high in Britain. As a result, Triumph at first refused to call it a new model, and never got round to changing the badges, although they eventually gave in to popular request and acknowledged it as the TR3A with its European introduction in January 1958. The change of nose panel also meant that the headlamps were slightly recessed for a smoother look—but other than that it was very little different from the TR3.

The first major change was as a result of Girling's development work on disc brakes. Much improved calipers were fitted from chassis number TS56378 in 1959, with a better balance being achieved by reducing the rear drums to 9 ins by 1.75 ins. By then, too, production had reached such heights that it became necessary to re-tool the body presses with the result that the centre section panels were made easier to stamp. These changes—made at chassis number TS60001—hardly showed outside the car, however, although they meant that the optional rear seat had to be redesigned and the boot and bonnet hinges were now mounted on plinths. The windscreen fixings were revised as well and the electrical system updated to incorporate Lucas snap connectors throughout. Larger, 86-mm, liners and pistons were also listed as an official option, although engines of the bigger capacity of 2,138 cc, had been available since they were first used by works cars in the summer of 1957. The advantage was not in power, but in extra torque—127 lb/ft at 3,350 rpm—and it was not possible to increase the capacity to take any more advantage of the international 2,500 cc class.

The TR3B

Following the introduction of the TR4 in 1961 to replace the TR3A, there was a demand from American dealers for another run of the 'classic' TRs', because they felt that the new car would appeal to a different sector of the market. As a result, Triumph transferred their tooling to the Forward Radiator Company, who were able to accept the order. The first 500 of these 1,962 cars, with TSF chassis numbers, had the 1,991 cc engine; and the final 2,831, with TCF numbers, had the 2,138 cc unit. Virtually all these cars—still called simply the TR3—had a new all-synchromesh gearbox designed for the TR4 being produced at the same time (which is covered in the next chapter). Although the layout of the gearbox was not changed, the extra 0.44 ins needed for the first-gear synchromesh meant that it had to have a new aluminium casing, which was not interchangeable. The first gear ratio was also raised to 3.14:1, giving an overall ratio of 11.61, with 11.92 for reverse, because more torque was available with the 2.2-litre engine, which was a standard fitting in the TR4. Minor modifications were also made to the remote control to reduce play in the gear linkage. The overdrive was unchanged.

These were the last, and most desirable, of the 'classic' TRs, because of their specification ... and because of the popularity of the TR4 in Europe, no right-hand-drive versions were made.

III
The Transitionary TRs

The TR4 with its new bodyshell, the TR4A with its ingenious new suspension, the TR5 and TR250 with a new engine, and the TR6 with new lines, marked the second phase of the Triumph Roadster's life. And because they all featured a good old-fashioned chassis with open-topped bodywork they were proclaimed the last of the traditional TRs—and, for a while, as the last of the Triumph Roadsters. But time was to show that these endearing cars were but a transitionary model on the road to the thoroughly modern machines that really were the last of the TRs.

Triumph were in considerable financial difficulty, through no fault of the TRs, at the time it became necessary to update the 3A, so, once more tooling costs had to be kept to a minimum and played a significant part in the design of the new car, the TR4.

Comfort was the main prerequisite of the TR4's body. Slooncar-style wind-up windows were a necessity now that the rival Sunbeam Alpine had had them for two years and it was only a matter of time before they were fitted to MGs and Austin-Healeys. And once Triumph had priced them out, they became even more attractive because it was discovered that they would cost less to produce than the TR3A's sidescreens! Wind-up windows meant that the doors would have to be of full height (rather than cut away), and thicker, to contain the glass when it was wound down; more elbow room was also desirable, so the body had to be wider. All this was quite in keeping with contemporary trends, and reinforced the feelings that such a change would also improve the appearance of the car by making it look more modern. Experiments by the competition department had shown that an extended track would improve the handling as well, so it was an easy decision to take in making the TR4 2 ins wider at 4 ft 9.5 ins overall. This resulted in the critical measurement across the seats working out at 47 ins, a gain of 2.5 ins achieved after abandoning the TR3A's door pockets. An extra 3 ins was also liberated inside the cockpit by moving the fascia panel forward and the luggage boot bulkhead backwards. No room was sacrificed for the baggage, though, because the tail was completely redesigned to make it longer and squarer, a more useful shape that gave 5.5 cu ft of stowage space. The seats were given an extra 3 ins of rearward travel with the extra width

The TR4 on test by *Motor Sport* with muddy tyres and optional spotlights knocked askew.

of the car also being felt in the area devoted to the occupants' legs. This made the handbrake marginally less intrusive!

The new bodyshell with its longer (13-ft) lines and lower bonnet and boot lid, was built in much the same way as the TR3 from steel pressings, with the bolt-on wings being retained as an investment saving and a good marketing feature. The body was mounted on the chassis as a single unit, however, which made the car twice as stiff torsionally as the TR3A. A deep gearbox tunnel, welded to the floor, with a steel instrument console connecting it to the main integral instrument panel above, contributed to this as did the revisions to the chassis, which provided a wider track of 4 ft 1 in front and 4 ft rear. The extra 2 ins either side at the front were achieved at minimal cost by welding long channel-section spacers to the outside of the existing box-section members, making the chassis more rigid at the same time. The extra rigidity enabled the suspension to be made effectively softer, for a better ride, and, hopefully, for better handling.

The spring rates were unchanged front and rear because the new car was about 60 lb heavier at 2240 lb, but the damper settings were a little softer. Otherwise, the suspension was exactly the same as before, with the extra width at the back being made up by lengthening the half-shafts and axle casing by 1.5 ins either side. The rear springs were slightly more cambered than before, however, because the extra body weight was particularly evident at the back. The wheel and tyre options remained unchanged from those of the last of the TR3As, except that when Michelin X radials were ordered, a 165–15 section was used in place of the earlier 155–15 cover to prevent the engine being over-revved in top

The revised rear end of the TR4 featured a large luggage boot that appealed especially to the American market.

gear. Overall, the new car benefitted from these changes even more because they left enough money to fit rack-and-pinion steering.

An Alford and Alder unit replaced the old worm-and-peg mechanism with an Impactoscopic steering column as pioneered on the Triumph Herald touring car range two years earlier. This gave 2 ins of adjustment for the driver and allowed the column to collapse under impact as a safety measure. The rack itself fitted in neatly behind the radiator—still pierced for a starting handle—and ahead of the engine. Apart from fitting a slightly revised 2.2-litre unit as standard and the new gearbox (described in the previous chapter), the only other mechanical modification was to reduce the rear brake's operating cylinders from 0.75 ins in diameter to 0.7 ins with a matching master cylinder to combat wheel lock under heavy pressure.

The main difference in the engine, apart from the use of 86 mm liners and pistons instead of 83 mm—which were listed as a rarely-ordered option aimed at 2-litre competition classes—was that the combustion chambers had chamfered edges. This reduced their squish effect a little, but increased the compression ratio to 9:1 to take full advantage of the better-quality petrol that was readily available by now in most countries. A 7:1 option was listed for the export territories where petrol was still poor, and the distributor advance and retard curve was modified to suit the new characteristics. Officially, the new engine gave only 100 bhp as before—but it was one hundred more honest horses because the readings were taken with vital ancillaries such as the generator in place. This was the equivalent to 105 bhp stripped, or 115 bhp by the exaggerated SAE ratings favoured by American manufacturers. Not that this made much difference to the way the car went—because the real power was cancelled out by the extra weight—but it helped the insurance ratings.

Michelotti's new body had exceptionally clean lines for one designed in the early 1960s; it also had frameless windows like his Triumph Herald. Although the TR4 was wider, its drag factor was not substantially higher because the bonnet and boot lid were lower (necessitating a long bulge to clear the carburettor tops), and the windscreen was curved, thus retaining the earlier ground clearance and the headroom for the occupants. The bonnet, with 'eyelids' covering the tops of the headlights (still set in from the front wings) was now hinged at the front for better access to the engine (most of the ancillaries were at the back), and extra security against being lifted by the airstream.

The rear compartment was partially upholstered, so that with an optional seat cushion, it could be used for children. This padded backrest doubled as a hood storage envelope. The hood was redesigned as well to make the wrap-round windows as large as possible.

The painted dashboard of the TR4 was, in some ways, even simpler than that of the earlier cars, but its face level ventilation was a real breakthrough. It worked very efficiently and predated the much acclaimed Airflow system used on Ford saloons by three years. Within the strict confines of cost, the Triumph engineers were responsible for some excellent innovations. At the same time, they did not waste money on unnecessary sophistication. The stiffening member between the dashboard and the gearbox tunnel that doubled as an accessory console can be seen here.

The ingenious new 'Surrey' hard top was offered at the same time as an option. It had a substantial alloy casting to surround the rear window and provide roll-over protection for the occupants in the event of an accident. A pressed steel roof panel was then bolted between the roll-cage and the windscreen's top rail. This could be replaced with a vinyl roof panel supported by a light folding frame, which could be stored inside the car in good weather. This was the 'Surrey' top, a description that went back to early English coachbuilding days. There were other ways of obtaining fresh air in the TR4, too. Face-level ventilation grilles connected to the scuttle flap and shielded by butterfly shutters, were particularly effective.

Other detail fittings that represented a considerable advance on the TR3A included a padded fascia surround, improved slides for the front seats, press-button door locks, a full-width rear bumper (which, unfortunately, meant that the spare wheel could only be reached through the luggage boot floor), and seat belt anchorages. Similar options to those available on the TR3A continued to be offered, plus provision for a brake servo mounted between the right-hand flitch plate and the scuttle. The instrument panel remained traditionally TR, but the overdrive switch had to be moved to the steering column to make way for the driver's side air vent. An additional silencer was fitted behind the rear axle line to calm the exhaust.

The factory did not have the time, nor the money, to introduce all the changes they would have liked at the start of TR4 production, but soon after—at chassis number CT4388 (for steel-wheeled cars), and CT4690 (for those with wire wheels)—the front suspension geometry was improved. This change, early in 1962, could be readily spotted because the top wishbones adopted a smoother shape. Smaller and lighter Girling 16P front brake calipers were fitted at the same time. They had similar pads, but they seem to have been just as efficient as the earlier brakes.

Late in the year, from body number 15076CT, new seats with flatter cushions and squabs—which needed new frames—were introduced. At about the same time, from engine numbers CT16801 to CT16900, Zenith-Stromberg 175CD carburettors were fitted for a trial run. These carburettors had been designed by Standard-Triumph using the best unpatented features of the existing SU carburettors, and produced by the independent firm Zenith because SUs were costing Triumph too much. SU, which was owned by BMC, who made the rival MGB, supplied carburettors to MG at a much reduced price, which made life difficult with the penny-pinching that had to go on in this ultra-competitive field. Stromberg was a name owned by Zenith, and used for a time before these carburettors became known simply as Zenith constant-depression, or CD, units. They had particularly good anti-emission characteristics and were to become popular on cars exported to America later in the 1960s. But Standard-Triumph, who had designed them, had the first supplies, which then found their way on to the TR4 as a standard fitting from engine number CT23594 and gave no noticeable change in performance.

The TR4 rolling chassis with its radiator in place, still featuring an aperture for a starting handle.

The roof of the Surrey top on a TR4 could be replaced with a roll of canvas, supported by a folding framework.

The Dove GTR4

The Dove GTR4 was produced to similar ideals to those of the Swallow Doretti, although not in such an ambitious initial manner. It was the result of coachbuilders Thomas Harrington, of Hove, Sussex, searching for additional work to supplement commercial vehicle body production and conversions based on one of the TR4's rivals, the Sunbeam Alpine. The first Harrington Alpine—a luxurious fastback version of the Sunbeam Alpine—was produced in 1961 and was an immediate success. Harrington chose the Sunbeam as a base for their GT conversion because they were Rootes main dealers. As soon as they had put this car into production, they looked for other models as a basis, and the new TR4 was an obvious candidate. Standard-Triumph had too many problems to market it themselves, so an agreement was reached with distributors L.F. Dove,

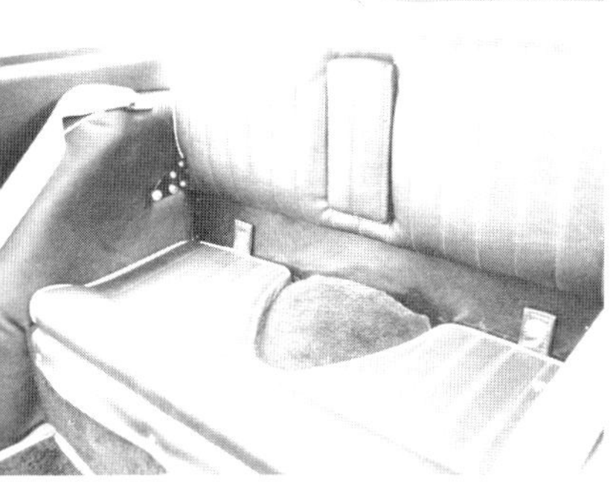

The rear end of the TR4 could be converted to accept the Dove hatchback hard top and extra folding seats.

of Wimbledon, South London, and the new car was christened the Dove (pronounced *Dovay*) GTR4 in keeping with its 'classy' image.

The GTR4, which, like the Harrington Alpine, was intended to be a cheaper and more easily-maintained version of the defunct Aston Martin DB Mark III, was designed to carry two adults, children and their luggage rapidly over long distances.

The bodywork was unchanged from the windscreen forwards, with the standard doors and rear wings being retained as well. The roof was completely new, however, sloping up slightly from the windscreen to a point just behind the front windows, above small rear seats. It then sloped down again in a rather angular manner to the tail. A hatchback door was fitted like that of the Aston Martin, with a vertical rear tail panel containing the repositioned fuel filler. The special rear side windows were hinged at the front for ventilation and the interior modified to take the rear seat. A new fuel tank was made up, of a quoted 15-gallon capacity, to fit under the rear luggage area above the spare wheel. Despite the 4 inch rise in roof height (any more would have ruined the lines and increased frontal area dramatically), only 2 ft 8 ins of headroom could be liberated above the rear seats. It was enough for small children, but not for large ones, or adults. The trim was to a high standard and Standard-Triumph extended their normal warranty to the car, which weighed a good deal more than the standard TR4 and cost a third more on its introduction in March 1965.

About 50 were sold before Harrington's were 'leaned upon' by the Rootes Group who were not happy about the way they were diversifying. Later in the year, Harrington's were taken over by Robins and Day, a group of companies owned by the Rootes family. The coachbuilding department was closed and existing stocks used up before the Dove GTR4 (invariably called just the *Dove*!) disappeared.

The TR4A

When criticism of the TR's dated suspension built up so much that it had to be changed, Triumph decided to adapt a new independent system that had been introduced on their Vanguard successor, the Triumph 2000 saloon, in 1963. The way in which the saloon car's suspension was adapted without changing the body was quite ingenious. The actual rear suspension was of partly swing axle, and partly trailing arm, design—the cheapest layout available without the perils associated with a pure swing axle system in which the wheels could tuck under when cornering, with hair-raising results. There was still a demand for the cheaper live axle rear suspension from the United States, so the new chassis had to be designed in such a way that it would accommodate both forms of suspension with the minimum of alterations. The result was a bell-shaped layout ahead of the rear axle line with the side members swept out from the front, mating with angled members which linked them to inner longitudinals under the final drive. These no longer stopped short to make a cruciform, but swept outwards to continue to the back as side members. The angled members, at 58

The chassis was revised for the TR4A to accept the new independent rear suspension. When a live axle was substituted with leaf springs, they were located between the mounting brackets in front of the trailing arms and the outrigger supports at the back. In this case, the independent rear suspension's bridges were also removed, but the rest of the chassis remained the same.

degrees to the car's centre line, carried diagonal pivotted trailing arms. These massive alloy castings located the rear wheels and provided a bottom mount for two coil springs, one each side. A channel-section crossmember like a bridge, mounted on the rear side members by towers, provided the top spring mounts. Another, smaller, bridge (mounted behind the axle line), located lever arm shock absorbers working transversely so that the luggage boot floor did not have to be changed. The Triumph 2000 used telescopic dampers, but there was not room for them on the TR4A without bodywork revisions. The differential casing was slung beneath the bridges by rubber bushes with more rubber being used for the coil spring mountings to reduce noise and vibration. The front bridge was omitted when the live axle was fitted with its half elliptic springs mounted on one of the trailing arm brackets at the front and another bracket at the back reinforced by a tubular crossmember which also supported a new twin exhaust system.

When the car was standing level, the trailing arm pivots were 5.437 ins lower than the wheel centres, giving a rear roll centre of 4.35 ins (5.53 ins lower than that of the TR4), which reduced roll-steer to a minimum. The front suspension geometry had to be revised at the same time to work in conjunction with this new layout. But it was a doubly worthwhile change because the new rear suspension also had the advantage of pulling down the tail (rather than jacking it up), under braking.

The front suspension roll centre was raised from 0.75 ins on the TR4 to 7.81 ins by repositioning the inboard pivots to reduce understeer even more, with 'bowler hats' on the spring mountings so that longer coils could be used. The rear wheel travel had been increased to 6 ins so that longer, softer, springs could be used there too. The result of all these modifications—achieved at minimal expense—was a much softer-riding car with tolerably good handling, even if the rear suspension geometry was not perfect in that it required a good deal of camber change.

The independent rear suspension added about 50 lb to the car's overall weight, which gave problems with straight line speed. It was becoming quite noticeable how the TR's performance had effectively stood still, but Standard-Triumph were having a lot of trouble trying to extract any more power from the engine and could not, as yet, produce a new one. So they did the best they could with what they had, bearing in mind a generally-anticipated tightening up of noise regulations, particularly in Germany. The exhaust manifold and pipes were redesigned to eliminate back pressure as far as possible without making the car too noisy. This new system used a cast iron four-branch manifold (which was cheaper and quieter than a tubular one) running into two pipes and a silencer with one pipe along the car's backbone splaying out into two silenced pipes at the back. The four-branch inlet manifold was recast with provision for crankcase ventilation as required by some American states, by Smith's 'anti-smog' valves. These were connected between the balance pipe and a breather on the overhead valve cover to maintain crankcase suction at a suitable level while providing a flame trap as well. The result of this development was an additional 5 bhp with 132.5 lb/ft of torque at 3,000 rpm, besides complying with the new regulations.

Externally, the TR4A was very much like the TR4, other than for different overriders, and sidelights moved from the grille to the sides of the wings where they were combined with indicator repeater lights.

When the TR4A was fitted with independent rear suspension, as it was in most cases, the letters IRS were tacked on beneath the normal badge.

With so much engineering work, there was not much more left for the body, but it was improved as far as possible with a new radiator grille and lighting that made up in ingenuity for what it lacked in investment. The sidelights, which had previously been partly obscured when the bonnet was opened were now combined with the indicators on the sides of the wings, where they could also be seen from the sides—as required in America. Most manufacturers only managed to get over this problem by using additional repeater lights. Once again, making a virtue of an investment deficiency, a stainless steel beading was run backwards from these exposed lights. The hood was redesigned for easier operation with its fabric permanently attached to the irons and new toggle clips for the screen fixing. The only drawback was that it now occupied much of the space behind the front seats when it was furled. But new, better upholstered seats and squabs were fitted with a glamorous polished veneer dashboard. The console was also redesigned at the same time, and now that the car had a new chassis the handbrake could be conveniently remounted on top of the transmission tunnel where it should have been in the first place. Years of leg-rubbing for the drivers of right-hand steering cars had been dictated by its old mounting on one of the cruciform members. Other deft touches included moving the lighting switches to a stalk on the steering column and badges that proclaimed the car as a TR4, with or without IRS. Triumph were still conscious that they really needed a new engine, so they did not feel justified in calling it a TR5.

The TR5

When they were faced with the prospect of a relatively civilised three-litre version of the MGB (the MGC), Triumph started thinking very hard about a

TR to compete with it. But they could not stretch the four-cylinder engine to three litres and the Triumph 2000's six-cylinder unit would not go that far either. So they compromised by stretching the 2000 unit by half a litre (because it was smoother than the four-cylinder engine at that capacity), and filling the power gap with fuel injection. For reasons of economy, the rest of the car could not change, with the result that they arrived at a similar solution to MG, with the MGC, and then found that instead of being rivals they were bedfellows!

Triumph took the 2000 engine up to 2.5 litres by the simple expedient of lengthening the stroke so that basically all they expected to do was to change the crankshaft, con rods and pistons. This gave them an unfashionably long-stroke engine, but which benefitted by having tremendous torque if not a great deal of power in normally-aspirated form. Dramatically-improved results could be obtained, however, by using fuel injection and a different cam with the minimum of trouble for the development engineers and the easiest diagnosis and replacement if anything went wrong. The only drawback was that such systems cost a lot—but they saved a great deal on development, the costs of which could also be spread by using the same unit in a higher-performance version of the saloon. The cost of the fuel injection could also be kept to a minimum by ordering the larger quantities needed for two cars rather than just one.

The fuel injection engine of the TR5 made an impressive spectacle.

The engine itself had been developed from a four-cylinder unit of the late 1940s, first appearing in six-cylinder form in the Standard Vanguard of 1960. Although it had a similar capacity of 1,998 cc to the four-cylinder shared with the TR, it was preferred for its smooth running. Wet liners had been abandoned, the bores being cast integrally with the iron cylinder block, without water spaces between them. The dimensions were slightly undersquare at this point, with a bore of 74.7 mm, and a stroke of 76 mm shared by its four-cylinder predecessor. The new straight six produced 80 bhp net at 4,400 rpm, with a forged steel crankshaft running in four bearings that had 2 inch journals. A rubber-bonded vibration damper was formed integrally with a crankshaft pulley to drive the car's dynamo, fan and water pump. This was immediately in front of a roller chain drive to the single camshaft running direct in five bearings on the right-hand side of the cylinder block, looking from the front. A rubber-bonded blade tensioned the chain on its slack side. Cast iron bucket-type tappets also ran direct in the cylinder block, offset slightly from the centre line of the cam to induce rotation and minimise wear. They operated the valves through 'knitting-needle' type pushrods which had a large spherical seating at their lower end and a ball cup, with screw and lock nut adjustment at the rocker end.

The cylinder head was also cast in iron with vertical in-line valves operating in a modified bathtub type of combustion chamber. The oil pump shared a shaft drive with the distributor.

The power output was raised to 90 bhp when the engine was transferred to the Triumph 2000, producing considerably less torque than the four-cylinder unit used in the TR at that point. Triumph needed the same sort of torque and at least 125 bhp to improve the TR's performance substantially, which could only be achieved at the expense of flexibility and reliability in the six's existing form. The cylinder spacing ruled out any bore increases, so there had to be a change in the stroke. The way in which this was done was a tribute to the ingenuity of the Standard-Triumph engineers. The depth of the cylinder block could not be changed economically, so it had to be widened to give room for a longer-throw crankshaft (which would improve the torque), with the extra capacity hopefully increasing the power sufficiently. The maximum convenient increase was 9.5 mm, which gave a 95 mm stroke and took the capacity up to 2,498 cc. The connecting rods and pistons had to be redesigned, retaining the same con-rod length, which meant that the gudgeon pin centre was much nearer to the piston crown than before. The new pistons were very short, and the lightest made by Triumph at that time, with two compression rings and an oil control ring above the gudgeon pin boss. The lower ends of the cylinder walls were notched to clear the longer con rod throw, but the water jackets were not affected. The new crankshaft was made a great deal stiffer than before with the bearing journals increased to 2.311 ins. An unfortunate side effect was that the big end bearings had to be rather narrow at 0.67 ins.

A new 'full width' cylinder head had been designed at the same time, with inlet ports in pairs above the exhaust ports. This took the power up to around 105 bhp in 2-litre form when a rather wild camshaft was used. But flexibility suffered too much, and when it was restored, the engine produced only 110 bhp, even in 2.5-litre form.

It was then that the Lucas electrical company's new fuel injection system appeared as what must have seemed a saviour to Triumph. The first attraction was because it was thought that its more precise metering might be needed to comply with America's new exhaust emission regulations, but then it was realised that it would also be able to tame a very wild camshaft. This would liberate far more power than the extra 5–10 bhp that could be expected from the fuel injection alone. When the saloon car racing cam with timing of 35–65–65–35 (against the Triumph 2000's 18–58–58–18) was fitted, the mixture control was such that the engine remained reasonably docile and idled satisfactorily—and produced no less than 150 bhp at 5,500 rpm. This was with valve lift increased from 0.312 ins to 0.366 ins, and sizes from, inlet, 1.303 ins to 1.443 ins, and, exhaust, 1.178 ins to 1.258 ins.

The injection system worked like this: petrol was drawn from the tank through a paper element filter and pressurised at 100 psi by a motor-driven pump. This was placed under the bonnet on prototypes, but moved to the luggage boot for production cars to keep it cooler. A pressure relief valve was incorporated in the motor unit to pass excess fuel back to the filter element. The pressurised petrol was forced into a metering unit, which had a rotor driven at half engine speed through skew gears on the distributor driveshaft. Fuel was then fed to individual nylon injection pipes by a mixture control unit responding mechanically to inlet manifold vacuum and throttle opening. This also produced extra petrol for cold starting. Cold air for the engine was drawn through a cannister cleaner ahead of a new water radiator, then channelled to a circular box, which fed the manifold through rubber hoses. A duplex chain replaced the earlier single cam drive chain, which had proved unreliable at high revs. A plastic fan was substituted for the metal one for the same reason, and an oil cooler offered as an option for people who visualised thrashing their TR along the new motorways which were springing up all over Europe. Further bonuses with this long-stroke unit included torque raised from 132 lb/ft to 179 lb/ft at 3,000 rpm and an overall reduction in engine weight of 6.5 lb.

The gearbox and overdrive were well able to cope with the extra torque, but the final drive and driveshafts had to be strengthened. The axle ratio was raised to 3.45 at the same time.

The suspension had needed stronger rear springs, and the trailing arms were modified, partly to clear new 4.5-inch wide wheel rims. Braking was improved by increasing the front disc diameter to 10.875 ins, with servo assistance as standard. A tandem master cylinder was fitted with dual circuits to meet the new U.S. safety regulations.

The gearbox had to stay in the same place, so the extra length of the engine was accommodated by bowing the chassis crosstube and moving the radiator forward. New engine mountings were needed and the numerous small pressings used in the front suspension mounts were amalgamated to make production simpler and consequently cheaper.

Two different exhaust systems were used on the fuel injection cars, one louder than the other. The quiet one was reserved for markets such as Switzerland where there were very strict noise regulations, but not offered elsehwere because it absorbed more power.

Unfortunately, the fuel injection could not be made to operate with sufficient precision to meet the new American emission laws without the addition of expensive extra controls. But the Triumph engineers were amazed to discover that by careful setting, revised Zenith carburettors enabled them to meet the new tests. There was a drawback, of course, as the engine produced only 104 bhp in this form, at 4,500 rpm (but with 143 lb/ft of torque), because it had to have a reasonably 10–50–50–10 mild cam. It also needed a lower compression ratio of 8.5:1 against 9.5:1, and as a result, the earlier 3.7:1 final drive ratio was retained, although the TR250, as it was called, was almost exactly the same in other features to the new fuel injection TR5.

The nose of the TR5 was just like that of the TR4A, even to its bonnet bulge (rendered unnecessary by the removal of the tall carburettors). In fact, the only change was a discreet badge.

Effective and simple, that's how the TR5 luggage boot looked.

The wire wheels of the TR5 were equipped with large retaining nuts that needed a special tool to help hammer them off, and radial ply tyres. A small 2500 badge and indicator repeater light was also mounted on the rear wings.

The interior of the TR5, especially the dashboard, was much more expensively trimmed than that of the earlier cars. This example has been fitted with one of the map reading lights so popular in the 1960s.

There was neither the time nor the money to redesign the body, but the interior had to be completely revised to meet the new American regulations covering safety. New switches had to be fitted for the starter, choke and lights, with less obtrusive window winders and hood clamps. The dashboard was remodelled with a padded surround and the sun visors made of flexible material; catches were also fitted to the seats to prevent them being thrown forward in an emergency stop. The steering wheel was given three padded spokes for safety's sake and now the price had to rise, the heater became a standard fitting. The hood—which was now coloured black inside to avoid reflection—had a new mechanism to make it easier to operate and rigid cantrails above each door glass with Velcro fastening to keep it firmly in place at the higher speeds of which the fuel injection car was capable.

The TR250, which had a special colour scheme to make it look faster, was also fitted with U.S. compulsory warning lights indicating brake failure (hopefully not to be needed), and a hazard warning system. Minor changes were made to the exterior trim of both cars, with new badges, and cheap imitation 'magnesium' wheel trims.

The TR6

As soon as the American marketing men, led by Bruce McWilliams, vice-president of the Triumph division of British Leyland Motors Inc, realised that the TR250 would not only perform no better than the TR4A, but would look hardly any different, they demanded at least a new body. Michelotti was fully occupied with other British Leyland projects and there was a temporary shortage of die-making capacity in Britain, so Triumph had to look elsewhere abroad. The problem was solved when the German firm of Karmann Ghia decided to expand and were looking for work to fill their increased capacity. They were set a seemingly-impossible task—by British standards—of designing a striking new body for the TR without changing any of the sub-structures (such as the floor and wheel arches), gaining approval from British Leyland's committee system (which could be tedious), and making the manufacturing tools in double-quick time. That they achieved all this in only fourteen months was a tribute to their ability and fortunate for British Leyland, as the Triumph bodyshape was beginning to look very dated. Karmann designed a completely new nose and tail while retaining the TR5's floor, scuttle, screen, doors and inner panels. A far simpler, full-width, nose was used with a bonnet unadorned by the power bulge that had been made redundant by the six-cylinder engine. It had a high-mounted radiator grille and raised boot line reminiscent of the highly-successful Ford Mustang that had been introduced in 1964. Oddly, the Mustang provided much of the inspiration for Ford's Capri, which was to be announced only a week after the TR6!

The TR6 Carb carried a union jack aggressively on each rear wing, with reflective tape round its hood to catch the lights of following cars. The rear rocker panel also carried a badge saying, simply, Triumph.

The European TR6 had a plain hood, no overriders, and a badge denoting the use of fuel injection.

Apart from aesthetics, the new body was better technically in that the luggage boot's capacity was increased to 6 cu ft from 5.1, with only an extra inch in length. But the hurried way in which it had been produced was revealed in a 200 lb weight penalty, although Karmann could hardly be criticised for that as bringing down the weight of a car takes a lot of time in development. Access to the boot was made easier in some respects by a wider, 43 inch lid, but more difficult in others, by a far higher vertical rear lip. This made the body a lot more rigid, however, and it was painted matt black no matter what basic colour was specified. Car makers were in the throes of a matt black phase at the time, as a change from chrome, the TR6's far more restrained radiator grille also being finished in this colour. So were the lower sills (which had a rubberised coating to combat stones and the ravishes of rock salt that was finding its way onto roads in increasing quantities), steering wheel, windscreen surround and wiper arms. As part of this styling change of the 1960s, transfer badges were fitted to the rear wings, which Triumph were happy to note, saved a few pence. Other exterior changes—apart from neat stainless steel mouldings along the sill line—were dictated by American safety regulations and included new wrap-round rear lights and repeater lights on the front wings. Further changes were aimed at making the car more comfortable: new seats were fitted, together with improved side location and perforations in the Ambla plastic upholstery to combat perspiration. The rear window in the hood was made detachable (by zip fastenings) for those people who used it as a sunshade, and a new hardtop, along MG lines, was designed by Triumph for customers facing worse weather. The lines of the Surrey top did not complement those of Karmann, in any case.

Mechanical changes were confined at this point to fitting wider, 5.5-inch, wheels with new Dunlop 165HR tyres (or Michelin XAS) and a 0.625-inch anti-roll bar at the front to improve the handling. It reduced the tendency to flick from understeer to oversteer if a driver lifted off the power when cornering hard. The extra track was accommodated by subtly flaring the wheel arches. At the same time, the fuel pump's relief valve was sited in a more protected location in the boot. The TR250 designation was dropped and the American cars called the TR6 Carb when the new models were introduced in January 1969.

The trim of the TR6 was further improved by ventilated upholstery. Its padded steering wheel centre can also be seen, with covered slots for optional head restraints.

Criticism of the cheap imitation wheel trims was countered by smart new wheels from chassis number 50,001 in the autumn of 1969, with satin spokes for the steering wheel, which had been found to be rather dull. The seats were also made adjustable for rake. Soon after, Triumph's new Stag sports car with a V8 engine was announced. This had to have a stronger gearbox with revised ratios, which replaced the earlier TR6 box in the interests of standardisation from mid-1971. Its ratios were wider, at 3.37, 2.99, 1.39 and 1, but nobody complained, least of all British Leyland's dealers, who had been clamouring for a more flexible car. At the same time, tightening U.S. exhaust emission legislation required the fitting of 175 CDSE (2) Strombergs in place of the TR6 Carb's earlier 175 CDSE units, along with the compression ratio reduced to 7.75:1 and a better-breathing 18–58–58–18 cam. The intake and exhaust manifolds were redesigned, with the result that the engine produced marginally more power—

106 bhp at 4,900 rpm! The torque was reduced a little, however, to 133 lb/ft at 3,000 rpm. British Leyland could have kept the extra 10 lb/ft of torque at the expense of power, but it was felt that the new wider-ratio gearbox, introduced from numbers CD51163 and CC89817, would make up for that.

More and more emission equipment was having to be hung on the TR, progressing towards an exhaust gas recirculation system and air injection equipment, with yet another type of carburettor, the 175 CDSEV being fitted to keep the power and torque figures reasonable from the 1974 model year. For the rest of the world, British Leyland responded to the dealers' demands for more flexibility by changing to an 18–58–58–18 cam from the beginning of 1973. These CR-series engines had their power rating recalibrated as 124 bhp at 5,000—a figure taken as produced from the clutch to meet tough new German consumer laws. At the same time, the much more modern J-type Laycock overdrive replaced the older A-type which had given such long service. The new unit had a higher, 0.797:1 ratio, and because nobody was using the TR seriously for competition now, it was wired so that it could be engaged only in third and top gears. A small black bib spoiler was fitted at the front to reduce lift and drag. The steering wheel was changed yet again and the instruments in detail. Within a year, the demand for the expensive chrome-plated wire wheels was so low that they were discontinued . . . the world economy was beginning to feel the pinch as never before when it came to sports cars!

The American safety laws were getting tougher all the time, but Triumph managed to scrape through impact tests by fitting large rubberised over-riders for the 1974-model year. They did not find their way onto the fuel-injection cars, production of which had ceased in February 1975. And by the end of that year, the TR6 Carb's compression ratio was down to 7.5:1 and its time was nearly up, production eventually ending in July 1976 as a new TR was phased in.

IV
The Latter Day TRs

British Leyland did not have an easy time designing their brave new sports car, the TR7, despite the decision to use as many proven parts as possible and the preponderance of regulations—mostly from America—as to what size, shape, and weight it should be. It was a classic case of too many cooks spoiling the broth although the final mixture came tantalisingly close to success. The biggest problem with the new TR was its shape; and the final solution grew out of requirements for bumper height, bumper impact resistance, crash and rollover reaction, and the one thing that no regulations covered: drag. That Triumph got this factor down to a lower coefficient (0.396 against the brick-like TR6's 0.44), was an achievement recognised in fuel economy and the risk they took with the styling.

Pop-up headlights, each powered by a Lucas windscreen wiper motor worked by a Fiat X1–9 style screw crank (which could be operated by hand if necessary), were an integral part of this philosophy. U.S. regulations, for instance, called for a minimum of 24 ins from the road to the headlight centres, and thc only way that British Leyland could get the drag factor down without creating undersirable lift at high speeds was to make the nose slope down as low as possible. Such a shape had an additional factor in its favour in that experiences with a British Leyland safety car had shown that pedestrians suffered less injury on average in collision with a soft-edged wedge than a blunt-front . . . and the designers did not know what kind of legislation they would face in the future. The bonnet, hinged at the front, had an interlock device (with hooks engaging in slots at the back) to prevent it slicing through the windscreen in the event of a head-on crash; a sensible example of the application of American safety regulations. This wedge-shaped theme was extended to the back of the car, with the result that it had an uncommonly deep boot for a sports machine, with enough space to swallow 9.5 cu ft of luggage.

In two of its dimensions (its 13 ft 8.5 ins length, and 49.9 ins height), the TR7 was almost exactly the same size as the TR6, but in its width, (5 ft 6.2 ins), and wheelbase (7 ft 1 in), it was totally different. The reasoning was that, seeing as a longer wheelbase two-plus-two seater version was planned, the two-seater's wheelbase should be as short as possible, just long enough to accommodate

Stylist Harris Mann presented an uncompromising shape with the TR7.

occupants up to 6 ft 6 ins in comfort. But because such people would be used to the comfort of an American saloon, the new car would have to be as wide as was reasonable to give plenty of elbow and shoulder room. The result was 3 ft 6 ins of legroom and 4 ft 5 ins of shoulder room for driver and passenger (3 ins and 7 ins more respectively than they had with the TR6). Again, British Leyland achieved something of a miracle in that the overall weight of this car was 2,240 lb against 2,390 for the TR6! This was despite having to meet the almost neolithic demands of the American safety laws which decreed that the car should be able to survive with all systems intact, a 5 mph impact with a large block of concrete.

These demands influenced the entire design of the TR7's monocoque shell, based on a platform chassis using strong sill and floor pressings. Although it looked like an afterthought, the roof was part of the design from the start with tremendously strong pillars to meet U.S. and Canadian safety needs. The sheer strength of this roof meant that an optional fabric sunroof would not weaken the car, but it caused a lot of problems when a open conversion was needed.

Extensive use was made of box sections in the TR7 shell, notably in the long members running forward to carry a front subframe for engine, suspension and bumper mountings. Deep sides for the engine compartment provided top location for Ford-style MacPherson front suspension struts. Other box sections were used for the leading edge door supports and ran backwards over the rear axle, making a mounting for its coil springs and supporting the rear bumper. Safety-related items, such as the battery and brake servo, were placed in the

The massive rear end of the TR7 coupé with its relatively small turret top.

reinforced engine compartment, well out of harm's way. The fuel tank was also very well protected, in a TR6-style location between the rear wheels, surrounded by steel bulkheads to separate it from the cockpit and luggage boot. The filler cap on top of the rear deck was designed in such a way that it stayed in place in the most severe accident. The doors were reinforced of necessity to meet these draconian regulations and contributed to an extraordinarily-stiff structure when secured by their anti-burst locks. Massive battering ram steel bumpers were designed to stand up to blocks moving at 5 mph in the United States and 3 mph in other places. They made the car 13 ft 8.5 ins long in America and 4.5 ins shorter in Europe because the bumpers didn't need to be so thick there. Both sets of bumpers were produced with energy-absorbing mouldings of urethane foam surrounding their hearts of steel, and sheltering beneath a polycarbonate cover at the front with nylon at the back to resist sloppy fuel fillers. These enormous bars were so strong that it was possible to fit the front side lamps and indicator lights inside them and still survive regulation thumps!

The X-shaped front subframe was rubber-mounted to insulate the bodyshell from road noise, locating the steering rack, an anti-roll bar, and two of the engine mounts. A rear mounting for the engine was fixed to the body, with a cable acting as a horizontal tension stay, and another stay by the sump to keep the power unit in place during the 5 mph shunts. One of the advantages of this system was that the steering trackrods could not move in relation to the lower suspension links, which provided consistently more accurate geometry and eliminated bump steer. It also made assembly easier. The bodyshell itself was quite stiff, 7,500 lb/ft of pressure being needed to twist it 1 degree, partly because the windscreen was bonded in by a heating process. Laminated glass was used as standard for export cars, all TR7s having stainless iron surrounds.

The interior of the TR7 was beautifully laid out providing you did not need a lot of room for oddments.

With the old TRs in mind, a truly monumental amount of wheel travel was provided. The MacPherson struts were chosen for simplicity, which meant easy service, which in turn pleased U.S. dealers. It also provided more efficient direct-acting cartridge-type dampers than before and gave more room in the engine compartment because its sides could be moved further out. This was important because British Leyland did not know how much more emission equipment they were going to have to squeeze in, and the projected Rover V8 engine—as an alternative to the Triumph Dolomite-based straight four-cylinder unit—needed more room in any case. The tall, vertical dampers, surrounded by coil springs, doubled as kingpins. They had a firm mounting at the top and a 'wishbone' at the bottom consisting of one transverse link and the actuating arm of an anti-roll bar. The steering rack was mounted at the lower level ahead of the wheel-centre line, with a telescopic, universally-jointed, steering column. The rack and the lower links controlling the movement of the wheels were mounted on the same pressing, which meant that there was no room for play; the steering column also used needle rollers in its joints, which kept everything torsionally stiff, the overall result providing a good feeling of the road for the driver without any unnecessary shocks. An excellent turning circle of 29.5 ft with 3.875 turns from lock to lock was judged to be ideal.

This front suspension turned out to be unique to the TR7, which might have seemed potentially costly, but it was intended to share it with a new saloon that never saw the light of day. The opposite applied to the rear axle, a beam lifted direct from the new saloon's predecessor, the Dolomite, on the early TR7s. Although the chief object of this rear suspension was to keep down the costs and to limit the number of moving parts for cheaper service, it worked very well. It not only gave the same historic—in TR terms—8 ins of wheel movement, but it contributed to a high-speed stability and traction that made the TR7 far superior to the Dolomite saloon on which so much of it was based. In other words, the sports car was worth buying if handling was more important than accommodation.

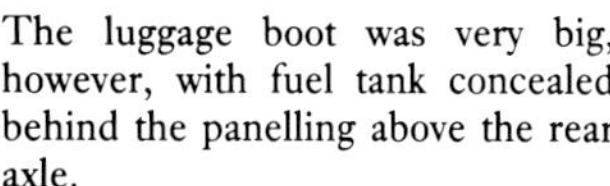
The luggage boot was very big, however, with fuel tank concealed behind the panelling above the rear axle.

British Leyland achieved this on the TR7 with a four-link system, two of the links being provided by long fabricated arms mounted to the body and the underside of the axle casing, and the other two—which provided transverse location—being mounted at an inclined angle between the body and axle. If you looked at them from underneath, their triangular formation for maximum rigidity was obvious. The inclined rods' rear mountings were on top of the axle to counter torque and, naturally, higher in the bodyshell in front of the axle. Vertical coil springs were fixed to the lower arms and the bodysides with upright telescopic dampers at the back of the axle. The attachment points of the shock absorbers were as far apart as possible to control roll, with the help of an anti-roll bar linking the two bottom arms.

The only real compromise in the development of this very basic form of suspension was in its bushing. The rubber needed to insulate the body from road noise and vibration, had on the one hand, to be stiff for good location (too much flexibility led to oversteer) yet, on the other, to be soft for comfort as so often the unitary construction of a bodyshell could boom like a tin box. Not surprisingly, British Leyland chose the middle course. However, progressive damper settings made up for a lot with the handling.

Despite its special suspension, the rear axle casing came direct from the Dolomite (or the sister Marina), with a 3.63:1 final drive and differential shared by the 1850 cc version of the Dolomite, the smaller Triumph Spitfire sports car and the self-same Marina 1.8 automatic transmission was also offered as an option, in which case a higher 3.27:1 axle ratio was fitted. This was shared with the Triumph GT6 sports car phased out to make way for the TR7, and 1,500 cc and 1,854 cc versions of the Dolomite.

The Dolomite's 8 ins × 1.5 ins drum brakes that came with the axle casing were used, married to 9.75-inch front discs with the U.S. compulsory dual circuit braking and a direct-action servo combined with the master cylinder. A pressure limiting valve minimised the risk of rear wheel locking; if the front circuit failed, this valve was automatically isolated to provide maximum braking. Should either brake circuit fail, a pressure differential warning light shone in front of the driver.

Pressed steel wheels of 5.5 ins section, fitted with 175–13 inch radial-ply tyres, were all that was offered for a start, to keep down the price while still giving decent handling.

The engine was based on one originally designed for the Swedish firm, Saab, a four-cylinder in-line unit with a cast-iron block and aluminium head. The cylinder block was canted over to 45 degrees to keep down its overall height and to fit in with a V8 development used in the Triumph Stag. In its four-cylinder form it had a five main bearing forged crankshaft with a single chain drive to an overhead camshaft acting directly on the valve stems via hollow piston tappets surrounding the springs. The cylinder head studs were positioned so that the head could be removed without disturbing the camshaft, cutting down on the labour charges for what would normally be an expensive job on an overhead camshaft engine. The head used cross-flow breathing with bathtub

The slant four-cylinder engine as fitted to the TR7.

combustion chambers. In its original Saab form, it had a capacity of 1,709 cc, which was raised to 1,854 cc for the Triumph Dolomite 1850. Then a 16-valve version was developed for the higher-powered Dolomite Sprint with its capacity stretched to 1,998 cc by boring out to 90.3 mm. Unfortunately this ingenious head could not pass the American emission laws, so the 1850's eight-valve version was mated to the larger-capacity block, which retained the original 78 mm stroke for the TR7. Once the new car had been launched, it was planned to introduce a Sprint version for European markets. Meanwhile the export-only TR7 was fitted with a 'Federal' engine on its introduction in January 1975. This meant that it had only an 8:1 compression ratio head to suit America's low-lead fuel—with a modified petrol filler that could accept only the special hoses which dispensed this fuel.

A pair of Stromberg 175CD SEV carburettors were fitted on a thermostatically-controlled air inlet operating through water-heated alloy manifolds on the left side—or 'top' of the engine—when seen from the front. The exhaust manifold, tucked under the cylinder bank, was made from cast iron for its cheapness and its sound-deadening qualities. The exhaust system presented a problem in that there was a characteristic boom at 70 mph—the normal British cruising speed—which was increased over 95 mph. Amazingly, British exhaust noise laws were more stringent than those of the Americans, and after a few cars had been produced, a more 'sporty' exhaust system was fitted at the request of U.S. dealers. It did nothing for the TR7's power output, but it sounded as though it did!

The extent to which the emission laws governed this engine could be seen from its closed-circuit crankcase breathing, air injection into the exhaust ports, exhaust gas recirculation valve with a service interval warning lamp, a charcoal canister to absorb carburettor and fuel tank fumes, and an electric cut-off valve to stop the fuel supply as soon as the ignition was switched off.

Electronic ignition was fitted because the US laws required long periods between servicing for those items which could affect emissions. The new Lucas 45DE4 system on the TR7 used a magnetic pick-up to trigger the firing impulses with all its electronics built into the distributor.

Triumph would not reveal power to torque figures for this heavily-dampened engine, but accurate estimates put them at 92 bhp at 5,000 rpm and 115 lb/ft of torque at 3,500 rpm. Although this engine suffered a good deal from the power-sapping laws, it had an advantage of being 90 lb lighter than the old TR engine. This kept the weight of the new car down to 2,241 lb and gave it about the same 54/46 weight distribution as the TR6.

A new bell housing improved the beam strength of the engine and transmission with an 8.5 inch single dry plate clutch on manual cars. This needed more pressure to operate than the normal 1850 Dolomite clutch because it had a specially-treated diaphragm spring to cope with the extra torque generated by the two-litre engine.

An all-synchromesh four-speed gearbox fitted initially to manual cars was a development of the unit used in Triumph's small vehicles, strengthened to cope with the extra torque. This gearbox used the overal Dolomite ratios of, top 3.63, third 4.56, second 6.47, first 9.65 and reverse 10.95:1. No overdrive was offered as a stronger five-speed gearbox was planned for introduction later. The rest of the four-speed box had been developed from the Marina's single-rod type which was also used in the Triumph Spitfire and MG Midget sports cars. A 3.63:1 rear axle ratio was adopted for maximum acceleration in the U.S., although it meant that the TR7 was substantially undergeared if used elsewhere. At the same time, a Borg Warner model 65 three-speed automatic transmission was offered as an option with overall ratios of 3.27, 4.74 and 7.82 with a 6.83:1 reverse, in which case the TR7 was fitted with a 3.27:1 axle to minimise the loss of performance resulting from the power absorbed by its torque converter.

The TR7's interior was totally different from its predecessors in that it was of thoroughly modern design. With a two-plus-two version in mind, British Leyland had made it an uncompromising two-seater so that as much room as possible could be devoted to its occupants, and their luggage (such as golf clubs), at the back. This meant that the seats were hard up against the rear cockpit bulkhead, leaving little room for odds and ends, such as overcoats, to be stowed. No doubt the designers considered that such items would be better off in the relatively large luggage boot that could be provided as a result of not allowing any room behind the seats. There was space, however, for small things, such as cigarette packets and maps in a variety of trays, a central console and a lockable glove box. The controls were extremely well placed for operation by the driver with most functions being covered by column-mounted stalks.

The heating and ventilation system was a combination of Austin Princess and Jaguar XJ Series Two parts, with a casing that could house either a plain air-blending heater or an optional air conditioning unit. When the air conditioning was fitted, an extra radiator heat exchanger was needed, linked to a pair of electric fans. It absorbed a lot of power, enough to reduce the cruising speed by about 2 mph the moment it was switched on! Four face-level vents were provided with another two in the footwells, and a four-speed fan.

The speedometer read somewhat optimistically to 140 mph with a tachometer red-lined at 6,500 rpm—enough for a thereoretical 129 mph—although the car was so far past its peak power at those revs that it could not have hit such a speed without a steep down gradient and a hurricane behind it.

In areas in which the TR7 was allowed to excel, however, the seats were as good as the handling. The squabs were adjustable for rake, with a total of 7 ins of backward and forward movement as well. They were upholstered in hard-wearing broadcord nylon, the interior as a whole presenting one of the most pleasing aspects of the car. Even the heavily-padded steering wheel boss required in the U.S. looked good.

In May 1976, the TR7 was released on the European market with 14 per cent more power as a result of not having to use all the American emission equipment and raising the compression ratio to 9.25:1 to take advantage of leaded petrol. Twin SU HS6 carburettors were substituted for the Strombergs now that the makers were in the same group as Triumph. In this form, the engine gave 105 bhp at 5,500 rpm with 119 lb/ft of torque at 3,500 rpm—and its overall weight was reduced by 2 per cent to 2,205 lb. Much of this weight reduction was due to lighter bumpers being fitted which also brought down the overall length to 13 ft 4.1 ins. Detail changes were made in other specifications, apart from offering the TR7—in manual form only—with right-hand-drive. A new, lighter, steering wheel was fitted, with a cheaper three speed interior fan, and no indicator repeater lights on the rear wings.

Meanwhile a five-speed gearbox being built for the large Rover SD1 saloon was phased in on export versions of the TR7 from the end of 1975, although it was not listed as an option until October 1976 when it could be fitted to all models. Whenever this gearbox was used, it was linked to the SD1's stronger rear axle, which was also fitted with larger, 9 inch by 1.75 inch, drum brakes. The combination of these two components was more than enough to cope with the TR7's torque, which could give problems on the four-speed cars with the lighter axle. The overall gearing of the five-speed cars, which had a 3.9:1 axle ratio, was lower than that of the four-speed machines, with a top gear of 3.25, fourth of 3.9, third of 5.44, second of 8.14, first of 12.95 and reverse of 13.37:1. This gave a far better combination of high-speed cruising ability with improved acceleration although it added 114 lb to the overall weight of the car. The heavier axle also extended the rear suspension more than was desirable in practice.

Ironically, as soon as the five-speed gearbox was announced as an option in Britain—chiefly, it must be admitted, as an exercise to qualify it for fitting to competition TR7s—demand for it had built up to such an extent in America that supplies ran out for British cars and it had to be withdrawn for right-hand drive vehicles between January 1977 and what amounted to a virtual relaunch of the TR7 in January 1978. However, European customers were given the option of the automatic transmission (with the lighter, lower-geared, axle) from October 1976—but it hardly seemed a fair deal.

In restrospect these cars are easy to distinguish, with chassis numbers prefixed ACL for early four-speed models, ACG for four-speed UK cars and ACG with an F suffix for the very rare right-hand-drive five-speed machines.

Soon after, from March 1977, all cars from chassis number ACG3001 had revised rear suspension to cope with the heavier axle—even if it was not fitted, as on the automatic ones. The springs were stiffened and shortened so that the rear rode an inch lower and 185/70 radial-ply tyres were fitted to everything except the TR7 auto. A trendy front spoiler was fitted as standard and a sunroof was offered as an option at last—Triumph having delayed such a move in the expectation of being able to introduce the convertible. Fancier wheel trims and tartan seats were added as well with grey plastic for the interior instead of matt black.

Again, these were relatively rare cars as the great strike at Speke stopped all production from September 1977, killing the projected Sprint and Lynx two-plus-two versions of the TR7 and holding up the convertible and TR8. A few cars were produced at Speke between March and May 1978, before production was transferred to Canley in October that year.

Numerous detail changes were made to the TR7 when production resumed at Canley with the five-speed gearbox and heavier axle as standard, and the wider tyres on all cars except automatics. Extra padding was included for the seats with a revised fuse box and cooling system that incorporated a hot-air flap valve in the carburettor intake. The sills and wheel arches were given a corporate anti-chip coating and the headlamp lift motors were sealed against water and road debris. The bonnet was given a small bulge in anticipation of the V8 version and the nose was crowned with a distinctive laurel wreath; the graphics were also tidied up at the back. Chassis numbers, which had ceased at 44328, were resumed at 100,000, with the prefix TCG.

The TR7 Drophead

As the Lynx was held in suspended animation, the Drophead version of the TR7 was prepared for export production from June 1979. It was not simply a case of cutting off the turret-like top even if the finished product gave that impression. The body structure had to be substantially strengthened to compensate for the loss of rigidity caused by the absence of a stressed roof. To do this, an additional box section was welded in between the seats linking the rear door shut panels, while the quarter panels in that area were extended downwards to anchor into the sills. In other words, instead of having a hoop above the driver's head—if you could visualise it that way—you had an inverted horseshoe at the back of the cockpit. The scuttle and windscreen surround at the front of the cockpit provided extra stiffening, but were inclined to shake over rough roads despite being strengthened along with the subframe. This condition was cured by a time-honoured method first seen on American Packard saloons before the Second World War and later adopted, among other manufacturers, by Rover, who were in the same group as Triumph. The front bumper bar was built to American specification with a box section steel armature pivotted in the middle and carrying weights on either side. The idea—which proved effective—was to carry a large mass at the extreme front to establish the same harmonic balance as the dashboard. As a result, the convertible weighed about 80 lb more than the fixed-head, and was longer than the UK model, although it was 0.4 ins lower because of the different lines of its folding hood. This was secured by eight fasteners and furled beneath a new storage cover. Cast alloy wheels that were fitted to the fixed head as standard were offered as an option on the Drophead. This convertible was then introduced in substantially the same form on the home market in March 1980.

The TR8

At the same time, the TR8 was launched in America. Mechanical changes were few because the car had been designed for the Rover V8 engine from the start. Apart from different engine mountings—although they were in similar formation to those of the TR7—it had firmer shock absorbers and spring rates, larger brake pads and the battery was moved to the luggage boot to help offset the heavier engine, resulting in an overall 57/43 distribution of the 2655 lb curb weight. The rear axle ratio was raised to 3.08:1 to take advantage of the extra power and torque.

The TR8 by universal acclaim, looked much more attractive with its hood down.

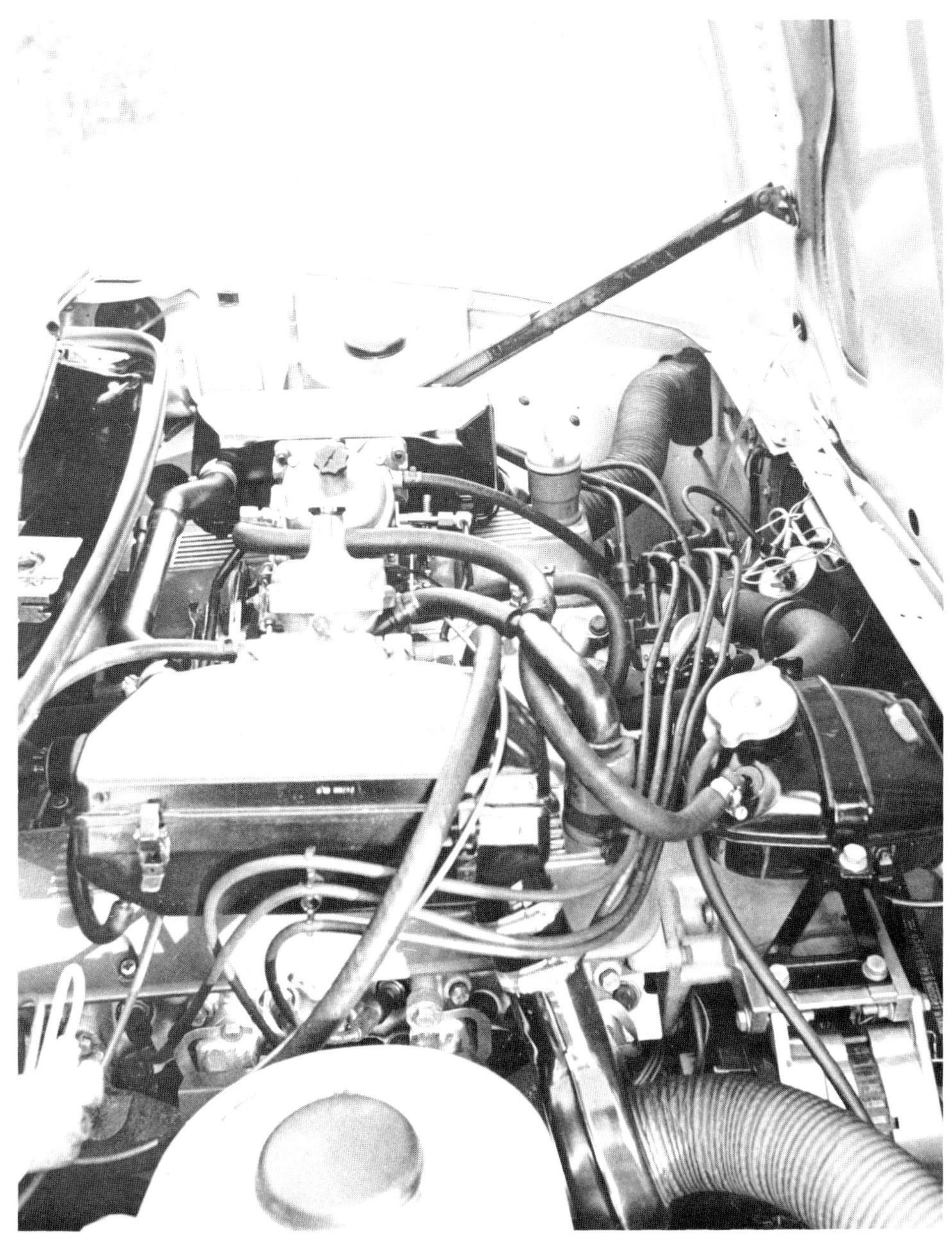

The TR8's engine fitted neatly beneath the bonnet with all major items readily accessible.

The engine, which had first appeared in the Buick Special in 1960, was discontinued by the American General Motors firm in 1963 when their compact cars became less compact, eliminating the need for a relatively expensive light-alloy engine. Subsequently the manufacturing rights were bought by Rover and the engine developed for use in British Leyland cars from 1967. It had the advantage for the European market of producing considerably more power and torque for little—if any—increase in weight over normal cast-iron engines and no more length than a conventional in-line four-cylinder unit.

This over-square engine with a bore and stroke of 88.9 mm by 71.1 giving a

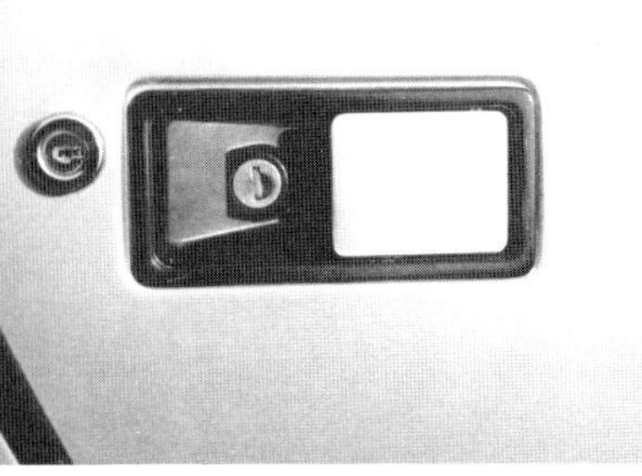

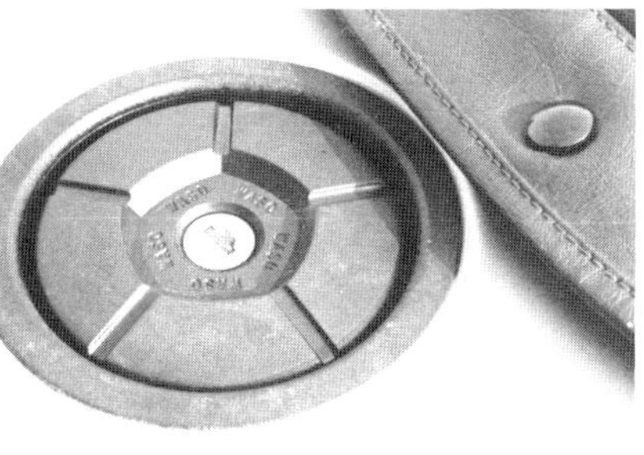

The interior of the TR8 was well up to the standards of rival cars, including saloons, but still distinctly sporting.

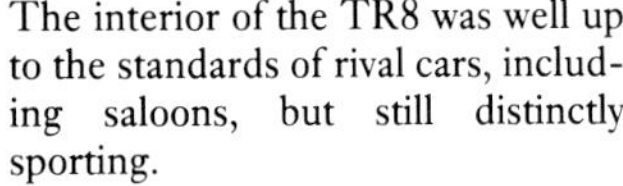

Door handles and the fuel filler were neatly recessed to meet American safety regulations.

capacity of 3,528 cc, was further developed for the SD1 before its installation in the TR8. It still retained its central chain-driven camshaft operating short, small-diameter pushrods and rockers via self-adjusting hydraulic tappets. These typically American devices were considered essential to provide a reasonably quiet valve gear in an alloy block which did not have the same sound-deadening properties as its cast-iron equivalent. In the British engine, the cylinder liners were pressed into place and located by stops at the bottom of the housings rather than by flanges on the tops of the liners. Good gas sealing was obtained by fitting the liners slightly proud of the cylinder block—shades of the old TR! A two-plane cast-iron crankshaft ran in five main bearings with a torsional vibration damper combined with pulleys for ancilliary drives at the front. The big ends of opposing connecting rods shared a single journal in the normal way and the gudgeon pins were a press fit into the little ends. The distributor was mounted above its drive in the centre of the 90-degree vee, with a belt-driven alternator on the left-hand side of the engine when viewed from the front.

Twin Stromberg carburettors were mounted on a pancake inlet manifold in the centre of the vee for all TR8s except those bound for California. The stricter emission laws in operation there meant that these cars had to have the more expensive Lucas/Bosch K-Jetronic fuel injection with a three-way catalyst and exhaust oxygen sensor. Inwardly, these engines were identical with an 8:1 compression ratio and their twin exhaust systems running back from under the banks of cylinders. The engine had received a great deal of development since the first installation in the Rover 3.5-litre saloon, however. The main preoccupation when developing it for the SD1—which used SU carburettors in its less-restricted European market—was to make it rev faster, 5,200 having

The bumpers were massive, of necessity.

been the former limit. It meant that the valving of the hydraulic tappets had to be altered to delay the point at which they 'pumped up.' After that, the breathing was improved with new cylinder heads which had bigger valves and single springs. Lucas electronic ignition was fitted as standard with an air intake temperature valve, the oil pump improved to give a higher output at low revs, a better steel (rather than cord) rear oil seal, fitted, and a water pump impellor and housing reshaped to reduce power losses.

In its TR8 form, this engine developed 137 bhp at 5,000 rpm with fuel injection, and 165 lb/ft of torque. The output was 133 at 5,000 with 174 lb/ft at 3,200 rpm with the Strombergs—a considerable reduction on what had been obtained with SUs. The 9.5-inch single dry plate clutch fitted to the SD1 was retained.

The optional alloy wheels became standard with new badges and a smart Motolita steering wheel. Nearly all these sadly short-lived cars were convertibles with only a few fixed heads. As British Leyland went through a traumatic time, production of the TR7 and TR8 was gradually transferred to Solihull with the two-litre car being fitted with Bosch L-Jetronic fuel injection for its final year in the U.S. In this form, virtually all exports were to California where its power output was rated at 89 bhp at 5,000 rpm, although performance was still down on the original 1975 car because its weight was up to 2,450 lb through standardisation of pressings with the Drophead. Production finally ended when the Solihull factory had to close in 1981.

Wide doors made access a relatively dignified and easy affair on latter-day TRs.

V

Contemporary Road Testers' Reports

Road tests of Triumph TRs, particularly the early examples, were exceptionally good. They never failed to emphasise what excellent value for money the cars were, besides faithfully recording performance figures. But perhaps their greatest value to us today is that they also gave a clear assessment of what it was like to drive a TR when it was new (rather than what it is like to ride in one now). They told of the days when a TR was treated like the cheap sports car it was, rather than as the classic it has become, requiring more of a kid-glove approach.

The first one to see much service in the hands of motoring journalists was a very early car, a TR2 with chassis number 6, engine number 9, and the optional overdrive on fourth gear, registered in Coventry with the number OHP 771.

The British magazine, *The Autocar*, were the first to lay hands on OHP 771, reporting in their issue of 8 January, 1954, that 'the sports Triumph not only provides an outstanding performance but it is also particularly good value for money as regards both initial purchase price and running costs, as a glance at the fuel consumption figures will show.'

The TR2's extraordinary frugality with fuel was highlighted by these figures: 32 mpg overall with an estimated 28–38 mpg, depending on how hard the car was driven. And after harping back to the 124 mph obtained at Jabbeke with an undershield and metal cockpit cover, *The Autocar* said that the performance was in no way disappointing. They recorded a top speed of 103.5 mph averaged out over two runs in opposite directions, and went to some trouble to explain how they did it. They said:

> 'From a flying start the car tested attained its maximum speed over a test distance of two miles with hood up and sidescreens in position. Over this distance no increase in maximum speed was obtained by using the overdrive, although it was possible that the absolute maximum on overdrive might be higher given an unlimited stretch of straight level road. The car was also tested with the hood down and sidescreens removed but with the normal windscreen in position, and in this trim a mean speed of 99 mph was obtained, showing, as would be expected, that the car is slightly slower when open unless the windscreen is removed and a full tonneau cover fitted.'

The car that made the Jabbeke run, with its metal tonneau cover and aerodynamic screen in place. The early globular bonnet badge can also be seen.

Ken Richardson sits in the early TR2 he used as a demonstrator in 1953 and 1954, complete with such details as globe badges on the knave plates.

Britain's Commonwealth took many of the original export TRs. These models left for Australia in 1954, with their brightwork taped over to protect it from damage during shipping.

Despite its low overall price of £912 as tested (with £249-worth of purchase tax, £40 for the overdrive, £10 for a heater, £12 extra for leather seats, and £6 for Dunlop Road Speed tyres), *The Autocar* did not consider the TR2 to be stark. They said:

> 'It is very well finished and equipped, and creates the impression even after only a brief acquaintance of being a well-balanced car that has that satisfying "all in one piece" feeling, an impression that grew as experience with the model increased.'

The problems of the day were also evident in the way *The Autocar* said that the TR only pinked slightly when its engine was pulling hard. At one time it might have sounded strange when it was realised that its compression ratio was a lowly 8.5:1, but in 1954 first-grade British petrol had not reached the octane ratings attained during the twenty years from the late 1950s. There was also no complaint about the position of the overdrive switch, it being 'conveniently placed on the facia,' because in 1954 no manufacturer had thought of putting it in the obvious position, on top of the gearlever.

The TR's handling also received full marks, which was not surprising, but what might seem surprising to later generations was the comment on its ride: 'The suspension is sufficiently soft to provide a comfortable ride, yet at the same time it does not permit excessive body movement, and there is noticeably little roll on corners.'

The Autocar were still living in the days of bone-shaking sports cars ... and they were not unduly alarmed when repeated applications of the brakes resulted in a 'rise in brake temperature that made it necessary to apply increased pressure'. They simply pointed out that when the brakes were applied hard 'perfectly straight black lines could be produced on the road surface'. Such were the standards of the day, with wonderful wide-open roads.

Hints of a furore and criticism to come could be gleaned from their comments on, first, the exhaust note: 'A healthy, but not unpleasant, bark at 2,400 rpm', and, second, the doors: 'The bottoms do not have sufficient clearance to enable them to be opened when the car is parked close to the kerb'. But overall, *The Autocar* liked the TR2, adding this gem on a 'surprisingly spacious interior':

> 'Driving comfort is important in any vehicle, but it is particularly important in a sports car, especially if it is to be used for competition purposes—no one would expect a cricketer to perform well if he were given a bat two sizes too small for him!'

Two months later, the redoubtable sprint driver, John Bolster, put OHP 771 through its paces for the youthful British magazine, *Autosport*, recording marginally better performance figures in its issue of 5 March, 1954. Bolster achieved 104 mph flat out in overdrive with 103 mph in direct top and acceleration times of 17.9 seconds for the standing quarter mile, with 11.6 for 0–60 mph, against 18.7 and 11.9 for *The Autocar*. But he paid the penalty in fuel consumption, obtaining only 25.4 mpg overall. This could not be considered representative, of course, but his introduction to the road test was almost prophetic. Bolster said:

> 'The Triumph TR2 is the most important new sports car which has been introduced for some time. First and foremost, it is easily the cheapest genuine 100-mph car on the market, and it brings this performance, with acceleration and roadholding to match, within the reach of the man of moderate means for the first time. Secondly, its excellent weather protection, large luggage space, and good traffic manners, render it entirely suitable for shopping and going to work.'

So far as the design was concerned, Bolster did not neglect details, observing that 'the spare wheel lies flat in a separate drawer, and cannot therefore scratch and soil one's personal impedimenta,' his mind, no doubt, harking back to some muddy experience.

He also lived quite happily with the bark of the exhaust, saying: 'It is not unreasonably noisy at the higher revolutions, but a resonance around 2,400 rpm spoils one's silent passage through urban areas.'

More seriously, he commented on the overdrive, in an era when contemporaries—notably Austin-Healey—were fitting devices to cut it in and out automatically:

> 'I am delighted to say that no automatic nonsense is fitted to the overdrive, and one simply moves a switch ... the change may be made on full bore without shock, and the engine copes manfully with the very high ratio of 3.03:1.
>
> 'Naturally the acceleration is noticeably less brisk, and it takes about five seconds longer to go from 80 to 90 mph. When travelling fast, I usually switch on the overdrive at about 95 mph. The car fairly flies up main road

The overdrive switch which Bolster found so handy was located on the extremity of the dashboard just behind the steering wheel rim. The indicators were operated by the lever on the steering wheel centre.

hills on normal top; for example, it exceeded 90 mph up Wrotham Hill before I had to shut off for the traffic lights.'

Those were the days when you rode on a car, not in it, like a gentleman on his hunting horse ... or on a ratio rather than in it. Despite the vigorous nature of his test, during which Bolster discovered that 'rear end breakaway may be finally provoked only if one takes leave of one's senses and enters a curve at a virtually impossible speed', he found it desirable to try the TR round a race-track, explaining that many potential owners would like to use such cars in competition.

Bolster lapped Silverstone's short circuit, windscreen erect, at 64 mph in the wet, which was fast enough to make the brakes very hot, and lead to the suggestion that competition-minded drivers should specify wire wheels for better cooling. He wound up enthusiastically: 'The high-geared steering makes it easy to avoid the common clot, whether afoot or awheel, and emphasises, once again, that a good sports car can be fundamentally a safer vehicle than a stodgy family saloon.'

The TR2's handling really could be extended on a long fast curve, with little suspension movement remaining in this case.

Bolster reckoned that the TR2 would be good for 30 mpg with more moderate driving, but the British magazine, *The Motor*, had other ideas. They gave OHP 771 a very thorough test in their issue of 7 April, 1954, recording 52 mpg at a constant 30 mph, 54 at 40 mph, 49.5 at 50 mph, 43.5 at 60 mph, 37.5 at 70 mph, 31 at 80 mph and 27 at 90 mph with a 34.5 mpg overall figure that they said verged on the fantastic. There was certainly no stodginess in the way they made the car perform, either, recording 0–30 mph in 4 seconds, 0–40 mph in 6 seconds, 0–50 mph in 8.2 seconds, 0–60 mph in 12 seconds, 0–70 mph in 15.8 seconds, 0–80 mph in 22.1 seconds, 0–90 mph in 30.4 seconds, a standing start quarter mile in 18.6 seconds, and a top speed of no less than 107.5 mph in overdrive, with 105.3 mph in direct top. Using direct top when accelerating from, say, 50 to 70 mph, could save up to 5 seconds; therefore the technique was to cruise in overdrive and switch down to direct top to overtake.

The Motor were in full agreement with the earlier testers on the Triumph Sports' strong points (they did not yet call it a TR2), but commented succinctly on the chassis. They said it was adequate for Britain, but disappointing on the fast and bumpy roads in France and Belgium. They warned: 'On really fast curves, it is wise to allow for the fact that due to light damping of the rear springs an unexpected bump can throw the car off its line to some extent.'

In the circumstances, they recommended that the optional large rear shock absorbers were desirable for long-distance travel, and added:

> 'Increased damping would also no doubt minimise unexpectedly vigorous shake of the front end and scuttle at speeds of around 75–80 mph which became increasingly evident towards the end of our extended Continental test, although the impression is formed that further stiffening of the frame or scuttle may be desirable.'

The Motor felt that the seats could do with more padding although they did an excellent job of holding the front seat occupants in place. Obviously, only very small people were suitable for these optional back seats.

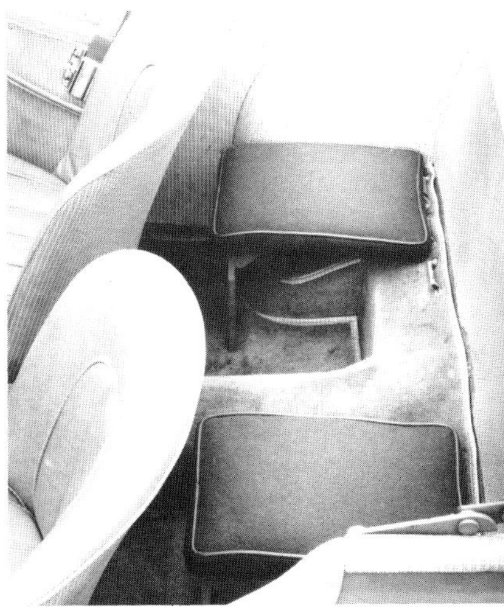

The Motor then went on to suggest, with feeling, that the seats could do with more padding, apart from commenting on the problems with the depth of the doors. They found the lack of door handles and the necessity to use a separate key for the cubby hole a nuisance. And so far as the exhaust was concerned:

> 'Unhappily, the system at present in use emits a quite ludicrous amount of noise at around 2,400 rpm, and in the overdrive gear this often corresponds closely to natural cruising speeds used at night or on rough roads.'

The report was an unusually critical one for those days, so *The Motor* felt that it was only fair to sum up:

> 'Although we felt obliged to criticize some details and characteristics of the Triumph in quite emphatic terms, we nevertheless rate this as not merely the best sports car available at its price, but also as one of the most promising new models which has been introduced in recent years.'

Road & Track were not so critical in their first full American test of the TR2, opining that the 'numeral name'—fast becoming fashionable in those days—stood for 'Tiny, Rapid, 2'. Although the test car had obviously been tuned for economy (to record 30–34 mpg), they still found the acceleration outstanding. They pointed out that the TR2 would outdrag any stock American car from a standstill and added:

> 'The acceleration seemed jet-assisted . . . but what we didn't expect was the fun element present with the driving. The TR2 is one of those rare cars that the novice sports car driver can slide into and feel comfortable and confident.'

This was a marvellous recommendation for a cheap car, and easily outweighed the fact that the performance figures with their overdrive model were not so good as those recorded in Britain, doubtless because of its weak mixture. Nevertheless, *Road & Track* recorded a top speed of 103 mph (only 96 mph in direct top), a 0–60 time of 12.2 seconds and a standing quarter mile in 18.4 seconds. Within a few years, the American sporting car scene would be far more interested in the 0–60 time than anything to do with economy, but while the Land of the Free remained delightfully unrestricted, there was only the by-now notorious exhaust note to worry about. *Road & Track* said:

> 'It will put a gleam in the eye of predatory police for miles around ... but for the real enthusiast, it's a true mating call and with the national and local confusion about muffler sound levels (especially from those cars with stock factory mufflers such as the TR2) it will be legal in some areas, frowned on in others.'

A nostalgic reminder of the times was contained in the quote:

> 'The general quality level of the car, inside and out, is of British standards. The plastic trim is of good quality and the dash panel layout is neat and efficient.' Those were the days...

And those were the days when Americans were still pleading for better bumpers on their imported cars, rather than dictating that they should be fitted. *Road & Track* said:

> 'The front bumpers with over riders seem adequate but the rear partial bumpers will create an open market for accessory manufacturers.'

The novelty had worn off by the time *Road & Track's* rival American magazine, *Sports Cars Illustrated*, published the test of a non-overdrive TR2 in November 1955. But they still liked it. Beginning with an answer to 'irresponsible rumours that the car didn't handle properly', they said:

> 'Our conclusions on the dangerous handling is simply that this little bomb is really loaded in the engine department and can easily be overdriven. There isn't a car in the world, with comparable power-to-weight ratio and as husky an amount of torque, that you can't get into trouble if you try. By the same token, the car is docile as a lamb when driven conservatively.'

SCI then experimented with the handling, discovering that:

> 'To drift, the TR2 requires a relatively high speed and a pretty violent cut at the wheel, coupled with some conservative work on the throttle. The back end is a bit light and if you let it, it will break away quite rapidly.'

Then, following some chauvinistic comments typical of the 1950s about 'the wife' and a baby carriage, the tester, Al Brannon, wrote:

> 'The second day we had the car, we also had thunderstorms. This gave us an opportunity to try the handling in the wet and also to experiment with the top and side curtains. The handling was good and seemed to be no more skittish than on a dry pavement. The top goes up, not without a bit of perseverance, and the side curtains really seal things up tight. In fact,

they're too tight for summer rain storms, causing the windshield to mist pretty badly. We tried cutting off the hot water to the heater and found that the fan makes a workable de-mister. With the top up, though, an outside mirror is a must.

'The following day we tried some acceleration runs and found that the car would consistently do 0–30 in 3.5 secs, 0–40 in 5.7, 0–50 in 8.1, and 0–60 in 11.8. We tried running over the red line to 60 a couple of times and in spite of a very slight uphill grade, managed to reach the mark in 10.5 seconds both times. In these runs we were somewhat appalled at all the power going into the wheelspin instead of acceleration, and feel that the car would not be handicapped by adding a couple of hundred pounds to the rear end...

'As a summary, it was the opinion of everyone who drove the car that it was, if anything, too potent. It is a car that should be able to hold its head up in competition with any of the 2-litre class and its price is well below most of its class.'

SCI were openly critical of the TR2's front, however, considering that the air intake was too stark, a view shared by the British magazine, *Motor Sport,* which had a relatively late test in a new wire-wheeled demonstrator, registered PHP 727.

Massive as was the scuttle structure of the TR, it was still subject to a certain amount of shake, as *Motor Sport* found. This was because it was not an integral part of the chassis.

It was near Christmas when the test took place, the report following in the issue of February 1955, and Triumph asked them not to take performance figures as a result. *Motor Sport* were quite happy with the way that the car performed, however, other than for its scuttle shake, considering that it offered astonishing value for money. Most of their criticisms centre on the difficulty in using minor controls when attired in a heavy overcoat and gloves. They evaluated the handling as being very good at 6/10ths, 1/10th on their scale being the pace of an elderly dodderer and 10/10ths being that of a 'dangerous motor-bandit hotly pursued by the entire C.I.D. in Ferraris.'

The Autocar were able to dispense with the heavy weather gear when they squeezed in a test of one of the later short-doored cars, complete with the optional hardtop and wire wheels, registered PRW 137, in the issue of 18 February, 1955. They did not comment on the new doors or the stiffer sills, but found the larger brakes very efficient and were well pleased with the hardtop. One of the most appealing features, in their opinion, was the large back window which gave rearward vision almost as good as when the car was open. The redesign of the exhaust system to eliminate the bark at 2,400 rpm was also well received. Although the new TR2, which also had overdrive, weighed 84 lb more than the earlier test car, it produced almost identical performance figures.

Characteristically, Bolster of *Autosport* managed to find a TR2 that would go faster, a club racing machine driven by veteran tuner Vic Derrington. This had larger carburettors and a free-flow exhaust system which was surprisingly quiet and which enabled Bolster to get the 0–60 mph time down to 10.8 seconds with a 17.6-second standing quarter mile. In conjunction with a top speed of 107 mph, the cost was a 20 per cent rise in fuel consumption (he reported on 16 September, 1955). Other modifications that were found to be particularly effective included a better-gripping bucket seat, stronger 64-spoke rear wheels, and the relocation of the battery in the boot to put more weight over the rear wheels at the expense of luggage space.

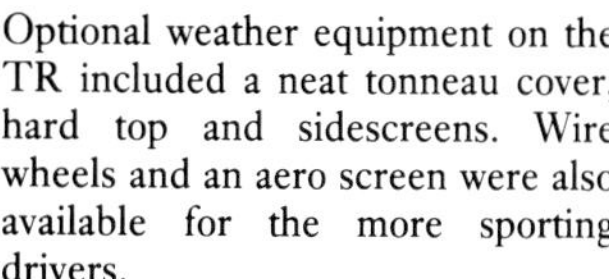

Optional weather equipment on the TR included a neat tonneau cover, hard top and sidescreens. Wire wheels and an aero screen were also available for the more sporting drivers.

15B
NRW 517

The Swallow Doretti

Excellent test reports that followed the Swallow Doretti's introduction in 1954 were marred only by criticism of its cockpit and lack of luggage space. *The Motor* were the first magazine to test a Doretti, reporting on 15 September, 1954, that its tubular chassis was, indeed, far stronger than most, allowing only a little 'working' between the heavily-braced scuttle and the relatively unsupported doors on the worst of Belgian pave. They explained further that:

> 'The small chassis deflections caused by the Belgian roads appear to be within fine enough limits not to upset the roadholding, even when bumps are met with just at the most awkward part of a corner. Modern, fairly soft, suspension depends on a really stiff base, and the Doretti has just that.'

The upright driving position of the Swallow Doretti was made even more evident by its nearly horizontal steering column. It looked lovely from the outside, but revealed itself to be very restricted inside when the spare wheel and tools were in position, and then there was little room to store anything other than the hood.

The dampers on this car, registered 609 CRF, were able to cope well with the pounding of the pave and standing-start acceleration times were accomplished with 'surprisingly little wheelspin.' The extra weight of the Doretti was reflected in generally slower times than those of the TR2, however, with a 12.3-second 0–60 mph, a 19.1-second standing quarter mile and a 100.2-mph maximum in direct fourth, 96.8 mph being achieved in overdrive. The overall fuel consumption of 27.9 mpg was higher, as well, than that recorded by *The Motor* with their TR2.

The driving position (comfortable only, said *The Motor*, for anybody who liked to sit bolt upright), left a lot to be desired. Another feature which they found particularly discomforting was the 'very bulky cylindrical (gearbox) cover, in size approximating to a five-gallon oil drum', which restricted foot room, and forced the driver's seat too near the door. They also considered the position of the overdrive switch in series with other identical switches to be confusing and suggested that the speedometer and rev counter might be better transposed. The rest of the car, apart from its minute luggage space, came in for praise.

The Autocar, in their test the following week, 24 September, 1954, echoed *The Motor's* comments and returned broadly similar performance figures with a sister car, registered 610 CRF.

Bolster claimed that the Doretti was fractionally lighter than the TR2 when he tested one in *Autosport* on 8 October, 1954, managing 102 mph flat out with an 11.6-second 0–60 time. He considered the Doretti a highly-attractive car, going as far as to say it was very pretty and adding, no doubt with such contemporaries as the MG TF in mind, that: 'If anybody still hankers after a "vintage" appearance. this should be a good car to convert him to the new look.'

He found the vintage driving position rather strange at first, but soon adapted to it and emphasised that there was 'quite a lot of luggage space behind the seats'. The total space was enough for a weekend, he reckoned, but not enough for a fortnight's holiday.

The doors were much more practical for carrying the odd small item than those on the TR2, but rather severe in their cut; the engine installation was as impressive as ever.

Even editor Bill Boddy, who was well used to vintage driving positions, found the steering wheel of 610 CRF too close for comfort in *Motor Sport's* test of November 1954, although he added: 'In such matters the Doretti has room for improvement, but after prolonged acquaintance a driver becomes used to minor inconveniences and gets much pleasure from the car.'

The TR3

Road tests of the TR3 continued to be uniformly good, even for the early models with their drum front brakes. Karl Ludvigsen discovered in the first road test report, in *SCI* in March 1956, that the extra power of the engine roughly balanced out the extra weight, his performance figures—of 11.4 seconds for the 0–60 mph, 17.8 seconds for the standing quarter mile, and a 100 mph maximum speed—being about the same as those recorded by Al Brannon's TR2.

The *SCI's* TR3 ran in its heaviest form, with steel hardtop, rear seat and wire wheels, and was equipped with overdrive operating on second, third and fourth gear. Ludvigsen found the gearbox a delight to use, although a hurried change from second to third could find a dead end in the reverse slot (a comment that had been made from time to time by other drivers, particularly ones in left-hand steering cars). He considered the seven-ratio set-up very useful, however, with only overdrive third, and direct fourth feeling at all alike. The whole car also felt a lot stiffer with the steel hardtop and its eight-bolt fixing. But the rear sidescreen holder, in particular, really got in the way of the driver's outside elbow. For those who liked the 'Farina-style' driving position—a modern style with arms outstretched that had become popular after one of its earliest exponents, Dr Guiseppe Farina, had won the world drivers' championship in 1950—Ludvigsen recommended the original non-adjustable steering column. The adjustable section of the new optional column did not allow it to be pushed in as close to the dashboard. He also observed that the steering was now free from the shaking which had plagued earlier cars and that the brakes did not fade with this wire-wheeled car. In conclusion, the *SCI* report said:

The nose of the TR2, or at least a prototype badged as such, after Belgrove had been at work on it ... and after the production engineers had prepared their replacement panel. To update a car's appearance, you simply unbolted one nose and substituted a new one!

'The TR3 represents the present peak of refinement of this type, and has much more to offer than the early cars. Several discordant elements remain, but they are not likely to perturb the enthusiastic driver.'

The Motor recorded notably better acceleration times when their test of a TR3 (registered RKV 335 and like that of *SCI* with the standard 3.7:1 rear axle ratio), appeared on 4 April, 1956. They set new standards with 0–30 mph in 3.6 seconds, 0–40 mph in 5.4 seconds, 0–50 mph in 7.5 seconds, 0–60 mph in 10.8 seconds, 0–70 mph in 14.6 seconds, 0–80 mph in 20.2 seconds, 0–90 mph in 28.8 seconds and the standing quarter mile in 18.1 seconds. Top speed (achieved in direct fourth) was substantially as that in the same ratio with the TR2 at 105.3 mph, but in overdrive top it was lower at 104 mph against 107 mph, showing the difference the optional 4.1:1 rear axle ratio would have made. Strangely, there was little comment on the way the fuel consumption had increased to an overall 27 mpg, although this was still good for a sports car. *The Motor* fully approved of the seven-ratio gearbox, although they commented:

The real change in the TR3 came with the introduction of disc front brakes—to the obvious appreciation of road testers everywhere.

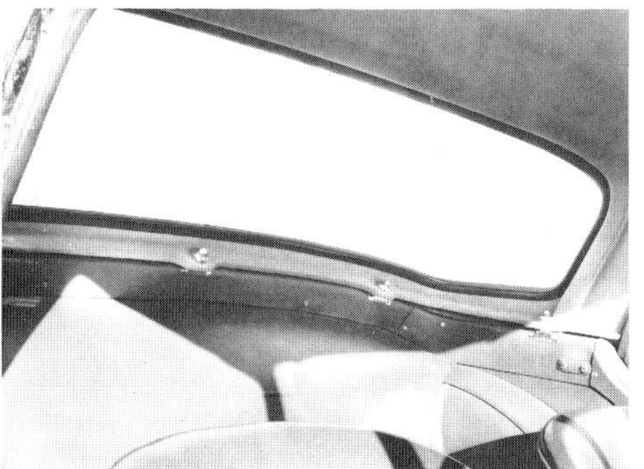

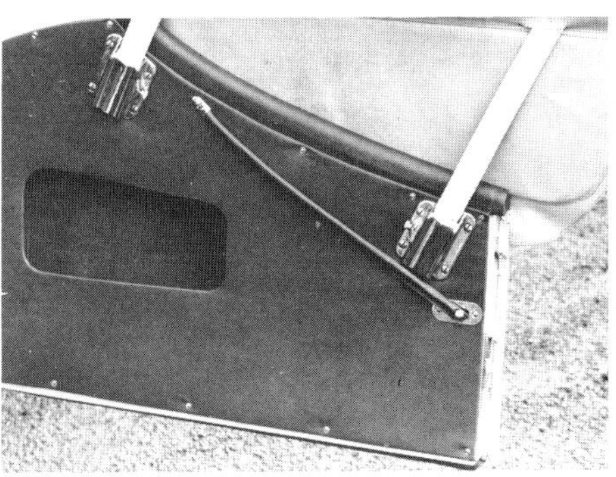

Three of the hard top's eight fixing bolts...

The prominent sidescreen holders and cord-pull door latch. Such a pull might have looked primitive, but it was light and effective and was used years later on Porsche's competition Carreras!

> 'In normal motoring, it is quite unnecessary to exploit the subtleties of these seven speeds to the full, but for competition work the availability of an exactly appropriate ratio can be of the greatest benefit.'

They noted that the chassis seemed to behave better at speed on rough and slippery roads, but did not say why, commenting only on the steel hardtop:

> 'On the whole it may find favour over the normal hood, for those who use their cars in closed trim almost all the year round, but it has positive disadvantages in space and noise without any great improvement in weather protection. Back draughts are notoriously difficult to avoid on small closed cars and it cannot be said that the Triumph designers have succeeded entirely in this respect...
>
> 'The new sidescreens are amongst the best we have encountered.'

The optional rear seat that aroused *The Motor's* interest and that of a surprisingly large number of customers.

They were enthusiastic also over the increase in body width, saying it added considerably to the car's comfort, but had mixed feelings over the optional rear seat. They said of this seat:

> 'For two very small children travelling behind parents of moderate height the arrangement is useful. For a larger occupant, such as a teenager travelling behind a front pair who require their seats in more rearward positions, the occasional seating is of very little use because knee-room is virtually non-existent, and a single transverse seat might have been of more general use.'

Road & Track were next to test a TR3, in June 1956. Their car was one of the first to reach the West coast of America, where they were based, and as a result was fitted with the older, instantly detachable, glass fibre hardtop because it was not anticipated that there would be much demand for the more permanent steel top there. *Road & Track* was intrigued by this fitting, pointing out that it 'dressed up the looks of the car considerably', but in spite of its contours being smoother than those of the normal soft top, it made no difference to drag when tested with a Tapley meter. They liked the new sidescreens and the rear seat, as well, commenting that it was not as cramped as might be thought—an unusual reaction, because, for decades, Americans had demanded more spacious interiors than European manufacturers usually provided.

Road & Track's car, which had the standard axle ratio, was not fitted with overdrive and proved to have a substantially higher maximum speed than their TR2 in the direct ratio, achieving a maximum of 104 mph. The 0–60 mph time was a respectable 12 seconds (*Road & Track* had long been against any form of 'brutality' in tests, almost invariably sticking to the rev counter's red line), and they commented on the growing interest in this standard that had been engendered by the influx of imported sports into America:

> 'Perhaps nowadays too much stress is laid on 0–60 times. Although the TR3 is fractionally quicker to 60, the standing start quarter mile is a better, fairer, test. With it there is practically no chance for human error or "fudging," and to shorten the quarter time by, say, five-tenths of a second takes quite a bit of doing.'

In this context, it is interesting to note that *Road & Track's* times with the TR2 and TR3 over the standing quarter mile were identical at 18.4 seconds. Fuel consumption, not surprisingly, was about 2 mpg heavier overall with the non-overdrive car, at 26–32 mpg.

Road & Track also commented on the growing trend for cars to be advertised at a low basic price, and then when the customer asked for one, he or she had little option other than to take a car loaded with expensive extras because it was the only one available. The German firm of Porsche were among those who provided the most flagrant examples of this pricing policy at the time. Of the Triumph, *Road & Track* said:

> 'There are a long list of optional extras that can run the price up, but there is hardly any American car owner these days who is not familiar with that pitfall, and with the Triumph, at least, the extras really are optional.'

Sports Cars Illustrated published the first full test of a disc-braked TR3, by Ludvigsen, in April 1957. Usually SCI's brake-fade test—which was similar to that used by all the specialist magazines— was considered to be a chore, but now Ludvigsen assumed the mantle of a pioneer and found it positively thrilling. He reported:

> 'From a dead stop, or nearly so, the machine is run up through the gears at

75–80 per cent maximum effort. At a genuine 60 percent, the clutch goes out and the brakes come on—hard, but not hard enough to break traction. The observer notes the maximum decelerometer reading, and as the car rolls to a rest, first gear is snicked in and away we go again. Ten times in a row—with a fast car taking about as long as it does to read about it . . . and this time we were really curious.

'First run was smooth—heavy pedal pressure but maximum stopping without a waver. Second was the same, like most other good cars. At the third we laughed—deceleration went up a point! It stayed up on the fourth stop, and went up again on the fifth. Still no swerve, still smooth, but the pedal was down a fraction. The sixth was slower, a driver factor, since the seventh was back up again. Each time we restarted now, in the frigid winter air, clouds of vapour billowed from the front wheel wells. They were hotter than any test brakes had ever been, but the ninth stop was as firm and fast as ever. Pedal feel was softening, and there were traces of swerve on the tenth halt, which was still among the best we've recorded. Discs were crackling hot, linings smelled to high heaven, but the darn TR3 stopped anyway.'

The rest of this test repeated the good impressions of the earlier TR3, except that *SCI* managed to get the 0–60 mph time down to 10.9 seconds by using first, second and second overdrive against 11.5 seconds with first, second, and third gears.

Road & Track then managed to get hold of a TR3 with all the competition extras, overdrive and 4.1:1 rear axle, wire wheels. Alfin rear drums, aluminium sump, and heavy duty shock absorbers, which took the price up from $2,665 to $3,039, the pound then retailing at about $3.90—a far cry from later years!

The TR3 was also tuned for maximum performance with a rich mixture, but although *Road & Track* took its new 'high-port' engine up to 5,500 rpm, rather than the red-line 5,000 rpm, the performance was relatively disappointing. They calculated that the change in gearing should have given a 10.8 per cent increase in performance, but an 8.6 per cent rise in weight—despite the lack of a hardtop—negated that. However, with the extra power of the engine they managed to raise their top speed to 106 mph with a 0–60 mph time of 11.4 seconds and a standing quarter mile in 17.9 seconds, achieved at the expense of an increase in fuel consumption to 18 mpg. Overdrive was not used for the acceleration tests, however, because it was slipping—but when it was engaged normally, the overall fuel consumption decreased to between 25 and 30 mpg. *Road & Track* concluded that as a 'competition-fun' machine, the TR3 had no equal in terms of perfomance per dollar.

With hindsight, the next test of the TR3, by *The Autocar* in their issue of 11 January, 1957, was quite revealing. The car, registered SKV 656, was one of the latest models, and fully equipped with steel hardtop, overdrive, wire wheels and spotlights, plus the standard ratio. They reported:

'Despite the power increase, and the smoother body shape with hardtop as compared with the ordinary hood of the first car we tested, some of the performance figures were not quite as good. However, they are a little higher than for the TR2 hardtop ... the main reasons for the present car not showing up quite so well are that the weight is now greater, and weather conditions on the Belgian autoroute [Britain at that time was still waiting for a motorway], where the acceleration testing took place, were decidely worse than those prevailing for the earlier tests. There was a stiff diagonal breeze, which was particularly noticeable at the higher speeds.'

Although *The Autocar* did not mention it at the time, this was the first published report of the chief problem with the steel hardtop, a feeling of less stability because of a raised centre of gravity for the car as a whole. *The Autocar* was quick to detect another change in handling, however, asking and answering:

'How does the TR3 hardtop behave on the road and in what way have the modifications affected its handling characteristics? One difference was unexpected: the stability of the back end on corners is not quite so good, particularly if the road surface is poor...

'A possible cause ... is that there is now a bigger, heavier, altogether stronger rear axle assembly ... General stability is of a fairly high standard, although driving can become a little tiring on fast, fairly straight roads when there is any wind. In such conditions the driver must keep the car straight by a conscious effort. A greater tendency for the car to follow its nose would then be welcome.'

The rest of *The Autocar's* extensive comments about the TR3 were complimentary, sticking to its well-known attributes and concluding:

'In its latest form, the TR3 is an exciting sports car, traditional to drive, fast, flexible and with first-class brakes. The steering is quick and light and visibility good. This latest model is as pleasant when it is closed up in the winter as it is in open form in the sunshine.'

Water splash test for the TR3's new brakes at the Motor Industry Research Association's track near Nuneaton, known as MIRA.

Triumph found this road test rather embarrassing, however, knowing that the car could perform better in less demanding circumstances. So they organised their test for *The Motor* with the same car in the summer, and were pleased to see far better performance figures in the issue of 3 July, 1957. *The Motor* managed a maximum of 110.8 mph against 103 mph, with an 11.4-second 0–60 mph (12.5 seconds for *The Autocar*), even the telling standing quarter mile time being 0.2 seconds less at 18.5 seconds. Triumph also felt that careful attention to tyres and pressures might alleviate the feeling of instability and asked Dunlop to make some suggestions to *The Motor*. The magazine duly reported:

> 'In deference to the speeds which would be maintained during performance testing on the Belgian motor road, the car came into our hands with the optionally-available Dunlop Road Speed tyres, and a request from the Dunlop engineers that a pressure of 40 psi should be used for testing, whereas for everyday driving a pressure of, at the most, 30 psi proved necessary for acceptable riding comfort. On dry roads the Road Speed tyres showed good cornering power and freedom from squeal, but in the wet they left a good deal to be desired, the back wheels sliding on slippery corners at the smallest touch of the throttle. Upon its return to England, the Triumph reverted to the normal Dunlop covers supplied as standard equipment, and the pressure was adjusted at 26 psi. The result, confirmed by experience with other TR models, was noticeably better roadholding at the speeds likely to be obtained on most occasions in this country, accompanied by some noise from the tyres in sharp corners, and slightly heavier steering.
>
> 'The two last features are further accentuated by adoption of the recommended pressures for "normal" driving of 22 lb and 24 lb respectively. Whether or not a differential between front and rear pressures is maintained is really a matter of personal taste. Softer tyres on the front wheels serve to increase the understeering tendency, which is inherent but not objectionable.'

Possibly due to the tyres and pressures—details of which were not revealed other than that the tyres were made by Dunlop—*Motor Sport* complained about the steering on SKV 656 in its test reported in July 1957. They said:

> 'When parking the driver finds the steering exceedingly heavy but it becomes almost too light at speed. It transmits little road shock or vibration, while there is mild castor-raction. It is, however, rather "dead" steering, lacking in immediate response ... corners can be taken fast, but a tendency to dart about spoils absolute precision, which vagueness of the steering does nothing to mitigate.'

Motor Sport then wound up its TR test by being thoroughly prophetic: 'It is selling splendidly in dollar markets and should continue to do so for a long time to come, especially if it could be re-styled...'

Front three-quarter, rear three-quarter, head-on, interior and profiles of *Motor Sport*'s road test TR3.

In those days, most British road testers worked in close conjunction with the motor manufacturers and were loathe to criticise a car too severely. They were also living through a time of rapid technological advance during which the standards they used for judgment were altered as quickly. All this was revealed by Bolster's report on his test of SKV 655, an open sister car to the hardtop model. Bolster, whose comments on the TR2's brakes and exhaust note had been rather muted, reported in *Autosport* on 27 September, 1957:

> 'I had to criticise the original TR2 for a noisy exhaust, but this has been eliminated, which greatly increases the pleasure of handling the car.
>
> 'In matters of suspension and roadholding, I am raising my sights all the time. Thus, a car which called forth extravagant praise a few years ago might be regarded as being merely adequate today. This is natural as techniques improve, and so I make no excuse for subjecting the TR3 to a very searching test.
>
> 'I would regard the Triumph as being a very safe car in the hands of the average driver. This is because it does not at first give the impression of holding the road particularly well. With experience, one finds that the adhesion is in fact better than it at first appeared, and the machine is always very controllable. Yet, for some reason which is not easy to define, it does not encourage the man at the wheel to take undue risks.
>
> 'The cornering power is not exceptionally high, but when the limit is reached and the car slides, it remains perfectly easy to handle. The rear end does break away, but quite gently and with no undue tendency to spin. . .

'I have spoken of the improved silencing. Another criticism that I made in my original road test concerned the brakes. The current car has the front discs ... which really do overcome all the fading troubles. In the past, the rear brakes of Triumphs have not always stood up to their work, but some time ago the drums were increased in size and all is well now.'

For some reason, Bolster's performance figures were a good deal poorer than normal and could not be considered to be a true representation of what a good TR3 should be like.

The TR3A

The British edition of *Sports Cars Illustrated* managed to obtain a TR3A that was so new it had not been registered for a test reported in February 1958. In fact, the only other one they had seen was a car registered VHP 529, on reconnaisance for the Monte Carlo Rally. Suspicions that their car was either a works development machine, or that *SCI* went only by speedometer readings (which were around 8 per cent fast on early TRs) were raised by their performance figures of a 115-mph maximum speed and a 9.4-second 0–60 mph. However, they considered the new grille to be a notable improvement along with the handles for the doors and luggage boot. A road test of the TR3A by the American edition of *SCI* a month later, in March 1958, was far more representative. Although their car was also new, the TR3A had been on sale in

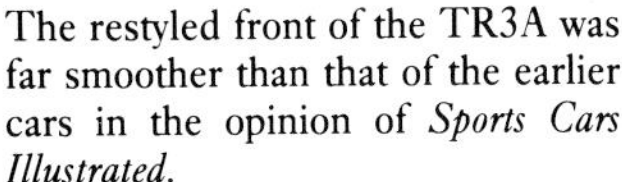

The restyled front of the TR3A was far smoother than that of the earlier cars in the opinion of *Sports Cars Illustrated*.

The TR3A's rear end changed in detail, too, with individual fared indicator lights and a central luggage boot handle.

America for some time then, and it was straight from the showroom, or as *SCI* put it, 'no super-tuned cream puff.' After a pleasant 2,000 miles running in this 4.1:1 axle non-overdrive car—which had only 35 miles on the clock when they got it—a top speed of 103 mph with a 0–60 mph time of 12.6 seconds and an 18.6-second standing quarter mile were recorded, with the comment that it was a car that would keep on getting better.

The mild restyling at the front was considered to be 'far smoother', although they felt grumpy about the sidescreens, saying:

> 'The exterior of the doors are curved surfaces, however the mating surfaces of the side curtains are flat. The result is that the surfaces meet only at the centre, allowing cold air to channel onto the back of the neck. We made the car comfortable by stuffing two wool mufflers into the gaps...
>
> 'On the other side of the ledger, the thing that impressed us most was the excellent quality control at the Coventry works. You get the feeling that if you own a Triumph for a hundred years, nothing is going to fall off of it. This, unfortunately, can not be said of all our domestic automobiles.' If only Britain could have kept that reputation...

The extent to which the performance of TR3 competition cars had been improved was revealed by *Autosport's* test of SAH 137, the ex-Sid Hurrell marque-racing machine owned by Neil Dangerfield, in the issue of 26 January, 1962. This car was fitted with a full race 2.2-litre engine, TR3A-style glass fibre

The sidescreens of the TR3A didn't quite follow the curvature of the doors.

Sid Hurrell's racing TR3A, registered SAH 137, was one of the top contenders in British club events during the late 1950s. The off-side headlamps have been removed from these cars to act as air scoops for the carburettors—a common modification at the time. Hurrell's example was also fitted with a centrally-mounted oil cooler.

body and competition suspension, complete with front anti-roll bar. The maximum power of the engine, which revved up to 6,000 rpm, was available between 4,000 and 5,500 rpm and was enough to take the aero-screened car, in overdrive top, up to a theoretical 130 mph. However, the roads were wet and icy, and the tester, Patrick McNally, felt ill at ease on a combination of Michelin X tyres that were worn at the back and better at the front, inflated to 35 psi all round. Nevertheless, he took the TR3 up to 120 mph in direct fourth with a mean 0–60 mph time of 8.2 seconds. His only criticism of this *Autosport* championship class-winning car was that its gearbox ratios felt too wide—a deficiency which he expected to be cured on the new TR4.

The TR4

Road tests of the TR4 continued to be complimentary when considered as a whole, although the redesigning of the body and the dated rear suspension came in for some criticism. One of the first tests was by John Blunsden for the British magazine *Motor Racing* in October 1961. He thought the new steering gear was a good compromise between the sensitivity demanded by a hard driver and the forgiving nature needed by the more leisurely. Blunsden was happy to observe that the new engine retained the excellent low-speed torque characteristics of the earlier unit and used it to good effect to record broadly similar performance figures of 11.6 seconds for the 0–60 mph, and a 17.8-second standing quarter mile, with 110 mph flat out. The car's overdrive was not used for these tests, which brought the fuel consumption down to 24 mpg; but Blunsden estimated that between 28 and 34 mpg would be seen in more normal use. He found the new synchromesh strong and the clutch pedal's travel a bit too long, but he was quite happy with the ride, which felt softer. The new ventilation system also worked 'extremely well'. Blunsden said:

One of the first TR4 cars to be built was registered 9132 HP and used extensively for Press demonstrations, with or without its number plates: it is seen here undergoing handbrake tests on MIRA's graduated hill.

'The new car has lost none of the appeal of the earlier TRs, but with improved comfort and performance, a stylish appearance and more subdued road manners, it represents the most significant advance since the series was introduced eight years ago. It should prove a winner.'

Douglas Armstrong was equally impressed when he reported on the TR4 in the same month for *Cars Illustrated*, the successor to the British edition of *Sports Cars Illustrated*. He said:

'The Italian Michelotti ... must be awarded full marks for the new bodywork. Although it is all new there is still a hint of the "TR look" but the car is now handsome whereas before it could only be assessed as neat and tidy ... Internally it has been brought up to a standard which puts it in the luxury sports car class. With the adjustable steering column the driving position is much improved. In spite of its increased body dimensions the TR4 still feels a small car externally when it is being driven, but the extra width inside the car is immediately evident. The handling is much improved and the car can be cornered fast, although there is still a suspicion of "TR weave" present. The clutch is sweet, the floor gearchange smooth and the engine as sweet as a limousine.'

The new ventilation system excited generous comments, particularly from Blunsden in *Motor Racing*.

Not everybody would agree with the extent of Armstrong's enthusiasm, but it must be remembered that his comments reflected how he felt in 1961 rather than how people might view the TR4 decades later. And the American journalists did not think of the TR4 in the same way as the Britons. *Road & Track* said in their issue of February 1962 that the shock absorber settings might be lighter than those of the TR3 'but they were by no means soft, even yet'. They also considered the steering to be rather dead at slow speeds although it was 'all that one could wish' at 70 mph; the higher first gear ratio on their non-overdrive car (which had the higher axle ratio, of course) also made a useful difference when plunging through traffic. They had mixed feelings about the styling, however, saying it was 'rather attractive in some respects, but it fails in others'. *Road & Track* like it better than that of the TR3, but hankered after something similar to the TRS which had raced at Le Mans. Styling aside, they commented on the body:

'On strictly practical grounds, there is no disputing the worth of the new bodywork. The car's squared-off stern provides the space for a relatively large luggage locker and a couple of much-needed inches of width have been added to the interior. The coming of true civilization was most apparent in the provision of roll-up windows. Naturally the side window arrangement has eliminated the cutaway door, and some hard-core enthusiasts will object to that. Nevertheless, most people do not really care for that cold-wind-on-the-kidneys effect and will consider the new doors, with or without sliding windows, a definite improvement.

'Our enthusiasm for the side windows was largely dissipated in the struggle that ensued the first time we attempted to erect the top. This top is

Douglas Armstrong waxed lyrical on the TR4's interior in *Cars Illustrated*.

weather-tight, has large windows and offers good vision astern but, by actual count, there were no less than 29 snap fasteners, a pair of hooks and a long metal slide—all of which must be worked in proper sequence before the top-bows are locked up into place. Time spent in "drill" would make the job reasonably quick, but it does seem that there is room for improvement in the basic system.'

Road & Track returned the same performance figures as *Motor Racing* except that they got the 0–60 mph time down to 10.5 seconds. Their new rivals, *Car and Driver* (which had taken over from the US edition of *Sports Cars Illustrated*) found their non-overdrive TR4 a little slower when they tested it two months later, in April 1962. They were quite explicit about the handling and ride, saying:

'The handling of the TR4 is perfectly predictable under all circumstances. The car gently but definitely oversteers. On easy curves the oversteer does not make itself felt to any extent, but on hard corners one does not have to go very fast for the rear end to try to help the car round the turn. If sometimes unpleasant, this is an important advantage on a winding road, both in reducing driver fatigue and as a safety factor in itself. On straightaways, however, the tracking is not perfect, and the car must be steered all the way.

> 'The ride, on a second-class surface, is something less than comfortable. The longitudinal semi-elliptic leaf springs are identical with those of the TR3, so the same choppy ride is inevitable. It was not uncommon for one rear wheel to be lifted clean off the road on a straight, but uneven, stretch. If this sort of thing happens on a curve, the car is automatically forced off the correct line. If there is one important disadvantage in the TR4, it is certainly the design of the rear suspension and the choice of spring rates. On a completely smooth surface, the car corners like an image of perfection, so the problem should be in no way insoluble. One cannot help wondering how a long-standing fault of the TR3 was permitted to live on in the TR4.'

All these comments were echoed by *Autocar* and *The Motor* when they published tests of the TR4 on 5 January, 1962 and 11 July, 1962, respectively. *Autocar's* non-overdrive model, registered 6179 RW, managed 102 mph with a 10.9-second 0–60 mph and a 17.8-second standing quarter mile, returning 21–26 mpg; *The Motor's* overdrive car with Surrey top, registered 6184 RW, achieved 28 mpg with a 109 mph maximum speed and similar acceleration times.

Bolster extracted 5,600 rpm from his non-overdrive TR4, whereas *Autocar* could not get their machine to pull above 5,000 rpm in top, with the result that he got the 0–60 mph down to 10.2 seconds for *Autosport* on 14 September, 1962, with a 17.4-second standing quarter mile, a top speed of 112 mph *and* 27–30 mpg! He complained about the 29 press-studs, but noted that the hood kept out the heaviest rain he had encountered in Europe.

The TR4 was a ready recipient for tuning equipment, as Sid Hurrell was to demonstrate with his new car.

Bill Boddy of *Motor Sport* complained in January 1963 at having to wait for the chance to test the Surrey-topped TR4, 6184 RW, but found it well to his liking, although the driving position seemed rather strange. He said:

'The seats do not seem at all abnormal, the cushion being flat and solid, the backs making a snug fit round the body. Yet after driving the TR4 nearly 350 miles between breakfast and dinner, I was not conscious of more than average discomfort, although the pedals offset to the right have to be contended with. A less pleasant aspect of driving the TR4, for a short-legged driver, is the long movement of the clutch pedal and to a lesser extent the positioning of the accelerator well over to the off-side, because this necessitates moving the seat closer to the steering wheel than would otherwise be desirable. There is only limited stowage room for the left, or clutch, foot. These objections apart, there are no discomforts with conducting the Triumph other than those habitual to a sports car.'

Rear three-quarter view of the Surrey-topped TR4 tested by *Motor Sport*.

Road & Track then had another crack at the TR4, reporting in September 1964 on a Stromberg-equipped non-overdrive car, which proved to have virtually the same performance as their earlier machine. They commented tellingly, however:

'The impression one gains from driving the Triumph is that it is an excellent machine for the average sports car driver or, alternatively, the Sprite or Spitfire owner who wants to trade up. We have criticized the car from the chassis and suspension standpoint and we can only assume that improvements will be made by Standard-Triumph along the lines of the Spitfire and the new Triumph 2-litre sedan, both of which feature independent rear suspension.

'However, the Triumph TR4 has many more virtues than vices. For $3,000 you get an honest $3,000 worth of sports car in the traditional

> manner, which will do anything that is expected of it. It is backed by a good service and parts organisation, and its conventional layout, good accessibility, and the straightforward design of its components presents no problems to the average mechanic, an important consideration for those people who live outside the metropolitan areas. And owners of Porsches, Jaguars and Ferraris might add that it is an important consideration even for those who live in the metropolitan areas.'

Meanwhile *Car and Driver* had tested the ex-Gates Sebring car in August 1963 with a standard overdrive machine for comparison. The competition TR4 had around 145 bhp from its Kastner engine, a 4.55:1 sprint axle ratio, limited-slip differential, torque rods, stiffened suspension, and wider Goodyear racing tyres. *Car and Driver* were not at all impressed with the competition machine's 'street' potential, pointing out that the tyres were useless in the wet and caused the TR to dart around inconsistently on rough surfaces; the suspension seemed to owe more to stiffness than science, and was only suitable for a billiard-table surface. The car oversteered less than the standard one and had overdrive only on third and fourth. But it proved to be one-tenth of a second faster than a Ferrari Superamerica they had tested over the standing quarter mile at 17.1 seconds with an 8.9-second 0–60 mph, and, more important, a 25.6-second 0–100 mph against the standard car's 41 seconds. Top speed on the 4.55 ratio (used for SCCA class D production sprints) was 115 mph although it was capable of 125–130 mph in theory, a 4.1 axle having been run at Sebring. *Car and Driver* summed up:

> 'The moral? The full-house, ex-Sebring TR4 is a very fast car not recommended for street use; the stock TR4 is almost as fast, yet much more civilized.'

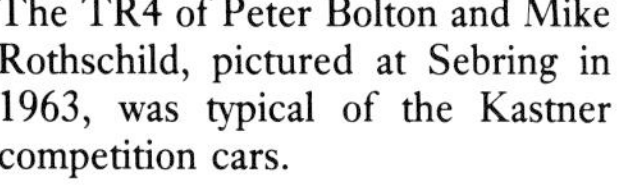

The TR4 of Peter Bolton and Mike Rothschild, pictured at Sebring in 1963, was typical of the Kastner competition cars.

Autocar then tested two modified TR4s, a Lawrencetune version by the firm which had prepared the works Morgans (fitted with TR engines), for international racing, and a full works Triumph, the rally car registered 6 VC. The Lawrencetune test, on 22 March, 1963, revealed a worthwhile improvement in performance although the car in question, registered 151 MRO, was not directly comparable with *Autocar's* standard TR4 test car because it had overdrive. It used the same 3.7 axle ratio, however. The Lawrencetune conversion—which cost £150 for the engine and £26 for suspension work—consisted of a modified cylinder head and special free-flow exhaust, twin Weber 45DCOE carburettors, an oil cooler, and, on the front suspension only, Koni adjustable shock absorbers and an anti-roll bar. The best results were achieved by using the overdrive which gave a 112.5-mph maximum, a 9-second 0–60 mph, a 28.9-second 0–100 mph (against 46.3 seconds) and a 17-second standing quarter mile, with 19 mpg. The standing quarter mile time was increased to 17.2 seconds when direct drive only was used for comparison with the standard car. The front suspension modifications were found to delay the onset of the TR's typical front-end weave until near the maximum speed.

The works rally car test on 25 October, 1963, revealed a far more savage machine. It had similar engine modifications to that of the Lawrencetune car, with a wilder camshaft, giving around 130 bhp. The suspension was much stiffer, however, and all the sound deadening material inside the car had been removed to save weight—with the result that the ride was awful (even if the handling was much improved) and the occupants were practically deafened. Although drastic moves had been made to reduce weight—by fitting glass fibre and alloy bodywork, for instance—the actual car weighed about 100 lb more than normal because of its heavy-duty springs, sump guard and oversize 18-gallon fuel tank. A 4.3:1 axle ratio from the Standard Sportsman saloon, helped improve acceleration times, however, giving an 8.5-second 0–60 mph, 26.4-second 0–100 mph, and 16.8-second standing quarter mile with an unchanged top speed of 112 mph. Something had to give, though, and fuel consumption increased to 18 mpg.

The Dove GTR4

The Harrington coachwork conversion on the Dove GTR4 was well received by the road testers. *Autocar* were particularly enthusiastic about it in their issue of 7 June, 1963, saying that it was possible to accommodate four adults inside the car if the two at the front did not mind sitting with the seats well forward, the two at the back 'adopting a slightly hunched attitude'. Obviously that all depended on the size of the adults, but for its design function, the GTR4 coped well with two adults and one or two small children in *Autocar's* opinion.

Their example, Dove's well-known demonstrator, registered DOV 1, weighed 450 lb more than the open two-seater they tested, partly because it was fitted with overdrive. It also had a balanced engine with gas-flowed head—which was noticeably smoother in operation than a normal TR unit—although it did

The Dove GTR4 received good reviews from the road testers, despite problems with the capacity of the fuel tank.

not depart far from standard specification. The weight penalty was reflected in poorer acceleration figures at the bottom end of the scale, the Dove GTR4 needing 12 seconds for the 0–60 mph and 18.4 seconds for the standing quarter mile. The superior nature of its aerodynamics were confirmed by a 0–100 mph figure of 43.6 seconds, however, and an 80–100 mph acceleration time of 16.5 seconds against 25.4 seconds for the soft-top car. Top speed was, perhaps, limited to 106 mph by a request to keep to the recommended 5,000 rpm rev limit. Overall fuel consumption of 24 mpg was artificially high, *Autocar* said, because the car was used extensively in heavy traffic; 25–30 mpg should have been possible with more varied use.

Bolster managed to improve the 0–60 mph acceleration time, with 11.2 seconds and a standing quarter mile in 17.9 seconds when his test of the same car appeared in *Autosport* on 12 July, 1963, although his top speed worked out at only 104 mph and the fuel consumption at 23–26 mpg. He found it difficult to believe that the car had a 15-gallon tank, as claimed, because he had to walk five miles when it ran out! He did not question the maker's claim of a weight penalty of only 56 lb, however. Bolster was highly complimentary about the car's appearance, saying:

> 'There is nothing improvised about this construction. Indeed, the shape of the car is so attractive, and the finish so good, that crowds collect wherever the machine is parked.'

Blunsden had the misfortune to have a Dove GTR4, registered APA 787B, that needed mechanical attention when he tested it for the American magazine, *Sports Car Graphic*, in October 1964. So his performance figures did not ought to bear comparison with the earlier ones—but the hardy nature of the basic TR4 was reflected in a 0–60 mph time of 12.4 seconds, a standing quarter mile in 18.6 seconds and a top speed of 108 mph! It would also confirm that the Stromberg carburettors on this car were accompanied by no loss of performance against the SUs fitted to DOV 1 because the mechanical defects on the Blunsden car included at least one piston. He commented favourably on the bodywork, especially in its detail design with fitted tool trays.

The TR4A

Road testers, generally, appreciated that the TR4A still represented excellent value for money at around £1,000—but, Americans particularly, asked why it had not been fitted with the new six-cylinder engine from the Triumph 2000. One of the earliest tests, by *Autocar*, was also one of the most complimentary. They said of the independent rear suspension fitted to their standard overdrive model, registered EDU 43C:

> 'The greatest improvement in the TR undoubtedly comes from the new rear suspension ... it is much softer and better able to cope with rough roads. Longer front springs give more suspension travel, and consequently

the ride characteristics have changed out of all recognition. Before, one could never forget the live back axle, which pattered and thumped about, especially if disturbed in a corner taken under power. Now the TR can be driven deliberately fast at obstacles it would have shied from before.

'On motorways the undulating waves from subsidences cause no recurrent pitching and it was only on our closely spaced undulations at M.I.R.A. [the motor industry's research track near Nuneaton in the Midlands] that we were able to get the back to kick up in the air. On pave there is a good deal of bottoming, but the car is not thrown from side to side and keeps a very true path.

'Cornering is transformed, and there is now a steady degree of understeer, with quite a lot of body roll. If power is applied early in a bend, eventually the tail will slide out, but this doesn't happen until well beyond normal speeds. Sometimes, when taking the double bends of a roundabout, for instance, there seems to be a slight rear wheel steering effect which upsets one's chosen line and causes the car to go through a kind of rolling choppiness.

'Part of this lack of precise cornering is due to the steering, which now has 3½ turns from lock to lock instead of 2½. It is considerably lighter than before, and it calls for no great effort to wind between locks with the car stationary ... however, at speed there is a certain delay in response to slight movements which seems to stem from the rubber mounting of the steering rack. Side gusts tend to displace the car noticeably.

'At maximum speed in a straight line the car is much more stable than the TR4 and all the previous wandering has been eliminated. Once the car is set up on a steady radius, like a fast motorway curve, it holds its line accurately.'

Autocar were well pleased with the other new features of the car and returned similar performance figures to those of the TR4, explaining that the heavier weight of the new overdrive model compensated for its extra power. The extra torque gave it slightly faster top-gear acceleration in the mid-range, however. The actual figures were 109 mph top speed, an 11.4-second 0–60 mph, and an 18.5-second standing quarter mile with a 0.5-second improvement in the top-gear test. Fuel consumption was 25 mpg.

Sports Car Graphic approved of the new independent rear suspension in an assessment published in May 1965 although their car was a prototype which had too-soft rear springs. They said: 'There was one advantage to our testing it this way; it really proved that the geometry under maximum wheel travel was excellent.'

It was the only such car in America then (about February 1965, allowing for the time it took to get the test into print), and was probably the same car that *Road & Track* used for their test, also printed in May 1965. They were equally enthusiastic about the rear suspension, even if it did feel wallowy, saying that it was 'little short of remarkable,' and adding:

'Although the optional i.r.s. will add about $125–$150 to the delivered price of the car, we can't imagine that many buyers will choose the TR4A without it. Equipped like our test car—which had overdrive, wire wheels, radio, seatbelts, windshield washer, heater, tonneau cover, whitewall tyres and independent rear suspension—the TR4A will deliver at about $3,500, plus tax, licenses and local transportation, if any. This adds up to what might be considered a lot of money for a fairly old-fashioned type of sports car that has been considerably civilized and refined but is still not as new as yesterday by any stretch of the imagination.'

In the circumstances, they felt it right to inquire why it hadn't been fitted with an uprated version of the 2000 engine at the same time . . . and recorded a top speed of 107 mph with a 0–60 mph time of 10.5 seconds and a standing quarter mile in 17.5 seconds. *Car and Driver* then got the TR4A down to 9.8 seconds for the 0–60 mph with their test published in the same month, but they still asked for a 2000 engine because they couldn't get the rear wheels to spin so easily with the new rear suspension. Their comments on the handling of this obviously too-soft car were similar to those of *Autocar*, and they added:

'You may notice, if you are a very sharp Triumph type, that the TR4A has a new top. No more will one be asked to erect a framework only slightly less complicated than a Coney Island roller coaster and then strap a cover in place. The new top yanks into place (virtually one-handed) in a flash with the top fabric all neatly attached. Pip on a few snaps, and then dog it down with the pair of over-centre latches above the windshield. Gloriosky, Zero! Unhappily, the time may come when you will want to return the top to its well; then is when the trouble may start. You see, in providing a top frame that scissors up and down, Triumph has succeeded in making one that will also function with marvellous effectiveness. Fling the top carelessly down, and you may find that the frame has scissored so many holes in the fabric that it looks like a poncho for an octopus.'

The content of the conservative *Road & Track* and the more radical *Car and Driver* were still much the same, but the language was becoming quite different. Not everybody was enthusiastic about the seats fitted to the TR4A, but they found a friend in editor Gregor Grant when he took *Autosport's* road test car, EDU 43C, to Monte Carlo-and-back from Britain for the issue of 10 September, 1965. He said:

'The designers must surely drive the cars themselves, for I could not possibly criticize seating, or the driving positions possible with the generous adjustment provided. They have obviously studied creature comfort as regards all weather equipment, for not a drop of water did that hood let in. . .'

Like Bolster, Grant was no mean driver, and recorded a top speed of 108 mph, with a 10.3-second 0–60 mph and a 17.4-second standing quarter mile. His fuel consumption figures must also be considered quite definitive at

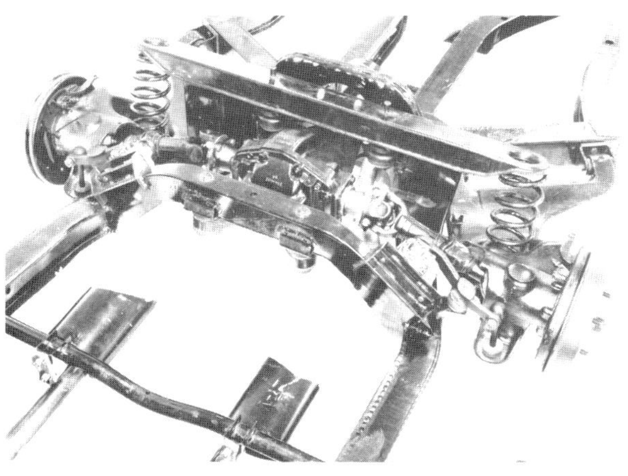

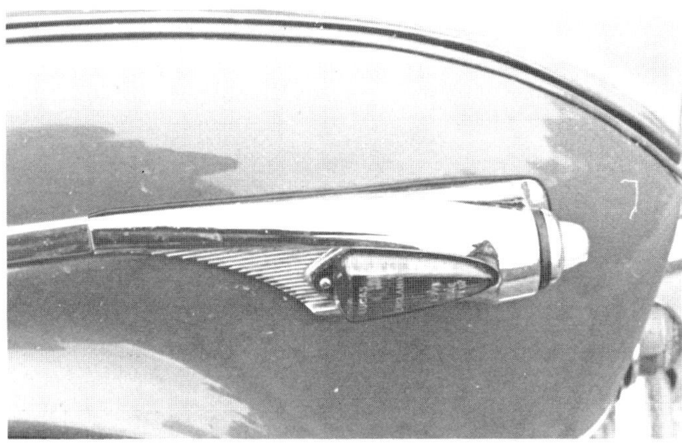

Motor considered the TR4A's new independent rear suspension to be a great improvement on the old live axle layout.

The combined sidelights and indicator repeaters of the TR4A were considered quite ingenious.

28–30 mpg for normal driving and 24–26 mpg for fast, now that car was well run-in.

Motor returned almost identical figures with a sister car, registered EDU 45C, in their issue of 18 September, 1965, saying:

> 'To say that the Triumph TR4A is a much-improved car which, for £1,000, goes very fast, stops very quickly, and is reasonably economical, paints only half a picture. From our own experience after 2,000 miles, this is not a car that always makes friends immediately but it is significant that those who drove it most grew to like it very much. The new independent rear suspension has improved the ride and roadholding, especially on indifferently surfaced roads, but the scuttle shake and body dither we have noted on earlier cars over really bad bumps are unfortunately still evident, despite a re-design of the back chassis members.
>
> 'A relatively big beefy engine combined with no fewer than seven forward gears is a good formula for providing a keen driver with lots of fun and short journey times. The performance is both vivid and relaxed and you could cruise all day at 100 mph without fuss, excessive noise or using too much petrol. Excellent brakes are inherited from earlier TRs and the handling and steering are enjoyable, if not the best you can buy.
>
> 'Apart from new seats which some drivers found disappointing, the civilized cockpit is comfortable, well trimmed and ventilated, and now protected by one of the very best soft-top hoods—except that when it is folded a family man can no longer pile his children in the back.'

The interior and seating came in for mostly good comments.

The TR5

The 150-bhp fuel injection engine in the TR5 was welcomed with open arms by the testers. *Autocar* were very enthusiastic about the increase in performance on 4 April, 1968, when they found that the new car was capable of 120 mph with a 0–100 mph time of 28.5 seconds, a full 20 seconds faster than the TR4A. And 'anything under 17 seconds for the standing quarter mile is exciting; the TR5 does it in 16.8 seconds...' They then went on to add, sagely:

> 'Unfortunately one has to pay for this extra urge, and the TR5 is the thirstiest TR so far. Our overall fuel consumption of 19.6 mpg is, of course, partly the result of much hard driving, but it seems unlikely that even the most restrained behaviour would wring much more than 25 mpg from it.'

Nevertheless, they were well pleased with the car, a non-overdrive model registered LHP 295F. They said:

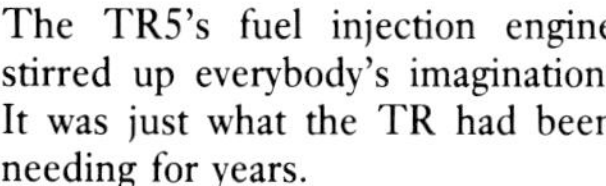

The TR5's fuel injection engine stirred up everybody's imagination. It was just what the TR had been needing for years.

> 'Compared with its predecessors, the TR5 is a complete transformation. As we have remarked before, the heart of a car is its engine and the TR5 has an eager unit which responds just as the sports car driver wants. The rest of the car is traditional rather than dated, well modernised so that overall and above all it is very much a fun car still.'

These feelings were confirmed by *Motor*, who recorded similar performance figures with another non-overdrive model, registered LHP 288F, in their issue of 4 May, 1968, and said:

> 'On the basis that high maximum and cruising speeds and vivid

acceleration are the essential ingredients of a true sports car, this magnificent power unit is the answer to the enthusiast's prayer. Once above its rather lumpy idle it explodes its torque on to the road with effortless ease to the accompaniment of a melodious howl from the exhaust which must delight even the most decibel-conscious ear. And, considering the margin of performance over the TR4A, the increase in fuel consumption is relatively small. Other improvements seem less significant beside the new engine ... but the powerful brakes are even better with bigger discs and a vacuum servo ... Steering and roadholding are enjoyable though not outstanding and the extra power tends to exaggerate the firm ride and tendency for the tail to dip when accelerating and cornering hard. Some of the scuttle shake and body dither on really bad surfaces, that we have criticized before, are also still evident.'

Bolster was equally happy when he tested yet another non-overdrive TR5, registered LHP 294F, for *Autosport's* issue of 31 May, 1968. He returned another set of almost identical performance figures and said:

'Without any doubt, this is the best Triumph yet. It is a car of exciting appearance with sporting lines, but it has the luxury and mechanical refinement usually associated with large and expensive saloons. Fuel injection adds interest to the specification but above all it improves the performance and the flexibility.'

Without doubt, the best Triumph yet, said Bolster of the TR5.

Motor Sport spent a hectic four days covering 2,084 miles while chasing the Gulf London Rally, in the same car that Bolster had used, for their test published in August 1968. Their comments were similar to those of the other journals, with special emphasis on the tyres:

> 'Leaving Manchester Airport at the start of the rally, we soon ran into torrential rain, and in these flooded conditions the Michelin XAS tyres showed up excellently, draining so well that we never had a nasty moment with aquaplaning, which most other people seemed to be experiencing. In just damp conditions, though, with a slick road surface, they did tend to let go, and with the car's inbuilt tendency towards understeer it was possible to slide into corners with the front wheels on more lock than necessary, but with 150 bhp driving the rear wheels these could easily be unstuck to bring the car round and point it out of the corner before "feathering" the sticky throttle in again to accelerate gently away. Under heavy braking also it was possible to lock the front wheels, but cadence braking, naturally, minimised the effect.'

That was all very well for the skilled driver, but the vast majority of people who bought the TR5 new had never heard of cadence braking, where the pedal pressure is released just before the wheel locks and then reapplied, let alone tried it. They would have been better advised to drive more slowly...

Cars and Car Conversions, which had succeeded *Cars Illustrated*, were starting to feel thoroughly nostalgic about sports cars by the time they tried LHP 288F in September 1968. They commented:

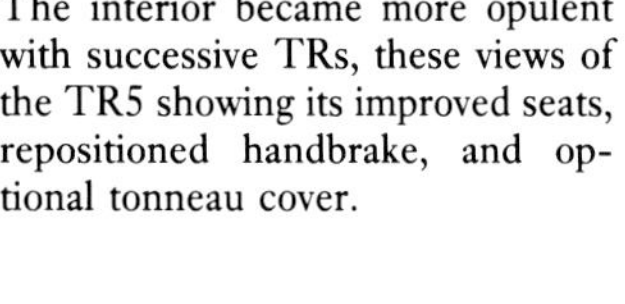

The interior became more opulent with successive TRs, these views of the TR5 showing its improved seats, repositioned handbrake, and optional tonneau cover.

'Time and again we've rambled on in these pages about the dying breed of sports cars, about how the modern sporting carriage is either soft, pansy, soggy and slow (unless it's a saloon, which is worse in a way) and about how no-one makes a car for young men with red blood in their veins any more. We've been doing that for years.

'And then what happened? Triumphs, or Standard-Triumph, or Leyland, or BLMH, or whoever it actually is these days, handed us a TR5 PI for a few days to go and have a road test in. And if no-one else makes a car which fulfils our requirements as a full-blooded sports car, they do. And this is it. Such few cars as did measure up to scratch for the job have, in the main, been pretty vintage in outlook—rather primitive where creature comforts are concerned, a bit fierce for the wife to go shopping in and strictly not for false-teeth wearers where ride is concerned. Most of them went well enough, but revealed a certain dated approach to the problem. But the TR5, apart from a rather old-hat body style combines all the attributes of a Man's Motor car with enough modern touches to swing the balance.'

The TR250

The Americans felt quite differently about the TR250, with only *Road & Track*, reporting in December 1967, not too upset that they didn't get the fuel injection engine. They said the carburettor power unit was nicely engineered—'you get that impression just by looking under the hood'—its smoothness giving the car a lot more refinement, with the extra torque adding to that impression. So far as the rest of the car was concerned, they said:

The TR250's new, smaller, steering wheel, and redesigned face vents, shared with the TR5, aroused good reactions from *Road & Track*.

'The people compartment has undergone some changes that are, we think, for the better. The instruments have been restyled for improved legibility, the seats have been reshaped and made more comfortable, the folding top now has an inner lining and there are new catches for the windshield. We also like the new steering wheel, not only because it is leather-covered but also because it is an inch smaller in diameter and has proportionately more space around it for such things as legs and knuckles. There is also a new set of vents that make the TR250 one of the best ventilated sports cars we've encountered.

'The wheels that come as standard on the TR250 are steel discs with attractive mag-styled trim covers. These, it seems to us, are perfectly acceptable in appearance and suit the looks of the car much better than the unattractive and unadorned disc wheels with which TRs have been equipped since time immemorial.'

The fuel injection metering unit of the TR5 was located behind the distributor at the top of the picture, feeding each port through individual pipes crossing the cam cover to the inlet manifold.

In performance, *Road & Track* found the TR250's acceleration to be very close to that of their TR4A with a 10.6-second 0–60 mph, a 17.8-second standing quarter mile and a maximum speed in overdrive top of 107 mph. Fuel consumption was better than the TR5 at 22–25 mpg.

Sports Car Graphic decided that the new engine made the zestful driver realise that the TR250 was a touring car at all times and could only be a 'race-car-in-hiding after many hours and dollars had been spent in preparation'. Apart from that, they added in May 1968:

> 'Our only gripe was in the new gear spacing. First and second are quite close together, which we found ideal when we wanted to drive the car hard, but got to be a bit of bother when lugging our way home on crowded freeways. The upshift to second seemed normal all too often and we wound up keeping it in first for extended periods. Conversely, second and third have quite a gap and charging up on-ramps to the freeway meant leaving it in second gear until near the 5,500 rpm redline to prevent an alarming lack of acceleration when dropping into third gear. Third and fourth are as close together as first and second, which produced a lack of deceleration upon gearing down from fourth to third at anything less than illegal highway speeds. But it is extremely smooth, all things considered…'

Bob Brown, in *Car and Driver*, was far more vocal about the TR250 in June 1968. As a former TR4 owner who had suffered a wheel falling off after an accident, he admitted not being a TR fan. He said it would need a rabid Triumph-lover to be happy with any TR250 because 'what you are getting for the extra money is a smoother but slower car'. However, he admitted that the TR250—which was 1.7 seconds slower up to 60 mph than *Car and Driver's* TR4A—was a lot smoother and more tractable, so he decided to blame the government, going on to describe a weird feeling on the over-run caused by their new anti-smog laws. Brown said:

> 'Lean mixtures, which are not conducive to maximum power, are essential for minimum smog emission, and if the TR250's jets were much smaller they'd be blanks. Normally, with the throttle fully closed, vacuum zooms up on the overrun and sucks raw gas out of the idle jets, enrichening the mixture and polluting the air. So Triumph doesn't let the TR250's throttle butterflys loose completely. When you get off the accelerator, the carbs are still propped open slightly. This means the engine loses revs very slowly, like a John Deere tractor motor with a 100-lb flywheel.
>
> 'After testing the TR250, we complained to Triumph about the engine's disappointing showing, and from the depths of their headquarters in Teaneck, New Jersey, came a car that was dubbed the TR4 and a half. It was something more than a regular 250, having the fuel injection cam and head, advanced ignition timing and a less restrictive exhaust manifold, but it used two standard carburettors instead of the TR5's FI. It turned the quarter in 17 seconds at 77 mph—1.8 seconds and 3 mph faster than the production model...'

The TR6

The TR6 featured new wheels and trendy transfer badging.

With the panning the TR250 received in the States, it was hardly surprising that Triumph produced another super-tuned model for *Car and Driver's* test in February 1969 in company with the other two major magazines. British magazines would have to wait a while for their TR6 test cars with the model having been launched later in its home market. *Car and Driver* realised that they had a special car—or were told so—but they were still full of praise:

> 'The TR6, we are moved to report, is an excellent automobile. It is bluff and straightforward—as its predecessors have been—but it is no longer Colonel Blimp. Subtlety has crept into British Eden, and the protectorate is the better for it. Still bereft of the fuel injection which made its British counterpart, the TR5, an energetic car beyond the dreams of U.S. Triumph owners, the new car is nonetheless the fastest, most comfortable, best-mannered Triumph ever to offer enchantment to the American buyer...
>
> 'The TR6 is a member of the family and instantly recognizable. But it's a little like being introduced to a strikingly handsome daughter in a

family of very plain, very earnest people you have known for ages. Who would ever have dreamed...?'

Car and Driver revelled in their TR6, finding the throttle linkage more responsive, the suspension better controlled, the brakes still brilliant, the understeer fine providing that you had strong arms, the hood and sealing much better, only the clutch and gearchange as heavy as ever. The standard of this non-overdrive car's preparation was also revealed in performance figures of an estimated 110 mph maximum speed, 9.8-second 0–60 mph, 17.2-second standing quarter mile and 20–22 mpg fuel consumption.

Road & Track managed 109 mph with their non-overdrive TR6, but had to be content with 10.7 seconds for the 0–60 mph, and a 17.9-second standing quarter mile. They still liked the package, however, commenting: 'This is one of the rare facelift jobs that comes off,' before adding:

'The vintage body makes itself known in the driving compartment: the seats, located inboard of the separate frame's siderails, are, of necessity quite narrow and shoulder room in more restricted than it might be with today's curved side glass...

'If Triumph were to put an all-new car on the market (a TR7?) the car would probably be too good to be true, and certainly the price would shoot way up.'

Sports Car Graphic, which did not appear to be quite in tune with a 12.2-second 0–60 mph and a 17.5-second standing quarter mile, were not quite so prophetic either, but they said the TR6 looked so good that Leyland might have trouble importing enough to meet the orders. Part of this problem was because the TR6 was a 'real sporting machine.' They explained: 'Gee, what a joy to be driving a sports car in the autumnal sunshine of Southern California. And what a honest sports car this is! None of this hokey about a 2 + 2...'

It was two months later, on 17 April, 1969, that the first British road test of a TR6, an overdrive car, appeared, in *Autocar*. Again, it was a very good, very quick car, recording a 119 mph maximum speed that was only 1 mph short of the lighter TR5. Its acceleration figures were even more impressive, the overdrive making up for the extra weight in this case to give a 0–60 mph time of 8.2 seconds against *Autocar's* previous best of 8.8 seconds with the TR5, although *Motor* had gone a fraction better with the earlier car. *Autocar's* standing quarter mile with the TR6 of 16.3 seconds also emphasised the help of the overdrive, as did the fuel consumption at 20–22 mpg.

Reflecting on the demise of the Big Healey little more than a year earlier, *Autocar* said of their car, registered PDU 520G:

'Even if the Austin-Healey 3000 had not been dropped, the TR6 would have taken over as the he-man's sports car in its own right. It is very much a masculine machine, calling for beefy muscles, bold decisions and even ruthlessness on occasions. It could be dubbed the last of the *real* sports cars, because it displays many qualities so beloved in vintage times. In spite of all this (although many would say because), it is a tremendously exhilarating car to drive anywhere.'

Motor could not quite match their 0–60 mph or standing quarter miles times with their identical TR6, registered PDU 515G, in their test of 7 June, 1969, but they did manage an exceptionally fast 0–100 mph of 24.7 seconds, before commenting:

'The big improvement ... was in the ride; the first impression in town is that the car just rolls along with almost no noise at all, from wind, engine or road and it is only bad surface deformities that generate shuddery thumps. It feels initially as if the suspension might be too soft but at higher speeds it is, in fact, pleasantly firm and gives a ride as comfortable as many less well suspended saloons. It can get a bit pitchy on close-coupled undulations but it is well damped and takes single humps and hollows without hitting the bump stops. There was no noticeable scuttle shake.'

Self-confessed TR enthusiast Ray Hutton—who had owned a TR3 in his youth—whisked PDU 520G away to the Continent for *Motor Racing's* test in November 1969 during which he achieved similar performance figures to *Autocar*, with an even higher top speed of 121 mph. With the TR3 in mind, he commented:

'The gearchange is quite heavy, notchy and positive, if not of the quickest; a few years ago it might have been excellent, but recent Ford products have set the standards by which these things are judged. Some of that man-sized energy is also needed for the clutch, which is nonetheless smooth in operation.'

Bolster had problems with his hard-worked demonstrator, when a universal joint broke during his acceleration tests for *Autosport*, reported on 23 July, 1970. It was replaced with a hard-top model, registered RWK 531H, however, and Bolster said that he could not decide which one he liked the best. He wasn't too happy with the front anti-roll bar on it either, finding it too stiff for his taste. 'On a bend that I entered at 110 mph, I found the car running uncomfortably wide and was unable to keep the nose into the apex, though lifting the right foot enabled me to regain control,' he said. 'At lower speeds, the TR6 feels better balanced, but perhaps I was expecting it to be the equal of the 2.5 saloon, which it is not.'

With such modern machines in mind, and the Stag especially, contributing editor Doug Blain did not have a good word to say for the TR6 when he tried one, registered RWK 434H, for *CAR* in October 1971. His feelings were summed up by a plaintive plea while testing:

'Who can try hard on the continent in a so-called sports car that gulps expensive petrol on motorways, bruises it occupants to the marrow on the back-doubles and understeers straight among the mountain hairpins?'

Plate 1 The clean simple lines of the original TR2 are emphasised in this picture.

Plate 2 The TR3 acquired a distinctive grille in its radiator intake.

Plate 3 The Swallow Doretti shows off its fine bodywork to advantage.

Plate 4 The TR3A was evidence of Michelotti's first involvement with the TR.

Plate 5 The TR3A still makes a highly-competitive club racer.

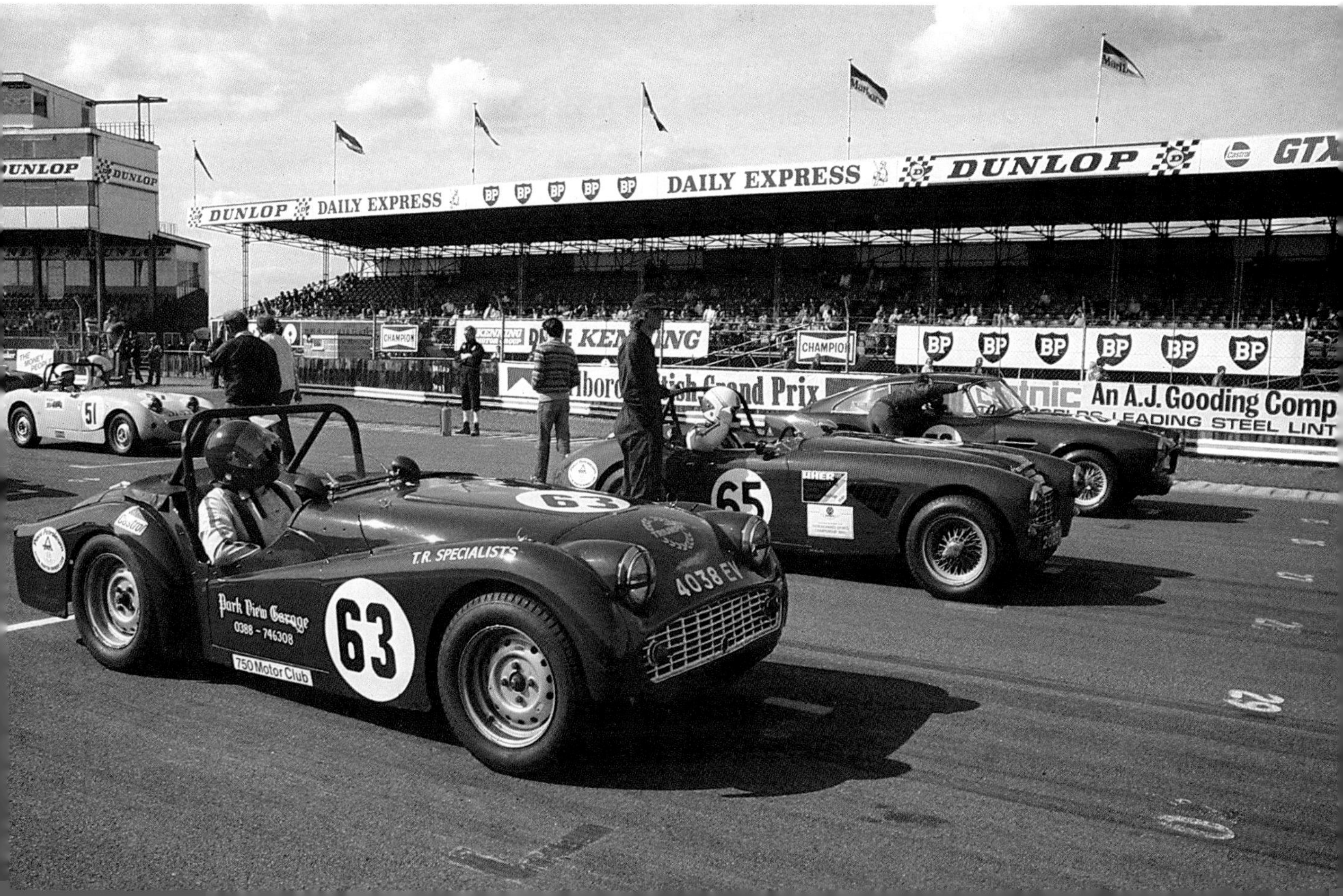

98
42
GT-10

Plate 6 (opposite page): The Kastner TRs made a great name for themselves in America, with this one running high on the banking at Daytona in 1966.

Plate 7 The TR4 rally cars were really rugged as privateer Harold Hamblin demonstrated in the 1963 Monte Carlo Rally.

Plate 8 The TR4A is pictured with its trend-setting Surrey top.

Plate 9 The Dove coupé offered much improved carrying capacity along the lines of an Aston Martin

Plate 10 (above): Concours fanatics can prepare the most immaculate engines as this TR4 unit shows.

Plate 11 (left): The front of the Dove remained exactly the same as the TR4 on which is was based.

Plate 12 (overleaf): Tony Pond gives his TR7 a baptism in the 1976 Manx International Rally.

LEYLA

Castrol
Leyland Cars

Plate 13 (right): The petrol injection TR5 is captured with a most appropriate registration number.

Plate 14 (below): Production sports car racer Nigel Bancroft proves that his TR5 is still fully competitive at Oulton Park in 1983.

Plate 15 (opposite page, above): The American specification TR6 featured far stronger bumpers late in its run.

Plate 16 (opposite page, below): The little that can be improved on the TR5 other than perhaps the substitution of TR6 wheels.

Plate 17 (above): Richard Morrant roars to another lap record in production sports car racing with his TR6 at Silverstone in 1982.

Plate 18 (right): Oh to be in England with a TR7, its top open to the world.

Plate 19 (opposite page, top): The long sweeping lines of the TR7 Drophead can be seen clearly in this picture.

Plate 20 (opposite page, bottom): One of the very rare TR8s that escaped in right-hand drive form.

Plate 21 (above): Pond at his best in the TR7 V8 on the Manx International in 1978.

Plate 22 (below): Still the TR7 V8s thunder on . . . with Roger Clarke's ex-Sparkrite example preparing for modified sports car racing at Snetterton in 1983.

Plate 23 (opposite page, top): One man's idea of a TR8, a TR7 with a strong Range Rover influence, picture in British off-road racing in 1983.

Plate 24 (opposite page, bottom): The TR8 is so versatile as this example showed in British Rallycross events in 1982.

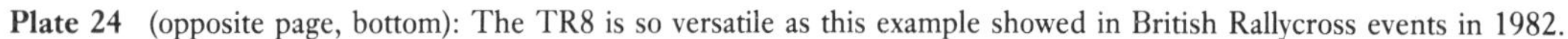

Plate 25 (right): Club runs are a pleasure for the TR Register...

Plate 26 (below):...and so are test days for the TR Drivers' Club.

Car and Driver then spent a lot of time analysing the kind of people who bought the TR6 when they next had the opportunity to test one, in November 1972. After talking to a stockbroker who bought one for his wife to keep her out of his Mercedes, a photographer who needed one for appearances, a long-distance commuter who felt that fresh air was necessary to unwind, a newspaper reporter concerned that convertibles were about to be outlawed, a police sergeant, a housewife who had heard of heeling and toeing, and a man who used to slalom a TR3, they decided that:

> 'Triumph owners see the discomforts as more than just the price they must pay for the tradition. They are an integral part of the tradition itself. Joe Bruce of the Wilton Imported Car Center says the Triumph buyer is not a discerning individual in the *Consumer Reports* style. Before selecting his new TR6, he either draws on a past experience with old Triumphs or no prior sports car encounters at all. It makes no difference that the competition has obvious advantages because he hasn't driven the alternatives. A Datsun 240Z may ride better but without a top that folds it's not a sports car in the Triumph buyer's eyes. Fiat 124 Spiders are surely quieter but what kind of image is there with those almost feminine lines? Only the Triumph, with all of its rude fittings and function, can deliver the classically British sports car they're after. And for that image, they gladly pay any sum and endure any discomfort.'

Their car did not appear to have been super-tuned, but it still produced good performance figures of 107 mph flat out, 9.4 seconds for the 0–60 mph and 17.4 seconds for the standing quarter mile on a quoted 101 bhp which made an interesting comparison with a 1973 model, registered RDU 998M, tested by the British magazine *Thoroughbred and Classic Cars* in January 1975, who obviously felt that it was already a classic. The softer cam on this car with late-model overdrive extended its 0–60 mph time to just over 9 seconds, with a 115 mph top speed. In fact, the engine 'seemed a little breathless and strained beyond 4,500 rpm, which is not quite how we remembered the earlier TRs,' said *Thoroughbred and Classic Cars*. Then they added on a line of thought that at one time held sway before it was realised that replacement carburettors cost more than a fuel injection pump:

> 'The petrol injection system obviously adds to the power and smoothness of the unit, but at the same time it does add cost and complexity, perhaps making it a doubtful proposition on a long-term basis—it is unlikely that its longevity can be compared with the American carburettor set up, for instance, and perhaps in the years to come we may well see enthusiasts for the "old" TR6 exchanging its petrol injection for more traditional methods of breathing.'

It was left for *Car and Driver* to provide the TR6's epitaph with a test in October 1976 when all but the last few cars were sold. After saying the suspension was as much a part of the past as pegged pants and Brylcreem, they added:

> 'This is really bothersome only if you are determined to judge all cars by contemporary standards. You can't just measure the TR6 that way. It's a throwback to another time, and even though British Leyland sees little commercial value in continuing to exploit that era, there are fine memories for the car enthusiast to celebrate. The TR6 really is the last heir in a long succession of big British sports cars. We're speaking now of cars on a plateau above the four-cylinder MGs and Sunbeams, the TR2s and Turners. Remember the big sixes, the sleek Jaguars, the delicate AC Bristols, the bluff and beautiful Austin-Healey 3000? They were the sports cars to which you moved up after you got your first taste of MG and liked it.
>
> 'For the last few years, the TR6 played that role. With factory backing, it won on the racetrack and, with the aid of pleasing cosmetics, continued to turn heads on the street. Unlike all of the other old sports cars—the MGB and the Midget in particular—the TR6 has suffered little in meeting bumper and safety standards ... It's a crisp package, one that combines both an appreciation of the past and an awareness of the future. Maybe that explains why British Leyland expects no difficulty in selling the remainder of the 6,000 TR6s that were shipped to the US this year, even after the discontinuation is public knowledge.
>
> 'It's an odd turn of affairs, this discontinuation, because you don't expect a manufacturer to stop making the one product people seem willing to buy forever, particularly when that product has the glorious tradition of the British sports car. What should one expect next? Certainly there will always be an England, but it now seems likely that this existence is doomed to some revised form.'

The TR7

The TR7 got off to a surprisingly good start with road testers when it is realised how much criticism its styling was to invoke. Most magazines only really slated the coupé five years after it was introduced when they saw how good the convertible looked by comparison. In 2,750 words extolling the virtues of the TR7, and giving it a typically warm American welcome, Executive Editor Patrick Bedard devoted only about 50 to the styling, in *Car and Driver*, including:

> 'The proportions are wrong; the body is too thick at the cowl and the passenger compartment is too close to the rear axle for there to be an engine of any size behind the seats. Nobody who has seen a Fiat X1/9 is going to fall for the deception...
>
> 'But there is no great loss, because the accommodations and the machinery under the skin make the TR7 an attractive alternative to any front-engined sports car, including the Datsun 260Z. And that is saying a lot.
>
> 'The TR7's strong suit is comfort. The cockpit is spacious (wider than either a Corvette's or a Z-car's) and the driving position is exceptionally

Even if the styling was open to doubt, the handling of the TR7 made it 'miles ahead of any Triumph sports car ever built', in the opinion of Patrick Bedard, of *Car and Driver*.

good . . . It's a damn convenient car and the designers have avoided most of the thoughtless mistakes that are found even in expensive cars. . .

'The TR7 is one of those care cars whose agreeable nature hits you as soon as you slide into the driver's seat. It just seems to work. And when you slip into traffic on your maiden voyage, you feel like you've been driving it for years. This is something altogether new for British sports cars. . .

'Make no mistake; the potential of this car is great. The bogus mid-engine shape falls somewhat wide of our sense of aesthetics, but it is certainly controversial and will appeal to those who want to be noticed. The interior appointments overshadow everything else in its class and performance is competitive. But more than anything else, the TR7 is available at a fair price.'

He took performance figures of 10.2 seconds for the 0–60 mph, 17.3 seconds for the standing quarter mile and a top speed of 105 mph that were not a lot different from those of *Road & Track* with one of the first true production cars—a '49-state' twin Stromberg carb model—the following month, in April 1975. *Road & Track*'s car was about 1 second slower in the acceleration tests, but the best part of 10 mpg better with 27.5 mpg overall fuel consumption, so the state of tune obviously influenced the figures. *Road & Track* thought the TR7's shape strange and stubby, but devoted the rest of their test to its good points, notably the handling. They said:

> 'If it's tough getting good results from engines these days, at least the U.S. government hasn't yet regulated handling. Here is where the TR7 is miles ahead of any Triumph sports car ever built. Generally it has a taut, all-of-a-piece feel that gives the driver confidence, and this is backed up by a lot of cornering power and good response characteristics. The rack-and-pinion steering isn't terribly quick for a sports car, but it is delightfully precise with r & p's typical lack of free play at the centre ... Understeer is its prevailing characteristic, but just enough to keep the novice driver safe while not enough to bother the expert.'

Autocar, now with former TR3 owner Ray Hutton as editor, was the first British magazine to give the TR7 a full test. In an unusually critical survey on 26 June, 1976, they pointed out how far removed the TR7 was form the TRs that had gone before because of the American influence. They said it was best to view it as a two-seater version of one of the *real* sports cars of the day, the Dolomite Sprint; 'Without the performance advantages—and the possibility of putting the roof down—the modern two-seater has to be able to provide something else that sets it apart from the normal run of cars. Hence on the one side, the controversial styling, and on the other its exciting interior...

Autocar was exceptionally critical of the TR7's styling, and said so.

'Leyland's designers have done well; the way the TR7 turns heads suggests that whatever one may think of the styling they have got the image right.'

Their TR7, registered LMT 456P (naturally one of the UK SU carb cars), proved to have better acceleration than the US models, recording 9.1 seconds for the 0–60 mph and 17 seconds for the standing quarter mile. Its top speed was 109 mph, but this was beaten by one registered LOE 113P tested by *Motor* for their issue of 11 September, 1976. *Motor's* car reached 111 mph with 28 mpg overall against *Autocar's* 26.4 mpg, but it could manage only 9.6 and 17.4 seconds for the acceleration tests. *Motor* were rather puzzled by the styling, and, as a result, said little, although they summed up:

> 'The TR7's strong points are its comfort and driveability, its spacious and attractive interior and instrumentation, and its excellent ventilation system—but let down by a noisy engine, dated transmission and not very good visibility.'

A noisy engine let the TR7 down, too.

The road tests of *Autocar* and *Motor* were carried out to broadly similar dictates, but in between came two distinctly individual tests. In one, by Leonard Setright, for *CAR*, in June 1976, there was a marvellous treatise on what it is like to drive a TR7. L.J.K. Setright, sometime lawyer and long-time motoring writer, said:

> 'Not many people have retained the nerve to go blasting down motorways at sustained high speeds, so it probably does not matter that the TR7 is not

The interior came in for praise, however.

the car for the task. It is not a good motorway car: it will reach 110 mph promptly enough, but at the corresponding engine rpm (a whisker over 6,000) it sounds fussy. In a strongly gusting crosswind it moves across a little, perhaps suggesting that the lip beneath the nose of that blatantly stylized cuneiform body is not as effective as it should be. On any other sort of roads, the TR7 is utterly happy and can be driven in as sporting and as exuberant a style as might be wished: while the ride is softly sprung and firmly damped to be perfectly easy at any speed, while the suspension absorbs ruts and bumps and hollows without betraying a tremor to the occupants, while the insulation from road noise and wind noise is so nearly complete as to defy comparison with anything else that might supposedly be in the same class of cars, and while the ratio of power to laden weight is never better than 100 bhp/ton, the TR7 can take winding roads with astonishing speed, coping with horizontal and vertical corners in a style so competent as to make very little demand upon the skill of the driver.

The trend of badging turned to shadow transfers on the TR8's rear panel.

> 'This Triumph is the kind of car that reaches high cornering rates without developing any quirks of behaviour. For most people—excepting those who are more concerned with proving something to themselves or their passengers than with covering the miles fast and objectively—that is the kind of car to have. It is not the ability to corner fast that really matters, it is the absence of any need to slow down: so the bend at the end of a country straight should not be the occasion for flurries of braking and gearchanging, nor for flourishes of opposite lock and fanfares of tyre-trumpets, but merely something that requires a slight smooth movement of the steering wheel so that the car tracks equally smoothly through the bend. There should be no other change—no shift of the accelerator up or down, no lift of a tyre from the road, no lurch of the torso across the seat, no change of speed or gear or engine note. The desired speed, already established is simply maintained; and if a corner has to be negotiated, then it manifests itself in no way other than a lateral acceleration felt by the occupants but not seen—no roll, no hanging out of the tail, no whinnying of tyres or jolting of bump-stops or that uncomfortable transverse bounce that suggests an anti-roll bar going into resonance. In modern times, that is as it should be.
>
> 'It is undramatic and it is safe. Throughout much of Britain, the traditional rolling English road limits cornering speeds by cramping visibility and confining lane width: even if you can see round the bend that the exit is clear, there is probably not enough room for the car to be put sideways and recovered. In such conditions, a car that will track positively through any country-lane corner as fast as conditions allow, as this Triumph does, is far more impressive than one that will get through as quickly to the accompaniment of fuss, doubts, and driver virtuosity.'

After that, there was little that could be said about driving a TR7, and *Motor Sport* had little opportunity, a 200-mile run in company with 19 other TR7s and 38 other journalists having to suffice. As it was, the *Motor Sport* men, Clive Richardson and Jeremy Walton, nearly set the front brakes alight shaking themselves well clear of the pack ... but they were left 'a little cold by a car that felt as though it was lacking in character because its roadholding and handling was too good for its performance.'

Bolster next reinforced the general opinion that the TR7 offered nothing more than a Dolomite Sprint in terms of performance, so it might as well have the 16-valve engine and the promised five-speed gearbox. But he managed to get the 0–60 mph time down to 9 seconds with a 17-second standing quarter mile for *Autosport* on 25 November, 1976, with a car registered GAC 866P.

Road & Track were quite complimentary about the TR7 when next they tried two cars, one a five-speed model and the other an early automatic. They commented on the two gearbox options on June 1977:

> 'The five-speed gearbox and other improvements are well worth the extra cost ... But the real highlight of the gearbox is the way it mates so well with

The luggage boot was as large as ever, but it was better trimmed than on the earlier cars.

> the engine's characteristics, giving the five-speed TR7 snappy driveability that was lacking with the four-speed.
>
> 'We were not surprised by the automatic. The idea of a four-cylinder sports car with an automatic does not excite us and the performance is leisurely at best. Moving off from a stop calls for burying the throttle and waiting. Keep your shirt on and eventually it comes together and begins to move along, but it seems to take forever...'

Their performance figures with these cars revealed that the five-speed TR7 (which had the latest 1977 86-bhp catalytic converter engine) was capable of 11.2 seconds for the 0–60 mph with 18.2 seconds for the standing quarter mile and 110 mph maximum, whereas the automatic was about 3 seconds slower.

The TR7 convertible

The TR7 convertible got a wonderful welcome, not only from the journalists who were overjoyed that it had not been outlawed after all, but by those who pointed out that it looked so much better. Now they could see what Harris Mann meant to do all along. *Car and Driver* started the rhetoric in September 1979 with Larry Griffin writing:

> 'At this very moment, purists the world over are probably breathing a collective sigh of relief because of the new roadster: saved from the comfortable life, and not a moment too soon! Bad news, cretins. The TR7 roadster is as cushy and pleasing as the coupé, a far cry from the cantankerous open-air creations that still scuttle out of the gates of many British and Italian factories. Today, Triumph reasons that there's no reason the sporty life should go down like a bittersweet pill, and the result

is a roadster with the cheery personality of a sunshine blonde, happy to skate fluidly through life with a bounce, a wiggle, and a wink all of its own. There is still just enough muscular mechanism remaining underneath that the TR7 won't catch on with the tight-pantsed lounge lizards who use musk by the barrelfull and curlers for their chest hair. The TR7 roadster is not for those who make a career of being fun, but for those who like to have fun.'

Road & Track ran a test on one in the same month and discovered that the heavier convertible was slightly slower than the coupé they had tested in 1977—returning a 0–60 mph time of 11.5 seconds and a standing quarter mile of 18.5 seconds. But they weren't too worried, observing:

'We're quite impressed with the TR7 in convertible form. The wedge styling with the top lowered, seems cleaner and crisper than on the coupé, the ragtop is well designed and weathertight, and open-air motoring with the top down, while perhaps not as intimate a feeling as in earlier Triumph sports cars, is still our favourite way to enjoy a sunny day on a country lane. With impressive fuel economy for this or any other era (27.5 mpg over the course of our test) the TR7 convertible must rank as one of the most comfortable, practical and entertaining sports cars on the market today.'

Autocar were just as enthusiastic when they tried another manual TR7 Drophead (as they perferred to call it), registered JRW 595V, on 15 March, 1980, saying:

'Those shapely lines and swept-back windscreens, would look rather silly if the TR7 did not have the performance they imply, but it is well up to scratch and the driver always finds ample acceleration in hand for swift overtaking or sweeping up hills. Good spacing of the gear ratios helps one to make optimum use of the power available, and the 2-litre Dolomite-based engine has a wide range of useful revs since it pulls strongly and very smoothly from about 1,500 rpm right through to 5,500.'

Autocar found, like *Road & Track*, that their TR7 Drophead was a little slower than its earlier equivalent so far as acceleration was concerned with 10.7 seconds for the 0–60 mph and 18.1 seconds for the standing quarter-mile, but faster so far as maximum speed was concerned with 114 mph thanks to its new gearbox. *Motor* couldn't quite manage that with a sister car, registered JRW 594V, which reached 110 mph, but they got the 0–60 mph down to 9.6 seconds with a 17.2-second standing quarter mile. They considered the TR7 Drophead a thoroughly enjoyable, well-developed and refined car with a lively performance and reasonable economy *and* you did not have the blind spots at the back. They said on 14 June, 1980:

'The design of the hood, with its three-quarter panels, has improved rearward visibility enormously compared with the fixed-head model, though the transparent windows are no substitute for glass and can lead to distortion.'

It was left to *Car and Driver* to give the TR7 its epitaph with a test of the convertible, a petrol injection model that yielded 3–4 mpg better fuel consumption, in October 1981. They said:

> 'The British sports car is dead. The last of the breed, the 1981 Triumph TR7 and its TR8 sibling, have finally succumbed to their perennially low sales figures. Even in semi-Socialist Great Britain, the world leader in featherbedding, the bean counters couldn't tolerate a negative cashflow forever.'

SCCA competition TR7

Such was the success of Bob Tullius's Group 44 TR7 in SCCA racing that *Road & Track* arranged to test it with a standard fixed-head car for comparison at the Road Atlanta circuit. The Group 44 TR7 had been prepared to the production Class D limits with a lightened bodyshell, competition suspension, brakes and steering and a 175 bhp engine. With Tullius at the wheel for the test, published in September 1977, it lapped the 2.5-mile circuit in 1 minute 38.8 seconds against the standard car's 2 minute 04.43 seconds. Both were fitted with the normal four-speed manual gearbox available at the time. Tullius said that he had never driven a standard TR7 on the track before and was surprised at how well it handled: 'You just throw it at a corner and it stays right there and does what you want', he said. 'When it goes into a corner, it gets up on its suspension a little bit, but then it takes a set and it's solid. Then you can stand on the throttle, work it with the steering wheel and it does the things it's supposed to do.' By comparison, the racing car was more positive. 'It doesn't really get up on its suspension,' said Tullius. 'It kind of drifts, within the confines of its handling parameters.'

Road & Track recorded a 0–60 mph time of 6.9 seconds, a 0–100 mph time of 15.3 seconds and a standing quarter mile in 15.5 seconds with a top speed of 132 mph in the D production TR7. At that speed it used fuel at the rate of 6.5 mpg.

The TR8

The tragedy of the TR8 was heightened when it is realised in retrospect, what a rapturous reception it received from the road testers. *Road & Track* took figures with a fuel injection Californian version and drove a '49-state' carburettor car for their test in June 1980. They said:

> 'There's hope after all. Just when it seemed as though we would never again see another mass-produced, lusty-hearted convertible sports car, here comes the Triumph TR8. You aren't going to have to trace down a Sunbeam Tiger or older Corvette after all, because you can now buy a brand-new V8 roadster, one that will outrun most every other sports sedan and sports car this side of $15,000. Just as encouraging is the source of the

The TR8, according to *Car and Driver*, had eight cylinders' worth of punch to ram the world through the windshield and out of the rear view window. Wow...

news. Its maker is Triumph, part of Jaguar Rover Triumph Ltd [as British Leyland's American operation was known]...'

They liked everything except the brakes, which didn't seem able to cope with the fullest extent of the performance, figures for which were 135 mph flat out, 8.4 seconds for the 0–60 mph, 16.3 seconds for the standing quarter mile and 15 mpg overall which they felt could have been improved with a longer test. The carburettor car felt just as fast as the fuel injection one. *Car and Driver* got really excited with their 'full rave review' in August 1980. They said:

> 'It's good: nothing less than the reinvention of the sports car, mate. You want a looker, you say? Well, peel back the ragtop and the 8's nifty doorstop shape will torque heads faster than a flat-rate mechanic. Maybe you're into Q-ships? The TR8 looks exactly like a TR7 except for twice-pipes and a few stickers. You want comfort? How about an interior that's practically draft-free, even with the top down? Seats that match the spine, a soft pad between your knee and the console, a dead pedal for your clutch foot, a steering wheel as satisfying as a graduation handshake. You want handling? There's enough grip here to make your ears bleed, the kind of agility that race drivers appreciate in off-season. Of course you've lived for torque in a

> sports car, the stuff that dusts the pavement under your rear wheels and cocks the tail sideways when you're feeling frisky. That's the best news with the TR8: eight whole cylinders' worth of punch to ram the world through the windshield and out the rear-view mirror. You need not be Saudi Arabian royalty to apply: this, perhaps the finest of all thrills from England, is a bargain at $12,000, plus one gallon of liquid gold for every 16 miles of your future highway happiness...'

The only thing they could criticize about the TR8 is that it could have done with 14-inch wheels and discs all round...

CAR magazine actually managed a test of the TR8 in December 1980, but it was by a Briton, Nick Valery, domiciled in America and headed up the West coast to Oregon. He extolled the car's virtues for 3,000 words with only a few more to describe delicious dinners en route, problems presented by the car being confined to a loss of brake fluid and windscreen wiper blades that began to melt when parked in temperatures around 110 degrees...

Competition TR8s

Meanwhile *Road & Track* had staged a triple test of Tullius's IMSA GTO TR8, North American rally champion John Buffum's TR8, and a standard car in their issue of November 1980. The Tullius Group 44 car was up to 360 bhp from a long-stroke 3989 cc engine with extensive modifications bringing the weight down to 2560 lb. Buffum's car was equally extensively modified although it looked nearer to standard, with a 280 bhp engine, but a weight of only 2390 lb. The standard car weighed in at 2655 16...

With a 4.55:1 rear axle ratio, the rally car was well equipped for the acceleration tests, returning a 5.3-second 0–60 mph time, 13.1-second 0–100 mph, a 13.9-second standing quarter mile and 107 mph at a 7,500 rpm maximum; but the extra power of the racing car, on a 3.9:1 rear axle told with a 0–60 mph time of 4.3 seconds, a 9.6-second 0–100 mph and a standing quarter mile of 12.7 seconds. Top speed was 150 mph at 8,400 rpm. Both used four-speed versions of the standard five-speed gearbox (the top gear having been deleted) with the race car using fuel at 3 mpg, and the rally car at 6 mpg on a stage and 12 mpg on the road. Everybody drove everybody else's car on the Riverside circuit, with Buffum saying of the GTO racer:

> 'Wow. It's got gobs of power compared to my rally car. And, of course, its suspension is a lot stiffer, to the point that it really doesn't roll when you get sideways. Sort of like driving a go kart, although the TR8 traits are still there.'

And Buffum on the standard TR8: 'It handles similarly to all TRs. There's some initial understeer that you can balance by tipping on and off the throttle. Play the throttle and steering wheel together, and it'll go where you want. In general, though, the stock car has more initial understeer than mine, and mine has more than Bob's.'

Tullius on the GTO racer: 'More than any other car I've driven, this one has a balance and agility that are close to perfection.'

And on the standard car: 'It has a lot of punch at the low end, but understandably it fades pretty quickly above 5000 rpm. I like the steering better than my race car because its power-assisted...'

VI
The TR in Competition

The Triumph TR enjoyed an amazingly successful competition career considering how little money was lavished on its development by the factory (in the case of early examples), and how it was stopped just when the later cars were set for success. Sir John Black started it by asking Ken Richardson if he thought the TR2 (still in experimental form) could beat the speeds attained by Rootes' rival product, the Sunbeam Alpine, on the Belgian motorway at Jabbeke. Richardson took a deep breath and said that he thought it could, and to quote the man who became Triumph's first competitions chief:

> 'The next thing I knew we were booked to run at Jabbeke at 7.30 in the morning of such and such a day. I was aghast and asked what happened if on that particular morning it was raining or a high wind was blowing. Fortunately it was the most perfect morning you could wish for with not a breath of wind, and after a false first start when a plug lead came off, we averaged 124.889 mph in high-speed trim and 114.890 with the normal windscreen and hood erected.'

Sir John never lacked the courage to take a decision—and Ken Richardson never spared himself to make sure that his cars were immaculately prepared. He had neither the budget nor the manpower to try to modify a car much, and certainly not the generations of understanding and genius that existed at MG; so for its high-speed run, the second prototype TR2, a left-hand-drive version registered MVC 575, had the bumpers, hood and sidescreens removed to present a cleaner aerodynamic profile. A small Perspex windscreen was fitted to protect the driver—Richardson—and an undershield and spats for the rear wheels. The undershield turned out to be ideal for high-speed runs providing they did not last long, otherwise there could be problems with the cooling; the spats were a serious production proposition that were only abandoned as optional extras when it became common to leave them off as an unnecessary hindrance to wheel changing in rallies. A rigid metal tonneau cover was fitted over the part of the cockpit unoccupied by the driver for the same reason. It was a common feature of record-breakers of the day, and some racing cars, too, but it was never fitted to production cars because it was too big and awkward to store when not in use. The Laycock overdrive was also used for the most obvious reasons, with Dunlop Road Speed tyres as the best available for coping with flat-out driving at that time. The early TR engines were notorious for consuming sparking plugs when under strain, so the hard Champion L10s were fitted—but otherwise the TR2 was absolutely what was to become standard! It was not possible to remove the undershield or to re-fit the bumpers in time for the 'standard trim' runs, but nobody minded. Sir John achieved his object on 20 May, 1953: a sensational send-off for the new model to emphasise its value for money. Orders now came pouring in.

It needed only Johnnie Wallwork's success in the RAC Rally in March 1954 for Standard to set up a competitions department under Richardson to give private owners whatever assistance they could. Wallwork's victory was no fluke because another TR2, driven by Peter Cooper, was second, and a third, with Bill Bleakley at the wheel, was fifth. The car's appeal became even wider when Mary Walker demonstrated how well it could be handled by a woman in the course of

Johnnie Wallwork (picture one) and Peter Cooper (picture two) gave the TR2 a great deal of good publicity by taking the first two places in the 1954 RAC Rally. It was the fourth such event organised by the RAC, and became known as the 'Rally of the Tests' because it amounted to a long road run between various sets of high-speed manoeuvres. Crews set off either from Blackpool in the north or Hastings in the south, with the Blackpool contingent spending the first night in Hastings and the Hastings entries in Blackpool. After completing the same tests en route, they all set off on a loop north through Scotland, ending up back in Blackpool for the grande finale. Thick fog and a tortuous route caused all but eight teams to lose penalty points on the road sections, with Wallwork pictured storming to victory on the Blackpool Promenade and Cooper competing a braking test at Goodwood.

winning the Ladies' Prize. Before this, sports cars with their heavy steering, oil-stained interiors and snarling exhausts, had been a dubious proposition for the average woman driver, with the exception perhaps of the mild-looking, small MG. Rally organisers were prejudiced against sports cars, too, introducing a points scheme to even out their advantage over saloon cars. Only eight cars completed the road section of this 'Rally of Tests' without loss of marks, and Wallwork's was the only sports car. After that, Richardson's tiny competition department devoted a great deal of time to developing the nimble little Standard Ten saloon for rallies, although they were grateful to see how well the TR continued to perform.

But on wide open roads, Standard had nothing to compare to a TR. Richardson said: 'The next thing I knew, Maurice Gatsonides and I were driving a TR2 in the Mille Miglia, finishing 28th out of about 365 starters. We had no trouble and just motored on the whole way beautifully, using about a quart of oil.'

Several other TR2s competed in the 1954 RAC Rally including the early road test car registered OHP 771, driven by W. B. Caldwell, and another, OKV 777, driven by Bob Dickson. These were officially private entries, but received a lot of works support. Nevertheless, they were completely standard cars, the Scottish Triumph dealer Dickson going on to finish 15th at Le Mans in the same car three months after using it to take 14th place in the RAC Rally! He is pictured with partner Edgar Wadsworth and their happy pits crew following the historic French race.

The car was one he used extensively in 1954: another left-hand-drive model, registered OVC 276, and equipped with 16-inch wire wheels partly to raise the gearing and partly so it could share Jaguar racing tyre supplies. It is incredible, and very creditable, to reflect that this was virtually the only modification that was deemed necessary to compete with the might of Ferrari, Lancia and Maserati over 1,000 miles of Italy's great national road race!

The Dutchman Gatsonides was to become a revered name in Triumph TR history as he was already in with other maker's teams. At the same time, other TR2s were competing in the Tulip Rally, with plenty of publicity being generated by the editor of *Autosport*, Gregor Grant, winning the best journalist's award for 17th place overall in Stan Asbury's car, OHP 676. And even then, Peter Agg was exposing what was to become an apparent weakness in TR2 stub axles as he lost a wheel in a high-speed trial at Silverstone. Never mind, tyres did not often grip so well in those days!

But a perfectly standard private TR2, OKV 777, driven by Scottish dealer Bobbie Dickson and its owner, Edgar Wadsworth, took 15th place at Le Mans in 1954 to the delight of the Britons in the crowd and the amazement of everybody else. None of the cars in front could be considered as anything other than pure competition machines, and they all cost many more times as much to buy than a TR2. It was hardly surprising that no fewer than six TR2s started Britain's oldest road race, the Tourist Trophy at Dundrod in Northern Ireland, three months later. But what was surprising was that they all finished in good fettle to win the prestigious team prize for the first team of McCaldrin/Maunsell, Lund/Blackburn, and Dickson/Richardson with the second team of Johnstone/Titterington, Brooke/Scott-Douglas, and Merrick/Tew immediately behind. As Bolster said in *Autosport* later:

> 'That six of these moderately-priced cars started, and every one of them finished at a respectable average speed, is beyond all praise; never has a team prize been so well deserved. It underlines the Triumph performance at Le Mans and must have made many people reach for their cheque books.'

The rallymen were not quite sure, however, even though Gatsonides and Rob Slotemaker had won a Coupé des Alpes with their TR2 for an unpenalized run in rare wintry weather during the French Alpine Rally in July. They were backed by Kat and Tak, and Richardson and Kit Heathcote for the team prize ... but it was not until the London Rally that the home demand reached massive proportions. This was the most difficult night rally in Britain at the time, with a non-stop 30 mph average over very poor roads. To the British club rallyman of the early 1950s, this was one of the ultimate tests. If the car that won was also practical to use every day, required little maintenance, and could be easily straightened out after a weekend's bash, that was the car for him. Wallwork obliged by winning convincingly with his TR2 in 1954, aided by the immaculate map-reading of Willie Cave over a very difficult route. It was during tortuous trials like this one and the Alpine that the seven-gear ratios were liberated to give

Meanwhile Richardson built three official works cars for competition, including one registered OVC 276, which he drove in the 1954 Mille Miglia. He is seen with the same car at the opening of the 1955 British club racing season in a sprint organised by the Combined Universities' Motor Club at Tempsford Aerodrome, Cambridge, between Oxford and Cambridge. He easily won the 1200 cc closed class with one of his Monte Carlo Rally Standard Ten saloons, but when he took the left-hand-drive TR2 out in the 2½-litre open class, he 'overcooked it', and spun off into the infield, leaving Derek Scott in another TR2 to win the class from Sir Thomas Beevor's Healey. Scott was so fast that his time was beaten only by Tony Crook's supercharged Cooper-Bristol and Leslie Marr's Formula Two Connaught in overall standings!

the right power and the right torque every time. Then it was a case of keeping the rev counter on 4,000 for as long as possible. Trouble with brake fade and front drums locking was nothing compared with the difficulties most other cars encountered and the handling was considered quite good while the back wheels were on the ground. It was helped in the dry by the advent of the Michelin X radial-ply tyres. They were notorious for letting go in the wet, but the TR2 was so fast between corners that a good driver could overcome this handicap and decimate the rival MGs. Austin-Healeys did not have enough ground clearance and Jaguar XK drivers were a rare sight in club rallies.

The balance of the brakes was soon improved by fitting the larger rear drums with fade reduced by the use of wire wheels pioneered on the Mille Miglia and Le Mans cars. But it was obvious that further improvements could be made and it was worth experimenting with the new disc brakes that had given Jaguar a runaway win at Le Mans in 1953.

Two systems were available: one by Dunlop, which had been used at Le Mans, and the other by the rival, Girling, which had proved successful on Lotus sports racing cars. The main problem with either of these sets was that they cost more than a brand-new TR! But Triumph reckoned that they could be mass-produced far more cheaply with a bit of development, so they decided on back-to-back tests with a team of three cars for Le Mans. One car for the fastest drivers (Dickson and fellow Scot Ninian Sanderson) was fitted with Dunlop's latest racing discs front and rear, which were also being used by the new Austin-

The TR2 rapidly became a popular club rally car as can be seen from the spirited way in which these competitors climbed the Devil's Staircase in Wales during the MCC Redex event in 1954.

6/7

Dickson and fellow Scot Ninian Sanderson took the works TR2, registered PKV 376, to 14th place at Le Mans in 1955. Their car is seen leading the ill-fated Austin-Healey 100S of Lance Macklin (which was involved in what was to be motor racing's worst crash), Peter Whitehead's Cooper-Jaguar, and Maurice Tringtignant's Ferrari 121LM—all of which retired.

Healey 100S road racing car. A servo had to be fitted in this case, but no servo was needed for the potentially cheaper Girling system fitted to two supporting TRs driven by Richardson and pre-war ace Bert Hadley, and by Leslie Brooke and Mort Morris-Goodall. These cars had Alfin alloy-finned rear drums and all three had the larger carburettors that were to be used on the TR3 for a little extra power. They also had Jabbeke-style plastic windscreens and normal soft tonneau covers over the passenger's seat. They were faster than standard, reaching about 120 mph along the Mulsanne straight, but not quite so quick as the EX182 prototypes for MG's new sports car, the MGA. The lighter, alloy-bodied, MGs, with a profile based on the marque's earlier record-breakers, came 12th and 17th. One of their team was eliminated as a result of a dreadful accident involving the Austin-Healey, a Jaguar and Pierre Levegh's works Mercedes, which killed 82 people. The TR team's achievement in finishing all three cars, with Dickson 14th, Richardson 15th and Brooke 19th after spending 1½ hours in a sandbank, was overshadowed as a result.

But the TRs were all set to demonstrate their reliability again in the TT until the leading car, driven by locals Brian McCaldrin and Charles Eyre-Maunsell succumbed to fuel pump problems. Nevertheless, Wilbert Todd and Ian Titterington took 21st place with Dickson and Richardson 22nd as the highest-placed production cars. The experienced Jack Fairman and Peter Wilson were 20th, however, in one of the lightweight versions of the MGA (which was soon to go on sale), and a twin overhead cam MG had proved far faster before retiring—so Triumph could not rest on their laurels.

As his brother Desmond fought for the lead with a D type Jaguar, Ulsterman Ian Titterington took his TR2 to 21st place in the 1955 TT with Wilbert Todd. The race, won by Stirling Moss and John Fitch in a Mercedes, was marred by three deaths from crashes. Many other classic races were cancelled that year in the aftermath of Le Mans, but the RAC were under considerable pressure to carry on with the TT, because it was the event's Golden Jubilee.

In rallies, though, they reigned supreme among production sports cars with a superb 90-hour drive in OVC 276 over some of Europe's toughest roads which gave Richardson and Heathcote fifth place in the Liege-Rome-Liege. This placing was considered a far greater success than any number of wins in lesser rallies, especially as two private TRs, driven by Liedgens and Rousselle, and Gatsonides and Bourelly, followed up in sixth and seventh places. Customer cars—frequently fitted with the new glass fibre hard top for warmth and convenience—dominated the entry lists of national rallies.

Naturally, the TR3 was even more attractive with its extra power, the model receiving a tremendous boost after the French Alpine Rally in 1956. In company with many motor cars and other rallies, the 1955 Alpine had been cancelled following the tragedy at Le Mans. Official feeling ran high against sports cars in the aftermath of the tragedy although the machines involved were all-out racers rather than more normal cars, such as TRs. In Switzerland, motor racing was banned and in France the government refused to allow any sports cars to take part in road rallies. It was a short-sighted decision because grand touring cars, such as the fixed-head Mercedes 300SL, were still allowed in rallies despite their far higher performance. However, Richardson—and Marcus Chambers, who was in charge of the MG competition effort—discovered a way to outwit the French government by getting their cars re-classified as GT machines. In the case of Triumph, this entailed the GT kit being offered with hard top, sliding sidescreens, door handles and so on and to certify that at least 100 had been made. In case of objections that the cars were not real grand tourers, it was decided to make the hard top from steel and bolt it to the body so that Triumphs could claim the TR3s were, in fact, steel-topped coupés, rather than flimsily-disguised sports cars. It was a happy coincidence when it was discovered that the rigidly-bolted steel hard top stiffened up the chassis a lot...

The Alpine was also a very happy event for Triumph because five out of the six TRs entered finished, annexing the coveted team prize, and the first five places in their class. To finish, let alone win one of the prized Coupés des Alpes, was no mean feat, and Triumph took six, including one for the team. Only 34 of the 79 entrants completed the 2,650-mile course over very tough mountain roads under regulations that would have eliminated every car in a modern rally. During the 1956 Alpine Rally, all cars had to be kept under *parc fermé* at night, which meant that any repairs had to be done during running time. The lights, wipers, horn, silencer and gearbox had to be in full working order at the end—and the tyres had to be the same ones used on the car throughout the rally. This one point alone caused a lot of problems and would have rendered any modern car uncompetitive. Richardson and Heathcote had to retire early with transmission troubles caused by an insufficiently-tightened wheel, but Gatsonides and Pennybacker took eighth place overall in the leading TR from newcomer Paddy Hopkirk and Cave (13th), and Kat brothers (14th), privateers Leslie Griffiths and Norman Blockley (16th), and Tommy Wisdom and his wife 'Bill' 17th.

In Britain, John Waddington and co-driver Mike Wood won five national rallies in succession and soon there seemed to be a TR in every form of club competition. The problems open sports cars faced in international competition also led *Autosport* to organise a championship to stimulate the continuing development of these cars which formed the basis of Britain's exports. Modifications 'within reason' were allowed providing the machines remained 'true road cars'. Needless to say, the Triumph TR3 was well to the fore in this championship, particularly one driven by Sid Hurrell. He took second place, in the 2,500 cc class behind overall winner Ken Rudd in an AC-Bristol, with D. F. Sidnell 24th in his Swallow Doretti! The championship's grande finale, however, went to an MGA which had more credit laps than Hurrell's misfiring TR2.

The main problem for competition TRs at that time was the lack of money for development by the factory. Already MG were planning to produce a twin-cam MGA and the AC, for instance, was based on a formula two racing car.

Although the Triumph management refused to sanction heavy development purely for competition, the disc brakes made up for a lot. Richardson's department made do with what they had, sending three of the 1956 rally cars to Sebring on the basis that they could easily be sold to keen American customers! In any case, the classic American 12-hour event had provided Austin-Healey with a lot of publicity and the trip was worthwhile on that basis alone without involving redundant rally cars. In the event, Richardson and Triumph's U.S. chief, Alan Bethel, thought that their main opposition was coming from an AC-Bristol until they discovered that it had been transferred from the GT class to the sports. Then Bethel, with Rothschild and Johns, went on to win his class, supported by Pennybacker and Bob Oker.

International rallies, which might have been a TR preserve at this time, were wrecked by all sorts of trouble, mostly political. The Monte Carlo and RAC were called off because of a shortage of fuel brought about by the Suez crisis of 1956, and the Alpine was stopped as a result of a bad crash in the Mille Miglia. Nancy Mitchell crashed a works TR, the one used by Richardson on the previous year's Alpine, in this event. Only the Tulip and the Liege were able to provide the TRs with good exposure. Many of the thrills on the Tulip came from a ferocious duel between the TR of Waddington and Hopkirk and a rival AC driven by Patten, an eventual class win going to the TR. The Liege, which should really have been called the Liege-Rome-Zagreb-Liege that year, was as savage and spectacular as ever. Once again, Triumph was the outstanding marque, with Bernard Consten and Picher taking third place overall, and leading the winning team of Gatsonides and Jetten (5th) and De Changy/ Liedgens (9th).

By then, extensive modifications to the Big Healeys were turning them into potential rally winners and Richardson wanted to do something about it by increasing the TR's engine capacity. The board vetoed this expensive suggestion, so for the Alpine in which the 2-litre class had been abolished and the two rivals had to run in direct competition, he had 87 mm tractor liners fitted secretly to give 2,187 cc. The result was a considerably improved performance and a dog-fight between the Big Healeys and the TRs, resolved in favour of Keith Ballisat and Alain Bertaut's TR3A, which won a coupé and proved best of 20 British works entries from BMC, Ford, Sunbeam and Triumph. The Irishmen Desmond Titterington and Brian McCaldrin were unlucky to miss a coupé by a split second with their TR. Consten was the winner in a very special Alfa Romeo Giulietta Zagato, prepared by the Italian tuner Conrero, that heralded the start of a new era in international rallying in which smaller cars than TRs would reign supreme. Nevertheless, the TR of de Legeneste and Blanchet vied for the lead in the Liege rally—renamed the Marathon de la Route—until it had to retire with a broken throttle, leaving Consten to win again with the TRs of Gatsonides and Gorris 5th and Liedgens and Dubois 6th. In 22nd and last place was another TR, driven by two senior officers of the British Army's motor pool at Bordon, Hants, Lt Col Crosby and Major Holmes. Their magnificent performance was rewarded by a win in the 2-litre class—all the other TRs had 2.2-litre engines—and a supporting role which gave Triumph the team prize. After that, the TR's days in the top flight of international rallying were numbered with the Austin-Healeys going up to a highly-tuned three litres and the imminent introduction of the BMC Mini. Clubmen soon had another choice, too, in the small Austin-Healey Sprite...

All sorts of cars tended to be pressed into service by manufacturers for the Monte Carlo Rally, including this road test TR3, driven by Peter Bolton and Peter Craven into a highly-meritorious 23rd place in 1958 when snow and ice decimated the field.

Triumph carried on rallying with some success—taking four class wins in international rallies and the team prize in the German and RAC events, with Annie Soisbault tying for the ladies' championship—but, with the factory's financial problems temporarily resolved, the works effort was concentrated again on Le Mans. Speeds had risen so much since the last time a TR had competed that it was obvious that they would need a new, more powerful, engine to qualify. It was either that or fit a completely different, highly-streamlined, body. Sir John's successor, Alick Dick, ruled against that because he considered that the maximum publicity could only be gained with a car that looked like a TR. It would also have to be of 2 litres capacity if it was to run in the same class as would have been entered with a standard TR. That is why he did not like Richardson's suggestion that the capacity should be increased. Rival cars, such as the Big Healey, had been allowed to use extensive modifications for their engines, so he could see no reason against going the whole hog and using a twin-cam like MG had introduced in 1958. If this proved successful, a top-line TR could be introduced with a twin-cam engine to compete with the new MGA.

Wallwork used his driving test ability to good stead to take third place with his works TR3A on the promenade at Monaco in 1959, and 73rd overall.

The twin cam TRs for Le Mans were quite unlike the products of almost every other manufacturer who entered the race. They were prototypes of cars that Triumph wanted to put into production, rather than outright racing machines that might eventually influence normal cars or the grand tourers that were so expensive that they could be built only in very small quantities. As a result, these models, called the TR 'S'—and later the TR3S to distinguish them from further efforts—weighed around 2,135 lb, making them almost the heaviest cars in the race, and certainly the heaviest for their capacity. This was partly because they used a six-inch longer chassis to accommodate their bulky new twin cam engine. The construction of this chassis showed a primitive disregard for modern design trends. Richardson's philosophy for improving handling was decidedly old-fashioned: screw up the dampers as far as possible and stiffen the springs. Designers such as Colin Chapman, of Lotus, had shown that far superior handling could be achieved with a very stiff chassis and much more supple suspension. The result of the Richardson method of suspension tuning was that something had to give—the chassis. This problem was made worse by the longer wheelbase of the Le Mans cars, so he tried to counter it by having reinforcing plates welded the entire length of the chassis. As it was, they would have probably got away with only local reinforcement to the engine bay in which the extra six inches had been inserted.

Triumph's TR3A works rally cars ran in substantially standard form, with few modifications other than the use of Dunlop Weathermaster tyres and Lucas 'flamethrower' spotlights until this car became one of the first to use the 2.2-litre engine conversion.

The Le Mans cars were completely different, although the 1959 versions retained the basic TR3A shape. In this picture, the Sanderson-Dubois car leads that of Bolton and Rothschild.

The TR3S body panels were made from glass fibre to a shape very similar to those of the normal production car. It had been previously assumed that this was to save some of the weight lost to the chassis, but further research has shown that this was far from the case. The glass fibre was three times as thick as the normal metal and weighed just as much. It would seem to have been no coincidence that this was exactly how one of the chief rivals in America, the Chevrolet Corvette, was made, leading to speculation that Triumph—with a body-building problem—were considering marketing a glass fibre TR. Except for oddments such as filler caps and extra lights, the TR3S was far more relevant to a future production car than anything to do with racing. Its new twin overhead camshaft engine was far from highly tuned, built more with reliability and ease of maintenance in mind than for outright performance.

It was of very conventional construction, taking most of its design philosophy from Jaguar's outstandingly-successful six-cylinder XK unit. In fact, the Jaguar engine had originally been intended for production with a four-cylinder option. Triumph's engine was built up by 'sandwich' methods with a large cast sump, lower crankcase, upper crankcase, separate cylinder block, and alloy cylinder head, the valves of which were opposed at 73 degrees. In true Jaguar style, the inlet valves were large with single offset ignition. To make servicing simple, all the auxiliary drives, for the cams, distributor, water and oil pumps, were at the front, with provision for fan blades on the nose of the crankshaft pulley. The timing gear covers were unusually prominent, giving rise to a nickname 'Sabrina' for this engine, with inspiration from the particularly well-endowed showgirl of that era!

With a bore and stroke of 90 mm × 78 mm, giving a capacity of 1,985 cc, this four-cylinder in-line unit had a potential for more than 200 bhp, but ran in conservative tune with a 9.25:1 compression ratio and two twin-choke SU carburettors to give between 150 and 160 bhp. Its overall weight of 438 lb looked good only by comparison with heavyweight units such as the standard pushrod TR engine. A rev limit of 6,500 gave the TR3S a top speed of about 130 mph, the only other alteration from normal TR competition specification being the use of disc brakes all round.

For some reason, Richardson's team decided that it was necessary to fit cooling fans; usually their preparation was immaculate, but in this instance test-bed running failed to reveal what would happen under more human conditions. The fan blades lost their balance and two of the team of three cars were eliminated as the blades broke up and punctured the radiators. Bolton and Rothschild had to retire after three hours and Sanderson and Dubois after nine—by which time the trouble had been identified and the offending fan removed from the car driven by Peter Jopp and Dickie Stoop. As engine trouble decimated the field, they moved up to seventh place before oil pump problems eliminated them with not much more than one hour to go.

Although the rally cars were as well-prepared as ever, their development suffered because of the Le Mans effort and they continued to run in almost standard form. In addition, the odds in some events were heavily weighted towards smaller cars and the Triumph team spent a lot of time preparing the new Herald for such events. This was all part of a change in the character of international rallying, with the long, tough, road sections that had suited the TRs so well being replaced with shorter, more clinical, tests that put them at a disadvantage. It was only natural that this should be so because the old rallies were really only thinly-disguised road races, and now there were more tourists to render such activities too dangerous. Nevertheless, Annie Soisbault tied with Ewy Rosqvist for the ladies' title with Ballisat and Bertaud winning their class in the Marathon de la Route. Further class wins in the Tulip, Acropolis and Coupés des Alpes, and the team prizes for the German and RAC rallies also fell to TRs.

The 'Zoom'-shaped TRS cars line up for Le Mans in 1960 with Richardson on the pit counter at the extreme left.

Le Mans again claimed most of the TR attention in Triumph's competition department during 1960 with four new cars being prepared. They were similar in construction to the TR3S that had raced before except that they now had a wider track, rack and pinion steering and different body lines from experimental projects labelled Zoom and Zest that were to reach fruition in the TR4. Little or no attention was paid to weight saving with the result that these later cars were about 150 lb heavier than their predecessors. It was also more than a standard TR3!

With fans removed, however, they proved far more reliable than the previous year; the three cars which ran finishing in 15th, 18th and 19th places for Ballisat and Marcel Becquart, Les Leston and Rothschild, and Bolton and Sanderson. Unfortunately they did not qualify on distance for inclusion in the results although they might have managed it had they not suffered from valve problems. It was another instance of race experience being superior to normal testing. The Triumph management were very disappointed, especially because they had put a great deal of effort into the project and were now in dire financial straights.

Ballisat and Bolton led in the Triumph team at Le Mans in 1961, their car being followed here by the Ferrari 250GT of Trintignant and Abate, the Austin-Healey Sprite of Sanderson and McKay, and the other TRSs.

The rally team kept the same cars as they had used the previous year, although their cause was not helped when they were beaten by a private TR driver, David Siegle-Morris in the Tulip, who had already won his class in the Monte Carlo Rally. Siegle-Morris, with his partner, Vic Elford, who was to become one of the fastest and most versatile British drivers, were then signed up by the works team for the Alpine. Although they won their class, the economic situation was then so grim at Triumph that this was the last that was seen of the works TR3A team.

The Le Mans effort continued, however, despite criticism from all comers, many from within the company. It was easy to pour derision on the great weight and ponderous appearance of the TRS cars—but Dick defended them on the basis that they made a genuine contribution to the company's research. He was vindicated, along with the competition department, when their three entries finished in 9th, 11th and 15th places at Le Mans in 1961. It was the only team to finish intact and at a speed around 10 mph faster than the previous year. For the record, the 9th-placed car was driven by Ballisat and Bolton, the 11th by Leston and Rob Slotemaker, and the 15th—which had to be held in the pits by Richardson for much of the last hour because of an oil gasket problem—by Becquart and Rothschild.

The TR3A continued to be a popular rally machine right into the 1960s, with Don Grimshaw and Alex Cleghorn seen here competing in the 1961 Monte Carlo Rally before being eliminated by snow. The TR's versatility was also demonstrated by the competitors in the Land's End Trial in the same year.

Soon after, with Britain in the grip of a credit squeeze and car sales suffering as a result, the competition department was closed, leaving an unused prototype TR intended for Le Mans in 1962. This car, built by Conrero along successful competition Alfa Romeo lines, had a chassis extensively modified to space frame principles established by designers such as Chapman. The power output of its Sabrina engine, equipped with twin Weber carburettors, was in the region of 200 bhp and the weight much reduced by the modified chassis and a neat alloy coupé body.

However, no sooner had the competition department been closed and Richardson departed with all his expertise and experience, than pressure from the sales department, with the support of engineering, got it re-opened! It was a very small-scale operation this time, under administrator Graham Robson, but achieved a great deal on an incredibly small budget. The Herald could not be made competitive with its small engine, so the main effort was concentrated on four lightweight TR4s. These were gradually developed with higher output engines and alloy body panels to provide some competition for the much-modified Austin-Healey 3000s which were enjoying great success in rallying. The TRs' best result in 1962 was a coupé in the Alpine Rally for Mike Sutcliffe and Roy Fidler, with Jean-Jacques Thuner missing one by only 90 seconds. Thuner managed ninth place out of 18 finishers in the Liege-Sophia-Liege with the Yugoslavian roads wrecking more than 60 other competing cars including the TR4s of Sutcliffe and John Sprinzel. The RAC Rally had also been transferred to tough tracks—forests—and suited the TR4 no better, with Thuner taking another ninth place. The TRs won the team prize, however.

By 1963, these works TR4s were up to 130 bhp with all sorts of modifications including limited-slip differentials, but they were inherently unsuitable for the changing face of rallying. Handicaps and unsuitable roads mitigated against them despite having the brilliant Vic Elford in the team. The Canadian Shell 4000 Rally in April 1964 marked the TR4's swansong in international rallying as the factory concentrated on the Triumph 2000 saloon and the small Spitfire sports car for Le Mans. Despite totally unsuitable prairie tracks which needed cars with a substantial ground clearance, Thuner and Fidler, supported by an inexperienced team of Gordon Jennings/F. Hornsey, and B. Rasmussen/P. Coombe, took second place in the team section with the TR4s and achieved the object of obtaining a great deal of publicity as the only sports cars to finish.

Meanwhile, TRs had been enjoying a great deal of success in Sports Car Club of America racing, which was officially for amateurs only. In SCCA events, cars of supposedly equal performance are grouped together, no matter what their capacity or weight. If any one car looked like dominating its class for a second season it was upgraded: nevertheless, TR2s and TR3s had a wonderful time in these races, held mostly on old airfield circuits, particularly when their disc brakes were introduced. One of the leading SCCA drivers, Rothschild, found his way into the Triumph works team in Europe and in 1959, a Triumph Racing Team was formed in California. The leading driver, 'Kas' Kastner, was

Meanwhile the works effort continued on a very low budget with the TR4 in events such as the Liege-Sophia-Liege rally during which the car registered 4 VC, driven by Mike Sutcliffe and Roy Fidler, is pictured, first, after colliding with a non-competing Volkswagen, and then after hitting a Rover as it followed it over the edge of the road in a cloud of dust. It was only then that the TR4 was eliminated.

The TR4s were far better suited to tarmac events such as the Tulip Rally—in which John Sprinzel and Graham Robson are pictured finishing 35th overall and fourth in class in 1962—than the rough forest stages in which a club machine is seen suffering.

also a very talented tuner who was eventually to concentrate on this aspect of the sport, with Bob Tullius as his driver. Tullius's TR4 won the SCCA's Group E in 1962 and was moved up to Group D where he promptly won again in 1963! Kastner's tuning was extracting 150 bhp from the TR4's engine by then, which was enough for Tullius to win the D production class again in 1964 and for a team of Kastner-prepared factory cars to take first and second places in the 2.5-litre GT class at Sebring for Bolton and Rothschild, Tullius, Kellner and Spencer.

By this time, Tullius had become recognised as the 'King of the Amateur Racers' running neck and neck with Dana Kellner and Charlie Gates in other TR4s. The TR2 and TR3 continued to compete in Class F of the SCCA series, with one veteran, driven by Dube and Kelder, finishing 14th at Daytona in 1965—a 12-hour endurance race won by a Ford GT40!

During 1965, the TR success story continued in America, with the well-established TR4 winning three out of six SCCA Class D divisional championships, and the new TR4A winning the only category in which it competed, the Pacific Division's D-modified. TR3s carried on winning, too, taking four Class F divisions. It was one of these cars that gave another rising amateur star, Brian Fuerstenau—who was to team up with Tullius—his earliest successes in SCCA racing. Other notable front-runners were Gates in a TR4A, Leon Herbert in a TR4 and Lee Midgely in a TR3A. In D Production, a new young driver, Steve Froimes, was also to make his name in a TR4, helping home a team of Dayglo TR4As to win the Pepsi Cola team prize in the 1966 Sebring 24-hour race.

These Sebring cars had Kastner-prepared engines slightly de-tuned from the 155–160 bhp extracted from SCCA sprint-type units. Although the TR4As continued to be reliable runners in SCCA production sports car events—even finishing a team again in the Daytona 24-hour race—most of the Triumph exponents switched to the more competitive Spitfire with the advent of the Porsche 911 as a direct competitor to the TR on the track. But by 1969, Kastner had got the SCCA to accept fuel injection for the TR6, and Tullius returned to TRs to enjoy considerable success against not only the Porsches, but Datsun's new 240Z in Class C. Other notable TR drivers included Jerry Dittemore, who had Richie Ginther's Porsche to contend with on the West coast. However, with considerable British Leyland support, Tullius and his Group 44 outfit on the East coast and Kastner on the West, carried on with the TR until 1972. At the end of the year, Tullius's car was shipped to Britain for the London Motor Show and soon after lapped Silverstone five seconds faster than the British production sports car record and only three seconds slower than that for modified sports cars.

The Kastner TR6 enjoyed a lot of success in SCCA C production racing once it had been allowed to run with fuel injection.

The marque racing in Britain that had been developed from the *Autosport* series had changed its name to Special Sports in 1968—but became better known as Production Sports. It was nothing like the Prodsports of the 1970s and 1980s, but the rather loosely-worded *Autosport* regulations were tightened up, when they insisted on standard body profiles—although wider wheels were allowed. TRs did not fare too well under these circumstances, especially since they were competing against highly-developed space frame MG Midgets and very powerful Austin-Healeys, although Richard Hawkins made a TR4A go very fast when this series became Modsports (for modified sports cars) in 1971.

Soon these cars were becoming too advanced for the liking of many people and with the sponsorship of Charles Spreckley, a form of historic racing called the Thoroughbred series, was started in 1973. The aim of this formula was to recreate the type of car that had raced in the *Autosport* marque events! It was in this atmosphere that the traditional TR rose to the top again, with Reg

Woodcock winning the three-litre class against a host of Morgans. Not surprisingly, his engine owed a lot to Kastner, although his suspension development and weight saving work was all his own. At the same time, Prodsports was reintroduced with far stricter controls on development to keep the cars as standard as possible consistent with safety on the racetrack, and with classes divided by showroom price. Shaun Jackson, with a TR6, trounced the opposition in the £1,201–£1,625 class to win 15 awards that year. Gerald Vaughan took over his mantle in 1974 for a very hard fight with Ron Hopkinson's MGB as Woodcock won the Thoroughbred championship a second time against a TR driven by Alan Ede, and other cars as varied as a Le Mans Frazer-Nash and the perpetual Morgans. Vaughan and Woodcock repeated the trick in 1975 as British Leyland prepared to re-enter the fray with the new TR7.

Reg Woodcock is pictured first, heading for yet another Thoroughbred historic racing title with his TR3 at Donington in 1982, and second, with the car in slightly modified form as TR Register team manager Graham Peach changes the sash in the Silverstone Six-Hour Rally race later in the year. The TRs took second place on handicap, and then it was all hands on deck to change the wheels and other parts to Thoroughbred specification overnight so that Woodcock could clinch that title from Mike Salmon's Aston Martin DB4 at Brands Hatch next day.

They were desperately keen to give the new car a good launch in Britain, and boldly announced in October 1975 that they would compete in every round of the following year's RAC Open Rally championship. With hindsight, it could be seen that such an announcement was premature and was made with little understanding of how specialised rallies had become since the days when near-standard TR3s were at the top. The RAC rally series, in particular, was totally different from the old-style rallies with long road runs: it was made up of events comprising a number of sprint stages—usually forest tracks—of no more than five miles. For any one car to be competitive, let alone shine, it had to be honed to a fine pitch because there was no margin for error. It had taken years, for instance, for Ford to develop their Escort to the degree in which it ran in 1976, and now the British Leyland management wanted the competitions department at the MG factory in Abingdon to do it overnight with the brand-new TR7.

It took until the Welsh Rally in May 1976 for the eagerly-awaited cars to appear at all, and they were relegated to the ranks of the also-rans by unexpected trouble with their Dolomite Sprint engines. As the weeks went by, it became apparent that the TR7 rally programme was nothing near like so staunchly supported within the giant Leyland corporation as might have been expected from the publicity. Other parts of British Leyland had their own problems and 'one-off' parts for the rally team got a low priority. No sooner had the team got their engines sorted out with new head gaskets than the cars lasted long enough to encounter suspension problems and it was not until September that Tony Pond and Dave Richards, and Brian Culcheth and Johnstone Syer, managed to finish an impressive third and fifth on the Manx International Rally, run significantly, on metalled roads. They were also using the five-speed gearbox which they had managed to get listed as an option for the road cars.

British Leyland were lucky to have a driver as determined as Pond, who persuaded them to enter a TR7 in the loose-surfaced Raylor Rally in October 'just to try things out for the RAC Rally the next month'. Pond drove like a demon, with Mike Nicholson, to win the Raylor outright! It was a very popular victory with the crowds on what had become Britain's biggest spectator sport because they wanted to see something different—a British sports car—doing well. Nevertheless, everybody, Leyland included, was surprised to see Pond lying second to Finnish ace Penti Airikkala on the second day of the RAC,

The TR5 still makes an excellent historic racing machine as can be seen from the very close duel between John Gray and Christopher Burbury at the classic Donington weekend in 1982.

before a puncture and eventual suspension trouble forced him out. Culcheth also had trouble with the rear suspension location and needed a new gearbox before finishing ninth. But at least Leyland had one victory under their belt and they had learned a lot. In lesser spheres, Woodcock remained invincible with his TR3, winning his Thoroughbred championship class again, although Prodsports—despite the rules—seemed to be becoming too specialised for the TR6.

The next year—1977—was more successful, although nothing near like so successful as it might have been, as British Leyland poured in far more money to compete in a combined British and European programme. Unfortunately, it was

Richard Morrant storms to yet another class win in his TR6 at Snetterton in 1983.

bedevilled with politics as responsibility for motor sport switched from Sales and Marketing to Product Planning and a new Motor Sport Director, John Davenport, was appointed. But the TR7 at last got the disc brake rear axle that the team—under leader Culcheth—had been pressing for, and Pond, with a new co-driver, Fred Gallagher, won the Boucles de Spa Rally in Belgium. At this time the TR7 was difficult to handle, with notchy steering at the limit, that was made no easier by the relatively restricted vision available from the cockpit. But Pond was on the top of his form and despite mud, snow and ice—none of which suited the TR7—he took third place in the British Mintex International, with Culcheth 17th. So far, so good, but this was also a time when British Leyland

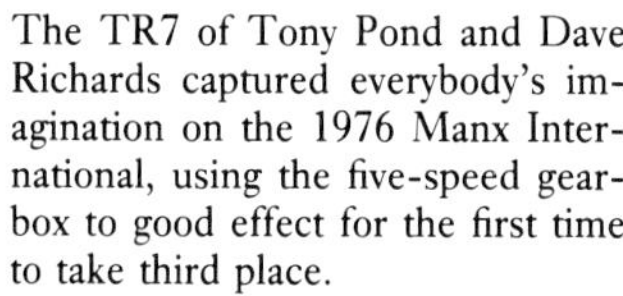

The TR7 of Tony Pond and Dave Richards captured everybody's imagination on the 1976 Manx International, using the five-speed gearbox to good effect for the first time to take third place.

was determined to press home its corporate image and the drivers were even banned from talking to the Press, who had to rely on public relations statements! As a result, the publicity gained by the TR7 was far more limited than it might have been. But Pond was still flying and took third place in the Tour of Elba, with Culcheth eliminated by a broken throttle. The rough tracks of Wales eliminated both TR7s, but with equally tough terrain north of the border, Pond took second place and Culcheth ninth in the Scottish Rally.

Despite the car's preference for tarmac events, Culcheth exploited its great strength to gain fourth place on the very rough Mille Pistes in France before putting up a magnificent drive for a second to Airikkala's Vauxhall Chevette in the Manx International. Pond had suffered from engine trouble and the internal politics dictated that Culcheth could not have the settings he needed for his car.

This works TR7 bore an unusual registration number, SCE 645S, because it was built by Safety Devices at Cambridge to bolster the Abingdon team to four for the 1977 RAC Rally. It took a hammering, however, being rolled by its driver Markku Saaristo, before continuing to 37th place overall.

It led him to say later: 'All the testing we had done showed that the alternative specification was faster and more efficient', which, coming from one of Britain's most experienced rallymen illustrated one of the main problems at British Leyland at the time. Everything had to be done according to the corporate plan, with no room for the individual—with the result that the TR7 finished second in such a specialised arena.

Four cars were entered for the RAC Rally as a climax to the season, but only two finished—one driven by Pond in eighth place and the other by Markku Saaristo 37th following a crash. Politics seemed to be affecting all forms of motor sport as never before, with considerable rule changes even in Thoroughbred racing; but nothing seemed to be able to stop Woodcock winning his class again with the TR3.

Despite the very rough tracks of the Scottish Rally in 1977, Pond and Gallagher took their TR7 to and excellent second place.

In the front rank, Culcheth left British Leyland, but his parting words had some effect as radical suspension development made the TR7 a potential winner, especially when more power could be expected with the homologation of the V8 engine from 1 April, 1978.

The new eight-cylinder car was called the TR7 V8 in deference to the marketing men who had only the four-cylinder to sell. With half as much power again, Pond took a good second place on the new car's debut in a Welsh Rallysprint. But it was hard work to drive, and Pond and Gallagher had to fight all the way to win the Granite City Rally in Scotland by 12 seconds from Nigel Rockey's Escort.

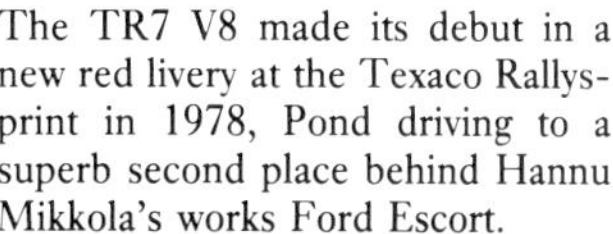

The TR7 V8 made its debut in a new red livery at the Texaco Rallysprint in 1978, Pond driving to a superb second place behind Hannu Mikkola's works Ford Escort.

Mechanical problems and an accident in the Welsh and Scottish Rallies left British Leyland needing a victory in the Ypres 24-hour rally, which Pond had

threatened to dominate the year before. This time he led from start to finish with the TR7 V8 in its element on the long, fast, flat roads of Belgium. At the same time, British Leyland had signed up John Buffum to compete in the SCCA Pro-Rally series in the United States with a TR7 in much the same manner as they had supported Kastner in circuit racing before. Buffum—the most successful rally driver in America—duly obliged by winning the SCCA series although he had to stick to a four-cylinder car because the V8 was not qualified for competition in the U.S. He also made infrequent visits to Britain and took eighth place in the Burmah Rally as Pond's TR7 V8 was eliminated by the old bogey of axle trouble.

Irishman Derek Boyd was teamed with Gallagher for the up-and-coming Ulster Rally, but was eliminated by a broken rocker shaft in his V8, and further engine problems in the Manx International—but a combination of Pond and the TR7 V8 proved unbeatable in this tarmac rally.

The car's reputation in this sphere was so high at that time that saboteurs loosened the gearbox drain plugs in *parc fermé* overnight before the Tour de Corse, and Pond and Jean-Luc Therier's cars seized up within a few miles.

Graham Elsmore took one of the works machines to second place on the Wyedean Stages before the year's climax in the RAC Rally. Pond and Gallagher overcame rear brake trouble to take a good fourth place with John Haugland and Ian Grindrod 12th, Simo Lampinen and Mike Broad retiring with clutch problems. But, as ever, Woodcock dominated his class in Thoroughbred racing with a car that seemed hardly to have changed since the late 1950s.

But British Leyland suffered a grievous blow when they lost Pond to Talbot, which was hardly surprising as this brilliant driver—without doubt Britain's best at the time—was anxious to try something less taxing than a TR7 V8. Elsmore took over for the Castrol *Autosport* series more to gain experience in what was considered a rather unwieldy car than with any hope of winning. But it was a tantalising situation as other teams had sorted out worse handling

Simo Lampinen and Ian Grindrod took 12th place on the Welsh Rally in 1979 despite being rammed by a non-stop competitor at the end of one stage.

problems and nobody at that time had anything like as much power. Privateer Terry Kaby also drove a TR7 V8, but suffered from having to prepare the car himself, which he often found wearing. Nevertheless, he finished fifth in the series, with Scot Ken Wood enjoying considerable success with a privately-entered ex-works four-cylinder TR7.

Accidents and mechanical mayhem wrecked the first part of the 1979 season for the works cars, although Per Eklund and Mike Broad managed an excellent second place in a snow-bound Mintex International. Lampinen and Grindrod survived being rammed by another competitor to take 12th place in the Welsh Rally before Gallagher was badly injured in a high-speed crash in Boyd's car during the Galway Rally. Eklund was at his best in winning the TV Rallysprint, however, from Stig Blomqvist's Saab Turbo, and took third place in the Scottish Rally with Lampinen 13th. Elsmore retired with overheating in this event, but he had better luck to win the Peter Russek Manuals Rally soon after in August.

Eklund and Lampinen were entered for the Thousand Lakes Rally in Finland, the former's car running on fuel injection. This gave all sorts of problems but he drove brilliantly to take eighth place. Gallagher was back in the co-driver's seat with Elsmore to take third place on the Manx International—but Pond was sorely missed.

British Leyland decided to take a leaf out of Ford's book for the RAC Rally in November, opting for safety in numbers. They entered four TR7 V8s and built a fifth for John Buffum, who had just scored a hat-trick of wins in the SCCA championship. His car was highly-experimental, with a modified fuel injection system that gave the engine 320 bhp. This made it the most powerful machine that had ever been seen in the tortuous British forests. It also produced far more torque and Buffum was at his best to run consistently faster than the official works entries before crashing out of contention in the notorious Kielder Forest.

The other drivers found their 290 bhp cars a handful, too, Eklund, Elsmore and Lampinen finishing 13th, 16th and 17th, with Kaby—in his first works drive—eliminated by oil pump trouble. It was the last event for Ford's Escort as a works car, but their seven entries dominated the rally. The crowds loved the TR7s though, with their rumbling V8 engines and menacing appearance that was rivalled only by a lone Lancia Stratos. As ever, there was nothing to seriously rival Woodcock in his class and he shared the overall Thoroughbred title with Jem Marsh's Marcos.

British Leyland pulled off a great coup in re-signing Pond for 1980, however, and retaining Eklund, with former Escort ace Roger Clark. The plan was for Pond and Eklund to concentrate on selected British and European rallies with Clark contesting the Sedan Open Championship in Britain with what was officially a privately-entered car. Once more mechanical problems intervened before Eklund took second place in a Rallysprint. During one event, the Criterium Alpin, the team had been forced to use Michelin radial ply racing tyres following trouble with their normal rubberware and found them so

The four works TR7 V8s received a standing ovation wherever they went in the 1980 RAC Rally ... Britons everywhere willed them to win, but luck was not on their side, with John Buffum, pictured here, retiring with only 2.5 miles to go following differential trouble.

successful that they were tried again—with chassis development taking a turn for the better—on the Manx National. At last it seemed as though the TR was reaching the pitch of perfection that British Leyland had hoped for in 1976. Pond and Gallagher had no trouble in winning convincingly on the tarmac of the Isle of Man. The car was not bad on the rough either, with Pond taking fourth place and Clark ninth in the Scottish Rally before Pond decimated the opposition—including two Porsches—at Ypres. However, Dunlop tyres were still competitive and worked well for Eklund to take a magnificent third place in the Thousand Lakes.

The Manx International was almost a foregone conclusion, with Pond and Gallagher winning by almost four minutes from Ari Vatenen's Escort. Suddenly, for the first time, the car was handling as it should and with a choice of Michelin

Privateers continued to rally the ex-works TR7 V8s, Bob Fowden on the 1982 Welsh Rally with OOM 512R, and Ken Wood in the Scottish Rally with SJW 548S.

or Dunlop tyres, Pond carried out back-to-back tests while taking second place on the Tour of Cumbria. Hopes were high for victory in the RAC Rally as Pond won yet another Rallysprint.

But misfortune struck on a greasy opening stage at Longleat wildlife park as Pond crashed into a lion's pen. He escaped with a battered roof and smashed screen, but there was no room for mistakes on a rally as tight and tough as the RAC, although he provided all the thrills in a dramatic climb back to seventh place overall. The other three entries retired with various maladies ... and suddenly British Leyland said: 'That's enough.' Just as the TR was reaching its peak, the rally programme was axed.

Ken Wood carried on with some success in ex-works cars, and Woodcock was as invincible as ever in Thoroughbred. A new name, Richard Morrant, emerged in Prodsports, mopping up lap records with a TR6, but the TRs at the top had run into the age-old problem: lack of factory finance.

VII
Strengths and Weaknesses

So far as sporting cars go, the Triumph TRs, especially the early ones with a chassis, are exceptionally tough vehicles. With the exception of one gearbox component, their mechanical parts are robust in the extreme. The steel chassis and bodies were very strong by the standards of the day, their only one weak point being their tendency to rust in a damp climate. The interior is only of average strength, but because of its simplicity it is very easy to replace. So, largely speaking, the Triumph TRs with a chassis—that is the models from the TR2 to the TR6—provide few potential problems to their owners other than those caused by corrosion.

Although the chassis is exceptionally strong, the days are gone when it could be relied upon to be the sound steel heart of almost any rust-ravished TR. After about ten years the chassis, in particular the outriggers and rear end which do not become soaked in engine oil, start to show signs of rust that can now be terminal, if not treated.

Also many cars have been fitted with replacement panels, in steel or glass fibre, for the body parts which rot away faster than the chassis. The result is that although there are now superficially good TRs around with sound body panels, they can often hide a rotten heart if nothing has been done to cure the rampant rust at the heart of the chassis.

As the chassis was made of such substantial steel it is often possible to reconstruct entire sections by specialist welding techniques, although the later independent rear suspension cars, with their more complicated curves, present greater problems than the earlier machines in this area. Such work is only really practical, however, during a major restoration in which the body is taken off the chassis.

It is quite possible, though; to replace corroded chassis outriggers without removing the body.

The built-in weak point is at the front, however. The brackets that provide the lower wishbone mountings on the chassis rails just behind the front suspension turrets, are not strong enough. They can bend quite easily if a wheel is struck hard on a kerbing stone, or even wrenched out of line if the car is reversed hard on full lock—such as happens quite frequently in a sporting

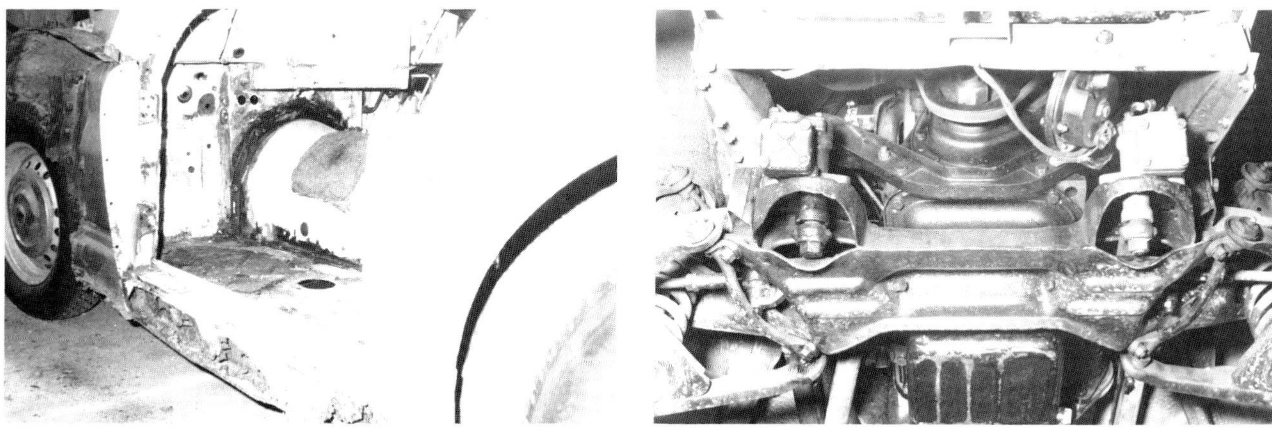

Rust attacks the bodies everywhere, particularly along the sill line.

The suspension mountings need especially careful attention for security.

driving test. The effects on stability, handling, and tyre wear have to be experienced to be appreciated!

The body itself is nothing near like so strong as the chassis on these cars. The problem faced when putting the bodies into production, in that large double curvature panels could not be afforded, has turned out to be both a strength and a weakness for the TR. The complex assortment of small panels, particularly around the wheels, provides far more nooks and crannies as sources of corrosion than might have been the case with large, all-enveloping, pressings. But this preponderence of relatively small parts does allow the outer wings to be detached, for instance (before they fall off!), which means that repairs can be cheaper and, with a car in perfect condition, ultimately much easier preventative maintenance. On the other hand, panels such as those used for the bootlid, bonnet and doors, are of thoroughly modern design and, as a result, expensive to repair, their saving grace being that they can be replaced as units.

The other main problem with body and chassis is that with a relatively solid base, it was possible for Triumph to make the outer panels relatively 'floppy.' No matter that the combination of the body and the chassis was stiff enough by the standards of the 1950s and 1960s; if they are separated today, the body—which is weak as a unit—can be exceptionally difficult to repair and even more difficult to refit to a replacement chassis. Nevertheless, it must be considered to be a strength of the early TRs in that you can take them to pieces so easily.

The four-cylinder engines may be among the toughest units ever made, but they are not entirely foolproof. Their main attribute is that they seem to be able to go on for a tremendous mileage without overhaul, and seemingly run well when, in fact, they can be in an extraordinarily worn state. The result is that components have a tendency to break without warning because they have run for an uncertain time without overhaul. Timing chain tensioners are a typical example. Bearings can also give unexpected trouble, which is not surprising when it is realised that one of the first signs of a worn engine can be manifested in the piston rings and it is quite easy to replace the rings, pistons and liners without touching the bottom end of the engine. As a result, a seemingly healthy engine can be running on bearings of great antiquity.

The six-cylinder unit, on the other hand, has inherent weaknesses, especially when considered alongside its predecessor. This is because it was a very long stroke engine at the end of a development cycle that started with a much smaller four-cylinder unit. The result is that it has rather narrow bearings and thin thrust washers, which wear more quickly than normal and can give unexpected problems. In cars fitted with fuel injection, careful maintenance is necessary and dirt can be sucked into the injectors. Repairs can be very expensive because of the precision with which its components have to be made. All the carburettors fitted to TRs are of well-tried design, however, and present few problems other than those associated with the wear and tear of advanced age.

The TR4A's rear suspension as it should look . . .

Clutches are as strong as those of any other similar car, and have only one inherent weakness: the release fork is located on its operating shaft by a pin which can shear inside the bellhousing. It should be wired on for security in case it falls down and damages something else. In some cases, the fork snaps next to the pin—and in either case, the unfortunate owner or driver is left without means of disengaging the clutch at the very least. If the car is travelling fast, it is wise to try to stop it by use of ignition key if you cannot change gear without a clutch.

The gearboxes are robust except for the first and reverse ratio shaft, which is just not strong enough, although its bearings were improved to some extent on later cars. This shaft runs in needle rollers and the front ones have a tendency to scatter and mutilate the shaft. Fortunately the overdrives rarely give trouble, apart from electrical problems caused by age and neglect.

The universal joints in the propellor shaft are subject to as much wear as those in any other car, but, if neglected, can cause some quite dramatic problems. On the independent rear suspension cars, worn universal joints set up such bad vibrations that the final drive can wrench itself out of its rather inadequate mountings, or, in even more extreme cases, with the solid rear axle cars, the rear end of the gearbox casing can split. However, such happenings should not be unexpected, and only deserved for anybody who drives a car in such a condition, because the vibrations can go on for around 5,000 miles before any breakages occur. There is a school of thought that if the final drive mountings were stronger, the unit's casing might go the way of the gearbox in such cases, or the gearbox trouble strike more frequently.

Play in the driveshaft joints on the independent rear suspension cars can also wreck the splines of the hubs fitted to take wire wheels. Rear wheel bearings are also difficult to replace on these cars, which was a weak point of design when maintenance is considered.

The disassembled state of this TR3A shows how easily the car can be taken to pieces.

The rest of the suspension is of such utterly conventional and well-tried design that there are no real weak points other than the enforced use of lever-arm rear dampers. These obsolete units do not maintain their efficiency for very long in comparison with later telescopic shock absorbers and they are expensive to replace.

Of these cars, the TR3A is probably the best purchase of the cars with the original shape, especially in its TR3B form for Americans. This is because it was the last of a line constantly improved in detail that benefited from having disc front brakes and a 2.2-litre engine. An exceptionally attractive point with the cars made from late 1956 was, of course, the disc front brakes although there is no reason other than for originality's sake that they should not be fitted to any other early TR. It is difficult to present a case in support of the earliest drum brakes, however, other than for originality, purely as a talking point, rather than anything active. And naturally the 2.2-litre engine is more attractive than the earlier 2-litre units because it provides a better performance.

A rear wing as it often looks . . . and as it should appear after repair.

On the other hand, the original long-door bodies of the TR2 were not that much less rigid than the later deep-sill versions and it is hardly worth changing them. The all-synchromesh gearbox is an obvious improvement when ease of driving is considered, and the wind-up windows of the TR4 are far more weatherproof and comfortable than the old sidescreens if in comparable condition. The original TR hood was definitely claustrophobic, and a potential traffic hazard, and again, originality is its only defence.

There is a strong case to support the live rear axle on the TR4s if maintenance and durability are prime concerns.

Obviously the six-cylinder engine is a major attraction with the TR5 and TR6, especially in its 'hottest' fuel injection form. But there is a consolation for TR250 owners in that they face far fewer maintenance problems. The chief attraction with the overdrive fitted to the later TR6s is that spares are far cheaper and more readily available—but the older units are outstandingly reliable. It is really a question of deciding exactly which sort of TR you prefer rather than that any one model has an exceptional number of strengths or weaknesses when compared with the others.

The TR7 and TR8

It is hardly surprising that the TR7 and the TR8 have totally different strengths and weaknesses to those of the earlier TRs; after all, they are of a completely different design, even if the concept was virtually the same. But what is surprising is that some of the inherent weaknesses in the TR7 were never eliminated. The TR8, however, benefited from having an engine that had been in production, on and off, since 1960, the development of which had been aimed almost entirely at reliability.

That could never be said about the early examples of the TR7! British Leyland had such a massive labour relations problem at Speke that the cars built there, with chassis numbers prefixed ACG, suffered the most appalling record for unreliability. In fairness to the BL designers, this was mainly as a result of poor quality control, but there were also inherent factors behind it. The cylinder head of the Dolomite-based engine was prone to move around on top of the block because of the curious layout of its securing bolts. This resulted in restricted water passages, the engine overheating (particularly if it was used hard, as with the case of many sports cars), and the gasket blowing. Moreover, there were two other reasons that this might happen: either the radiator could block up, restricting the water flow in a similar way to head movement, or if the cooling system was not properly topped up, that would blow it as well. When this happened, it was not enough to simply pour coolant into the nearest handy place, the expansion tank. The system had to be bled by filling it through an opening near the thermostat housing to stop the infiltration of air, and subsequent overheating. Later cars had a modified head gasket and revised torque settings for the cylinder head securing bolts, but the faults were never completely cured.

The TR7 also lost a lot of the backwoods appeal of the early TRs, particularly those with the four-cylinder engine, because its valve clearances were difficult to adjust and the ignition system—especially the distributor—was extremely awkward to maintain in the restricted space under the bonnet. The result is that many TR7s are run out of tune if they have not had skilled servicing, and then the engine suffers.

The V8 unit is a different matter in that virtually all its inherent weaknesses had been cleared up by the time it found its way into the TR8. But it can still suffer from low oil pressure at idle because of the way it is designed. It also has a rather small sump and the tappets are worked by oil pressure, so problems can develop when the car is cornered hard with the engine at high revs. It can also blow its rear main oil seal if maintenance of the crankcase breathing system is neglected, although this problem has been much reduced since a revised seal was fitted before installation in the TR8. The TR8's engine uses the lowest compression ratio pistons for a V8, so it should not give problems with low-octane petrol. In this, and with so many other points, particularly because it is so understressed in the lightweight TR8, the engine must be considered to be one of the car's strongest points.

The gearboxes certainly are not. The five-speed is far better than the four, but ultimately first gear gives up trying to cope with the torque of the V8. It is plenty strong enough for the four-cylinder engine, but even then it baulks badly until the oil is warmed up and can suffer damage with insensitive treatment. The four-speed box is generally notchy, gritty and unpleasant to use, especially when it is old. The synchromesh, particularly on second gear, also has a limited life. There are few problems with the well-developed automatic gearbox, however, other than an occasional tendency to leak.

The rear axles are a strong point, being quite reliable, although they often become very noisy with wear. But they seem to be capable of surviving for a considerable mileage in such a state. The propellor shaft universal joints present the same potential problems as those of the earlier independent suspension TRs.

Good solid sills are needed to hold the early bodies together.

So far as the body and chassis unit is concerned, it is massively strong when it is in good condition. But it is wise to remember that it can have a drastically limited life if it is neglected in a damp climate. It is of above-average durability for a mass-produced car though. Whereas the panels in some manufacturers' bodies crumble in about five years, or even less, the Triumph's seem to be capable of about seven years in similar circumstances. Corrosion starts behind the front and rear wheels, and especially around the vulnerable wheelarch lips. This is because these lips are exposed not only to road debris and salt, but are easily clipped during tight parking manoeuvres. Ultimately, the corrosion spreads to the wings (inner as well as outer), the sills, and the luggage boot floor, before moving forward towards the areas generally soaked in engine oil, which last longest. The boot seems especially prone to water leaks and the lid and doors are rather like those of the earlier TRs: they do suffer from corrosion, but at present they are easily replaceable. So are the hingepins on the doors, the weight of which makes them sag when subject to prolonged wear.

The front apron is prone to a great deal of corrosion if paint chips—which are very common because of its exposed position—are not rectified immediately. The whole nose of the car suffers, too, from the poor visibility afforded by the high cockpit sides and the low seating. It can be extremely difficult to judge the edge of a TR7 or TR8, with the result that damage around the bumper areas and the wheelarch lips is common. The bumpers certainly are not weak, but visibility is definitely a weak point with this design.

The swage line along the sides also makes panel repairs very difficult and needlessly expensive. Early paint-flaking around the headlight covers has been largely cured by better finishing, but the electric motors that lift the lights can still suffer from the effects of water; in addition, a general lack of maintenance in this area can make them very sluggish in operation. The unprotected inside surfaces of the luggage boot have also resulted in dents appearing on the outside of many cars when heavy or sharp-edged objects are carried unsecured in the boot or simply thrown in. The position of the boot lid lock and the fuel filler capalso lead to common paint damage. The interior, on the other hand, is very durable, suffering only from scuffing because the car is relatively small and low. But in the future, interior parts are likely to be much more difficult to remanufacture on a small scale that those of the earlier cars because of the complex tooling required.

Meticulous assembly is needed to ensure that all the panels line up properly.

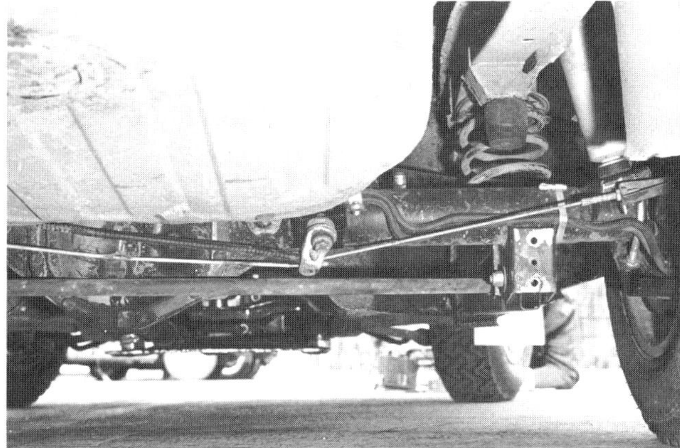

The rear suspension mountings of the TR7 and TR8 can be vulnerable to accidental damage and should also be checked for wear in their rubber components.

The steering and suspension is heavily dependent on the quality of the mounting bushes, particularly those at the back, which wear quickly. They should be replaced as frequently as tyres, a factor that few people realise or will admit. The suspension struts also wear but at a no higher rate than those on any other car using such a system. Their mountings at the top of the inner wings must be in good order or the car is rendered unsafe. The rear suspension brackets, which originally gave so much trouble, are just as vital and could become the Achilles heel of these cars when they are much older. With similar installations in other cars, the brackets generally become suspect after about nine or ten years when other forms of corrosion are evident. There is no reason to expect that the TR7 and TR8 will be any different. If terminal rust is to be avoided in a damp or salt-laden climate, it certainly pays to take preventative action against corrosion. In exceptionally hot climates, such as in some parts of California where many of the cars were sold, the interior plastic and the wiring can suffer from the heat, especially if the convertible is left with its hood furled for an hour or more in the sun. Overall, though, if it is in good condition, a TR7 or TR8 is an exceptionally strong car because it was designed to meet American safety regulations that were expected to be far more severe than those introduced.

The TR8 Convertible is without doubt the most attractive model, although only a handful were sold outside North America. Its only weak point of any great significance is the lack of disc brakes at the back. Next to that, it is a straight choice between a convertible or a fixed-head TR7 and that is based purely on personal preference, although the less-glamorous fixed-head could become more attractive to some in future years as its top endows more strength on what might be a suspect shell. The five-speed cars are much more appealing than the four-speed, with only a very small number of Dolomite Sprint-engined TR7 prototypes having been sold. It is quite feasible, however, to convert any TR7 into a TR7 Sprint or into a TR8, especially as originality is not, at an early stage in their life, of supreme importance to their value. It is only when the ready supply of original cars dwindles that this factor achieves an overwhelming influence. Obviously, with conversions it is best to stick as far as possible to factory specifications—but they were quite straightforward and it is not a difficult task. So, at present a replica Sprint-engined TR7, or even a neat TR8, is likely to be of greater value because of its rarity—a value that might never be eroded because of the desirability of such conversions.

The undesirable aura that surrounded early Speke-built TR7s ought by now to have evaporated because most of there faults were due to bad workmanship and should have been rectified in their early life.

VIII
Common Problems

The early Triumph TRs, with their separate chassis and relatively unsophisticated mechanical components (fuel injection apart), can be deceptive cars. They look quite easy to restore, but they can pose extraordinary problems. The mechanical parts are straightforward: it is simply a case of following the workshop manual bolt to bolt. But the body can be a real horror. This is because you have to take it off the chassis to do any extensive renovation and the common enemy, corrosion, usually ensures that this is necessary. Even in the hot and dry climate of Southern California, where so many TRs were sold, there are problems: most of the cars are now so old that if they are unrestored they have probably suffered substantial accident damage at some point which can also mean taking the body off—although if the body is still strong, it is a much easier task.

The main problem is not so much taking the shell off, however, but in getting it back together again accurately, and with even more difficulty, making it fit a restored chassis. No two chassis seem to be exactly alike, which makes the substitution of a repaired chassis even more difficulty. Another factor that poses problems is that the majority of replacement panels are reproductions. This means that they have to be made by far more primitive methods than the original factory parts—which were produced on huge and very costly presses, and which never fitted together very well in the first place! Fortunately, the major suppliers of reproduction body panels have a good reputation, but it is an inescapable fact that you cannot buy a whole pile of parts for a TR body, bolt, rivet, screw, braze and weld them together, and then expect them to drop neatly into place over the freshly repainted chassis. You have to be prepared to build up a replacement, or extensively repaired, body a little bit at a time—often incorporating some renovated parts from the car's original body—carrying out all sorts of minor adjustments and modifications along the way: the result can only then be a major success.

With the notable exception of the hot climate cars, the first thing you have to assess is how much of the body is left, and what it is made of: sound steel, rotten steel or glass fibre replacement parts. It is not too difficult to remove the outer wings, particularly if you are willing to hacksaw or drill out their securing

The scuttle makes a good starting point for reassembly on a restored chassis.

bolts. You might also have to angle grind out welding repairs made so often to the bottoms of the wings. But check the condition of the doors first, and do not remove them in haste. They can make excellent templates if their gaps are right when the wings are returned to the car. It's a good idea to remove the windscreen and surround at the same time, for safety's sake, but it can be very difficult; there are bolts behind the instrument panel that will try anybody's patience to remove. But remember, it's better to cut, drill or burn out a bolt than to risk damaging any surrounding metal or the captive nut which holds it in place. And when replacing such bolts, use an anti-corrosion solution to make sure that you never have this problem again!

Then have everything sandblasted to remove all the old paint, sealer and whatever might be below a deceptive surface. It is essential to hire a skilled operator for this task as a sandblaster in any other hands can leave precious panels looking more like the moon surface than anything Mulliner's made. Flanges can be destroyed that, although corroded, might be of great assistance in the frequent dummy rebuilds that are needed before final alignment. At the point where the car is down to the bare metal, an anti-rust preparation should be applied to ensure that it stays that way at least until it is repainted—which can be a long time, such is the work required to restore a TR body.

Only then can you think about more basic dismantling, such as removing the doors, exhaust system, radiator, horns, handbrake assembly, engine ancillaries, gearbox tunnel and wiring loom. Photograph or sketch the position of everything as you do it: with the TR2,3,3A or 3B for instance, the steering rod steady bar locates on the battery box stay underneath the instrument panel. If

As as-new standard is worth aiming for during the complete restoration of a TR2.

you strip the rod off without thinking, and then look at it again months later when you are about to replace it, it looks as though it ought to fit on top of the stay—but it shouldn't, it should go underneath, with packing washers on top. Refit it the other way, and you might get heavy steering at low speeds.

You then have to decide how to take off the body: in one piece, two or maybe more. It's best to keep it in one piece if you can, but it may not be possible, particularly if the sills are rusted. It is also worth considering fitting new inner front wings while the body is still in place so that when the front is taken off, it remains reasonably rigid. This will also help when it is time to return the body to its eventual resting place. The petrol tank does a great job at keeping the rear end from flopping about, but it is downright dangerous to leave it in place while the repairs are carried out at that end, so make up a template as a substitute. The template doesn't have to be metal: a strong wooden frame will do. If the body is strong enough, though, it can be lifted off with the doors shut. Otherwise, another possibility is to make up a wooden frame to bolt inside the cockpit to hold everything together in its original shape while the body is removed. It all depends on the space to hand and the state of damage.

Then it is time to give the chassis a really detailed examination, including possibly stripping it down and sandblasting to make sure there is no paint left in any nook or cranny. Should there by any corrosion, or damage—to the front wishbone mountings for instance—this must be repaired with new metal as a base rather than by plating over damaged areas. Such repairs require very accurate and skilled welding and are best left to the experts. It is vital that the alignment of suspension and body mountings is retained or restored. It is also a good idea to reinforce the wishbone mountings, and the final drive mounts on independent suspension cars, at the same time.

Should you be using a substitute chassis, rather than just repairing the old one, make sure you realign the body on the one that will eventually become the heart of the car. Do not be tempted into using the old one as a jig for body rebuilding while renovations are carried out on the 'new' chassis; they are probably different in some minute way which can make life very difficult later. And because of the way in which such chassis flex, work on alignment with the power train in place and the chassis rails supported at the wheel centres—otherwise you might have terrible difficulty in getting the doors to fit. Triumph did not have this problem when they were building the car because they used big

Trial reassembly is worthwhile before parts receive their final coats of paint.

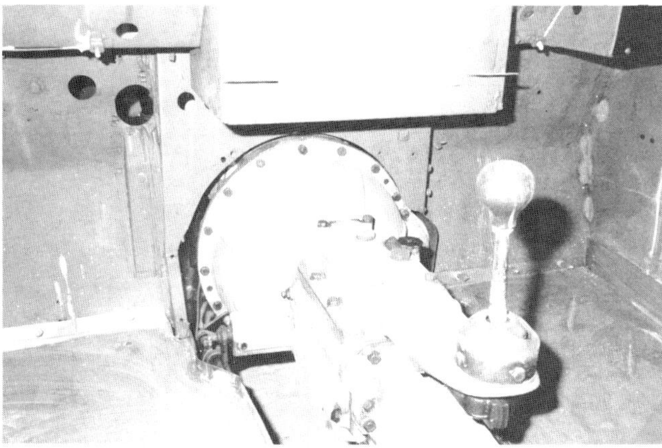

jigs. If the body is as corroded as many of them are, lift it off in two pieces, and then—after the mechanical side has been renovated—fit new floor panels very carefully. Then you can line up everything from this point. The sills follow next, with equal care being taken to fit them exactly in place.

It is worth checking the alignment of the front suspension turrets to see that there is no accident damage, while the body is off. The same goes for the rear suspension mounting brackets on the TR4A, 5, 250 and 6, because inaccurate geometry can cause awful handling problems. It is also wise to replace such items as the pin that locates the front of the rear road spring on the half-elliptic cars. This can be very difficult to get out whole the body is on and the spring needs changing! With such a major rebuild as a body-off job, all springs, shock absorbers, seals and piping should be replaced as a matter of course; retaining them is a false economy. The chassis is also much easier to work on, of course, when it is bare: fitting a new coil spring at the front—which requires a special compressor—is much easier when there is room to straighten your back. The fuel tank should also be examined in great detail because it often rusts out slowly from the bottom.

But once the chassis and mechanical parts are in immaculate order, and the floor and sills in their correct places, the front bulkhead and inner wings can be attached to them. Take care to allow for the fibre body mounting pads and use only new ones on final reassembly. It is essential to use new door hinges every time the body is assembled, not just at the end, because it is impossible to realign the doors properly otherwise.

A juggling act is needed with self-tapping screws, rivets, clamps or tack welding before the front door post can be welded into its exact position. The doors are used to ensure that the rear post is fitted exactly right, taking great care that it does not sit too far out. This is essential because the post dictates the line of the rear outer wings. The spare wheel tray and rear floor areas are involved in this process as is the entire rear end of the body. The point at which the rear wheel arch, door post and sills meets is highly stressed and the weakest part of the body, so it must be an exact fit. Self-tappers to hold the parts in a temporary position are an invaluable aid. The bootlid should also be fitted in place at the same time to ensure that its aperture is correct. When eventually everything is welded up and in good order, the body can be removed for the last time for painting and rustproofing. If repairs to the opening panels need only partial reskinning, it is wise to remember that this sort of welding requires a lot of skill.

From the mechanical point of view, the early TRs are amazing cars. There is hardly anything that is likely to cause undue concern to today's owners, other than front suspension trunnions that wear out relatively quickly and the fuel injection system which was at one time notorious because so few people knew how to service it. You have to remember that it is a precision-engineering job that relies on absolute cleanliness. So never let the petrol tank of a TR5 or TR6 run completely dry, or sediment might be sucked up into the pump with expensive results! It's a point worth watching when a car is being restored, too . . .

The TR7 and TR8

The average TR7 or TR8 was too young at the time of writing this book to suffer from many of the problems that the earlier cars are experiencing—though in time they will undoubtedly suffer from rust. The most common problems affecting those that are still being used as an everyday vehicle are to do with maintenance, particularly those that have the four-cylinder engine.

Detail shot of the inner scuttle side with sill attached.

The engines are robust and capable of high mileages before an overhaul becomes necessary, although the four-cylinder unit is tricky when it needs attention to its head. Tappet adjustments on the TR7 is by the pallet shim system and because it is a fairly major operation, it tends to be neglected. The ignition timing can be troublesome, too, because it is awkward to loosen the two locking bolts that secure the distributor body. You need special universally-jointed tools! The water pump is also difficult to reach in its position under the inlet manifold. You can save yourself quite a lot of money, however, by working on the cylinder head should it be necessary; there are only a few tips you have to remember. It's mostly a case of following the workshop manual: disconnect the fuel lines, drain the coolant, disconnect the battery and high-tension leads; then take off the distributor cap, with the leads. Remove the six bolts securing the inlet manifold, and take it off complete with the carburettors. Remove and clean the cam cover. You can then see the problem you're going to have removing the valve springs. But you can get over it this way: cut a short piece of metal tubing that will fit over the collets holding the springs in compression. Then saw an aperture in one side of the tube at the bottom that is big enough to accept the ends of a pair of thin-nosed pliers. By using this special tool in conjunction with an ordinary spring compressor, you will be able to hook out the collets through the slot in the bottom of the tube.

The other thing that can catch you out is disconnecting the camshaft's chain drive. With the engine turned to top dead centre on the firing stroke of number one cylinder, line up the marks on the bearing cap and camshaft. Then take one nut off a bearing cap and use it to secure the boss on the camshaft pulley to the spring steel bracket so thoughtfully provided by British Leyland. If you don't do this, the chain's tensioner will take up the slack and the chain cannot be refitted without stripping a lot more off the engine. Once you've done this, the rest of the bearing cap nuts are removed, the sprocket is released from the shaft, and the caps are taken off. Note their identifying numbers. Lift out the camshaft and remove the tappets and shims, sticking to the order in which they came out when you are returning them. Loosen the cylinder head nuts in the reverse order to that given in the manual for tightening, and then take out the cylinder head studs (using a lock nut at the top), because they are not perpendicular to the block. You can get at the exhaust manifold nuts from under the car. Then its off with the head for cleaning, checking and so on, taking care not to scratch its soft alloy. The valves are adjusted by removing or adding shims to the required thickness to give a specified gap.

The workshop manuals often advise you to refit two of the studs in the head bolt holes as an aid to realignment. This may prove difficult in the confined space under the bonnet, so line up the gasket using two bolts through the head—done up finger tight so that the gasket can be lined up. Be sure to realign the camshaft before refitting the head to avoid damage to pistons and valves. Should the head have warped due to overheating, it may be possible to have up to 0.020 inches skimmed off it, but more than likely it will have to be replaced.

The best advice to avoid this possibility is to watch the temperature gauge like a hawk and to check the cooling system for leaks and blockages at least twice a year—and don't allow the alternator drive belt to become slack. The rest of the car is relatively straightforward with attention needed to the rear suspension rubbers and greasing the steering rack, with special care to make sure that its gaiters are not split.

The V8 engine is very reliable providing its oil level is maintained accurately and the plug leads don't fall off or get burned through by the exhaust manifolds! But, like the four-cylinder unit, it is essential that anti-corrosion inhibitors are maintained in the coolant, otherwise there can be a lot of problems with blocked passages in the alloy heads and blocks. These conditions can be very expensive to rectify.

Structural corrosion is not a major problem yet in the average TR7 or TR8, although it pays to check the front suspension turrets very carefully even in Californian cars; a build up of road debris around these points traps moisture with the result that they rust through—so check here for any signs of corrosion, or expensive repairs will be needed later. Other rust traps which could prove costly on an otherwise immaculate car are at the base of the windscreen pillars, the trailing edges of the wings and under the sills, and in the luggage boot. More cosmetic areas are at the bottoms of the doors and around the wheelarches, but these could become expensive later.

Naturally there are certain similarities between repairs to the bodyshell of the TR7 and TR8 and those to the earlier cars. The convertibles in particular need a lot of support if major repairs are to be carried out to their floors, for the most obvious reasons. It is best to support the car as fully as possible underneath, with special attention to the areas of the wheel centres so that the correct stressing is retained. When much of the floor has to be repaired even on a fixed-head, it is worth considering building a temporary angle iron internal frame and welding it in place—there is rarely enough room for bolts and you have to fill in their holes at the end anyway—before any metal is removed from the floor. Reference points marked on this frame before removal of the old metal can then be used when the new material is welded back in. It doesn't take long to make one of these frames and it can be particularly valuable when suspension mountings are involved because their positioning must be of the utmost accuracy.

When removing old panels with a tool like a chisel, try to leave a reference point, such as a flange or part of the old panel, which will provide either a mounting or a reference for the new panel. At this point it is worth warning amateur workpeople to wear thick gloves to protect themselves from the lacerations that inevitably accompany cutting metal with tools gripped in bare hands. Do not use a welding torch unless it is absolutely necessary at this stage because its heat can distort surrounding metal. It can also set fire to old underseal with potentially disastrous results!

Marry up new panels before removing the old ones to see how much you have to leave for mounting. If several panels have to be replaced, approach the job in a similar way to restoring one of the earlier TR's bodyshells. Don't throw away any of the old panels that you have cut off because they can be useful for giving location points for trim mounting holes and so on. Just hammer the sharp edges flat and cover them with heavy adhesive tape for safety and ease of handling.

In general, it is a wise policy to repair the floor first and build up, or out, from there to minimise the possibilities of distortion. Some parts, such as inner sills, can be quite efficiently fabricated from a flat sheet of steel if you have the old ones to copy. Other parts can be built up with small pieces of metal, particularly if the damage is localised. In case of difficulty in obtaining replacement parts, it is worth thinking about cannibalising an old bodyshell if it has similar parts in better condition. Use the existing doors, lids and bonnet for refitting and adjustments in the same manner as with the earlier TRs.

Do not weld patches over rusted areas if the panel is at all stressed. It is far better to cut out the old metal and to weld in new so that the rust does not continue. But sometimes, particularly on unstressed panels, it is best to weld in a new plate behind a corroded area and then grind out the rust and lead-in the depression. Where visible, spot welds will be more attractive to later generations of concours judges if that was the way the panel was originally attached. But some items, such as repaired suspension mounting areas, must be seam welded for safety.

Once the inner panels are positioned correctly, the outer ones should be mated loosely before final fitting—and you'll need plenty of clamps with a car like a TR!

IX
The Men Behind the TR

The story of Triumph after the Second World War involves most of the people in the British motor industry. But of even those directly employed by Triumph, when they were making the TRs, only a few were at all involved with the car's design or development. This was because the TRs were of secondary importance to, first tractors and saloon cars, and then just saloons.

The first TRs owed their existence to two men: Sir John Black and development engineer Ken Richardson, for whom the Russian word stakhanovite (for a worker who increases his output to an extraordinary extent) might almost have been coined.

In the background, playing vital, but less spectacular roles, were the multi-talented stylist Walter Belgrove; the humourless Ted Grinham; the managerial whizzkid, Alick Dick; and the supremely cool, calm and collected engineer, Harry Webster.

Later came Italian car designer Giovanni Michelotti; bluff North countryman, Stanley Markland; salesman Sir Donald and later Lord Stokes; manager John Barber; accountant, Alex Park; stylist, Harris Mann; gifted old-school engineers, Spen King and Lawrence Dawtrey; and the dynamic modern manager, Sir Michael Edwardes.

The most horrifying tales are told about Black, climaxed by a quote from 'a colleague' related in Graham Turner's book *The Leyland Papers*: 'He could be the kindest or the cruellest man in the world, the gayest or the most depressed, a heavy drinker or a total abstainer. He lived on a razor's edge and nobody knew which side he would fall.'

Donald Stokes

The depths of passion displayed by this former military man were extraordinary. Decisions could be dictated entirely by mood: he demanded, almost created, the TR to hit back at Jaguar's nimble-footed chief, William (later Sir William) Lyons and the tiny family firm who made Morgan sports cars. Using the TR he wanted to cream off Jaguar's American market; and he kept Morgan alive with engine supplies in the hope of killing them later and then feeding off their reputation.

John Paul Black, born in Kingston, Surrey, in 1895, rose to the rank of Captain during the First World War, and married one of the daughters of car magnate William Hillman. She had five sisters and their descendants included

DUNLOP
TIM HOLDER

DUNLOP

Alick Dick and Spen King. It could be an incestuous business, making cars in Coventry. Black's ruthless talent took him rapidly to the top of the motor industry as managing director of Standard by 1934. He inherited not only a reasonably efficient mass production facility, but also great tracts of undeveloped industrial land around its factory. With demonic energy, he expanded production in every direction except sports cars. His right-hand man was the tough Ted Grinham, but as strong as was Grinham's personality, Black's was stronger, and he dominated the man who became his technical director in 1936. In turn, Grinham showed a cordial dislike for most other people who he thought might threaten his position, notably the talented artist, Walter Belgrove, Standard's chief body engineer since 1935. But Belgrove could look after himself, and together this incredible trio were at the head of a very highly stressed management until war intervened in 1939.

Black, with so much industrial land available, seized his opportunity to participate in the government's 'shadow' factory building for plane production. He came out of the war as an industrial hero having been responsible for the building of a truly monumental number of fighting fuselages, and an excellent modern factory as a tangible reward. The relatively small firm of Triumph had been bombed out of sight, with their dying embers bought up and lashed into life as a prestigious new name for Standard. In years long gone, Standard had meant the standard by which others were judged. In the brave new Britain after the war, when everything was to be de luxe if you could get it, standard meant something else altogether: a very basic product. Black's fortunes were to be made by very basic engineering, but nobody would glory in that at the time: so Triumph was an attractive name to have acquired. Black might have been on the verge of madness, but he was no fool in decisions like that.

On the other hand, he could do some stupid things. He was quite happily supplying SS (later Jaguar) with mechanical components before the war and watched with glee as they consistently beat the rival touring cars made by MG. It was good to have a stake in success, and to give one in the eye to Lord Nuffield, whose empire made MGs and was one of Standard's major rivals in the saloon car field. But when Grinham produced the basic and versatile engine that powered not only the new Vanguard saloon, but the money-spinning Ferguson tractor, Black sold the tooling that had made his old six-cylinder engines, to Lyons. Standard did not need it any more . . but Lyons was sharp and knew that Black (Sir John by then) might change his mind when he realised how valuable it was to Jaguar as a stopgap until their new engine was ready. Lyons paid promptly, sending his cheque round by messenger. As soon as Sir John realised what he had done he demanded the tooling back and flew into a towering rage when Lyons refused. Hell-bent on revenge, Sir John swore to produce a sports car that would show Lyons who was master . . .

He had always been keen on such cars personally, having owned one of the beautiful SS100s made by SS before the war; and one of the attractions of the Triumph name was its sporting image bestowed by pre-war technical director Donald Healey.

But sales of the hastily-designed Triumph Roadster built between 1946 and 1949 failed to take off because of its uninspiring performance; even MG's tiny TC could leave it standing! Grinham wasn't interested in sports cars and refused to co-operate and do anything about giving it more power, so Belgrove was told to give it a new body. As more and more political problems intervened, so the new Triumph Roadster was a long time in the making; suffice to say that by the time it appeared in 1950, Lyons had introduced the brilliant new Jaguar XK120, with styling and performance that made it a complete waste of time to even think about producing the stodgy Triumph Roadster.

It was at that point that Sir John turned his attention to the tiny family firm of Morgan, who were using the Vanguard engine. If he couldn't produce a rival with the performance and styling of Lyon's XK120, maybe he could get even by demolishing MG's stronghold in the small end of the market. At this time, it was difficult for the uninitiated to tell the difference between a Morgan and an MG, except that the Morgan was available only in minute quantities, and the MG was being made by the thousand. Imagine Sir John's anger when Morgan resisted his advances, and it was not hard to imagine the surprise of interested observers when he continued to supply them with engines (although he had done this with Lyons, who still had a use for the Triumph Roadster's four-cylinder unit even after the tooling coup). But really, you could never tell what Sir John would do next. With the sober side of his judgement, he considered that it was better to eep his engines under somebody elses bonnet, with the prospect of consuming them later, than to let somebody else, like Ford, Austin, or Morris get the lion's share.

It was into this fraught environment that the Triumph TR was born. Savage as might have been Sir John's intentions, the other side of his personality commended caution. He thought only at first of producing about 500 of the new car each year, and as cheaply as possible. One of the reasons it had not been worth producing Belgrove's previous Roadster was that it would have cost a fortune for the tooling needed to make it on a larger scale. But when it was evident that there would be a substantial demand for the cheap new TR, Sir John knew when to back a hunch.

He was a master of hunchmanship, that showed itself in his love-hate relationship with Harry Ferguson for whom he made the tractors. In the summer of 1953, Ferguson—who marketed the tractors himself—had prosposed a merger with the giant Massey-Harris agricultural combine. The board of Standard-Triumph did not want to get involved; then would rather have remained entirely independent, and not exposed to such pressure ... into this scene stepped Sir John, announcing with a sweep of his hand that he had just signed a new 12-year deal with Ferguson! But such was the power of his personality that he not only maintained his grip on the board of Standard-Triumph but became chairman soon after. Then came the crash: he was badly injured in an accident with the Doretti and his influence began to wane soon afterwards. But he didn't lose his venom, and when he decided that Grinham was about to depose him he began to think of ways to sack him. Without a doubt,

Grinham fancied the job, but he had done nothing wrong and a great deal of right from the engineering point of view. So he had little trouble in turning the tables on Sir John and mobilising the board to converge on Sir John's home to sack him. Sir John realised that his race was run and resigned, the accident being blamed for his bad health ... he never found another place in the motor industry and died, a bitter man, on Christmas Eve 1965. Ironically, however, Grinham didn't get the job; it went instead to Sir John's personal assistant, Alick Dick, in 1954.

This was a hefty blow to Grinham who had spent much of the previous five years grooming himself for promotion, concentrating more and more on management, and leaving the engineering to his effective deputy, Harry Webster. He had been the company's chief engineer since 1931, technical director from 1936, and deputy managing director in 1939. He had a relatively good war with the De Havilland Aircraft Company, but when it was over, he could land only his old post as technical director in 1945. Dick being on the ascendent by them. Naturally this did nothing for the disposition of Grinham, who continued to have poor relations with the rest of the work force and Belgrove in particular.

Grinham, a strict disciplinarian, had extreme difficulty in tolerating Belgrove's freedom of spirit, but could do nothing about it as Sir John played one off against the other. A reactionary he might have been, sour and embittered he certainly was, but that aside, nobody could knock his engineering ability, especially the astoundingly simple and durable Vanguard engine based on a pre-war Citroën design. Few people seem to have had quite such a talent for low-cost engineering, and on this, Sir John and he were in agreement: when all around him were suggesting that gearboxes should have four speeds Grinham said they had enough torque to get away with three and Sir John was in wholehearted agreement; they cost less.

With such an approach to life, it was hardly surprising that Grinham had no interest in high-performance motoring. So he handed over responsibility for that side of engineering to Webster and hired Richardson to do the donkey work. That he then had to resign himself to being the eternal supporting act when Dick took over from Sir John in January 1954 must have been difficult for him to accept.

His ancient adversary, Belgrove, had started at Triumphs even earlier than Grinham, in the late 1920s, as a coachbuilding apprentice. He was an excellent example of what a polytechnic education could do for you. There was no real design section then, individuals working on specific parts of a new car, which was then assembled piecemeal at the end with no real cohesion other than a rambling brief from somebody like Black, Belgrove's talent for three-dimensional drawing soon took him to the top as chief body engineer in 1935 under technical chief Healey. His life presented a considerable contrast to that of Grinham who was making his way to the top at the same time; Belgrove loved to shock the conservatists, claiming never to have been very much influenced by anybody else, and being quoted as saying: 'The public were not ready, as indeed they never are,' for one of his designs. He had every talent needed for a body engineer of the 1930s, he could draw beautifully, and design a body very quickly; his ability as a sculptor gave him an instinctive feeling for the extra dimension that so often escaped the grasp of other engineers; he also had a rare gift of self-preservation and his diplomatic approach worked well with Sir John.

This was because Sir John gave him more freedom to express himself than his theoretical boss, Grinham. Belgrove, for all his protestation of never being influenced by others, was not above following Sir John's directive to sketch American cars parked around their embassy in London, as a guide to what the lines of the new Vanguard should be! Belgrove was that diplomatic—he was well capable of doing his own thing, as could be seen from the stillborn Triumph Roadster, but at the same time he could convince people that he was following their plagiaristic principles. In day-to-day dealings, he is remembered as a scrupulously fair man, but it was a sense of fair play that extended to making sure that he got the credit he felt he deserved for his work.

It was only an engineering talent the likes of Belgrove's that could have created the TR on such a low budget: he skirted around Sir John's directive for a traditional sit up and beg body by producing that was not only better but also far more cost effective. But once Sir John was gone his days were numbered; he weakened in a war of attrition with Grinham and walked out on his job in 1955.

But if Grinham was the cause of some people leaving, he was also responsible for hiring and nurturing some good people too. Webster was to go on to great things and Richardson was certainly an absolute bargain so far as Triumph were concerned.

Richardson was born in a village called Bourne, Lincolnshire, as the First World War was about to be declared, and grew to maturity with the legendary ERA racing cars that were built there by hill climb ace Raymond Mays. Like Lyons, but on a far smaller scale, Mays had used Standard parts to make touring cars of his own. Grinham had known this young development engineer for a long time when he telephoned to invite him to sort out the TR. The call was timely: Richardson was ready for a change as Mays's new BRM racing car project was going from bad to worse despite Richardson's almighty efforts. He had driven these ambitious cars thousands of miles to no avail as their advanced engineering let them down; and the only reward in sight for Richardson was even more test

Ken Richardson in his favourite habitat: behind the wheel.

driving as always the stars were preferred when it came to racing. He was the ideal test driver, a very hard worker, a very sound mechanic, but above all a man who did not have accidents. A safe bet, thought Grinham. His dour approach to development suited Grinham so much that Richardson's first abrasive comments on the TR1 were not enough to stop Sir John hiring him. After that, he worked and drove as only he knew how, to turn the TR1 into a car to be proud of. His reward came in the establishment of a competition department. With only Grinham to answer to, Richardson was in charge, and since he did as he was told, didn't demand anything exotic like a new engine, and just made sure the cars were perfectly prepared with a minimum of staff and no undue expense, Richardson was Grinham's idea of the ideal employee. Richardson in turn was prepared to work like a slave for what he wanted—to drive with the great names (Maurice Gatsonides), in the great races (the Mille Miglia). Eventually, he found his ideal partner, 'Kit' Heathcote from Kenilworth. His spartan approach to life as a team manager, driver, and publicity man, was highlighted by this quote on the 1955 Liege-Rome-Liege Rally in which they finished first in class, fifth in the general classification, and took the Newcomers' Award on a daunting debut:

> 'It was 98 hours' non-stop. For days and four nights. The longest stop you got was 45 minutes, so there was really no time to eat. Kit and I started off with some bags of apples and bananas and when we'd finished those we just went hungry ...

When Kit quit rallying, so did Richardson as a driver. He had more onerous responsibilities as the Le Mans project came to an already stretched department. But he never spared himself, nor anybody who worked with him, and that caused a lot of trouble. He said of the time that the competitions department was established:

> 'I had to take men made redundant from other parts of the company. They knew nothing about competitions and they were all in different unions, so when somebody picked up the wrong tool there was an argument. I told them they could forget unions while working in the competitions department. As a result, all Standard-Triumph's 17,500 workers were threatening to come out on strike. So I advised the directors to close down the competitions department at the works and to move it up to the service department at Allesley. This was far better, for I could have six or seven men I wanted from the service department and there was no further trouble...
>
> 'I enjoyed my 10 years with Triumph very much. They were jolly nice people to work with. Grinham ordered that nobody, just nobody, was to interfere with me or my people. What I wanted done I had done and nobody could change it.'

As a result, nobody knew what he had been up to all those years when the competitions department was closed. The six or seven men who had produced so much were dispersed and all the experience and knowledge went out of the door with Richardson. His successor, Graham Robson, had no real chance, even having to type his own memos on a meagre budget.

Meagre budgets were always a problem to Alick Dick, the man who succeeded Sir John. He had shown himself to be an astute businessman when everything was going well for Standard-Triumph—or as well as anything goes in the motor industry. He was capable of making all the right decisions when expansion was the name of the game, and only to come to grief when times were hard. Dick, one of the many relatives of the Hillman family, began his working life as a Standard apprentice, before operating in close conjunction with Sir John. He became his personal assistant in 1945, rising to assistant managing director in 1947 and deputy managing director alongside Grinham in 1951.

It fell to Dick to present the case for resignation to Sir John on behalf of the board, a difficult task which he handled in his typically cool manner; and it was only a logical move to make him managing director—at the age of 37—on Sir John's demise. His appointment was welcomed by just about everybody who had known Sir John and management immediately became a much more open and logical process. He was regarded as a far more reliable person, whose decisions were based on common sense rather than primarily on emotion, and he fitted in well with the motor industry's establishment at the time—spending lavishly on public relations budgets (which overall did not cost much)—and frugally on competition development, which could be far more expensive in total. His business principles were sound and it took a credit squeeze to unseat him and bring down Standard-Triumph at the same time.

The main problem that he inherited was that of Britain's Big Five car makers at that time, his product—with the notable exception of the TRs and the tractors—provided the least return on capital invested. This made it hard to raise money in competition with the rest. And this lack of financial muscle meant that the other big manufacturers, BMC (which included the TR's rivals, Austin-Healey and MG), Ford, Rootes (which made the Sunbeam Alpine) and Vauxhall, were better placed in the vital manoeuvres for expensive components such as body panels. As a result, Dick spent much of his time being courted, or courting, other manufacturers with a view to merger.

Within days of taking office, he was involved in talks with the Rover concern, led by Spencer Wilks (who, like Sir John, had married one of William Hillman's daughters), and later with the Rootes Group (controlled by the Hillman family), but both foundered for a variety of reasons. In the meantime, Massey-Ferguson, the combine which had bought out Harry Ferguson, were causing Dick some problems, and when they objected to the number of Standard-Triumph overheads being absorbed in tractor production, Dick had the wholehearted support of his board to get rid of Massey-Ferguson by selling them the tractor interests for £12 million in 1959. It was generally considered that as he had to raise a lot of capital somehow, he had done well to get rid of an unpleasant bedfellow at the same time; his only problems were that it cost the group half its output, slashed its cash flow and left heavy overstaffing. If he was pushed sufficiently hard, Dick would sack people, but he didn't like doing it and redundancies were few. Instead, he chose his only alternative—to try to find something to replace the tractors and to spend the newly-raised cash in such a way that Standard-Triumph could remain independent, or at least come out on top in any merger. So Dick gambled on a new car to replace the tractor, called the Herald (after his yacht); and at the same time he increased production dramatically of the money-spinning TR3A, hoping that his sales force could sell all Standard-Triumph could produce. The Le Mans TR project was authorised as the cheapest way of publicizing the marque on the racetrack and developing a new engine at the same time to keep the TR ahead of the opposition on the road.

Rover had made renewed attempts to link up with Standard-Triumph, but the deal foundered on management structure; Dick would not take a back seat. He also decided that his major priority was still to sell Standard-Triumph in as advantageous a manner as possible, because the capital he had raised did not go far. He had bought Hall Engineering in Liverpool to ensure body supplies, Alford and Alder for suspension, Forward Radiators, and a plant in Belgium to

Webster used the Le Mans twim cam engine for a variety of experiments, particularly in a new process of die casting that was to be used to good effect in the Rover V8 production unit.

get into Europe, in addition to expanding production space in Coventry. On reflection, he was to say later, it was not money well spent because a credit squeeze in 1960 left Standard-Triumph in a worse position. Contraction, rather than expansion became the order of the day for a domestic car maker, and Dick—who had found troubled labour relations distasteful—became even more determined to sell his firm. In the end, he got a good price for it, from the Leyland truck firm, which was seeking to expand into cars to sell alongside its trucks abroad. Standard-Triumph's new production facilities were also attractive. The American firm, Chrysler, were also after a British car maker with which to compete with their rivals, Ford, and General Motors (which owned Vauxhall). Leyland's chief, Sir Henry Spurrier, lost his temper after it became evident that Dick's firm could not live up to its cash expectations and decided to get rid of all the board. So Dick quit in 1961 with the telling comment on his public relations bill: 'I was trying to sell the company and a bloke bought it.'

In the meantime, the Italian stylist, Giovanni Michelotti, had been signed up under contract to Standard-Triumph to become one of their major assets. His company in Turin was quite capable of turning out a new prototype in a matter of weeks, whereas the British were likely to take far longer and cost a lot more; he was responsible, first, for a 'dream car' styling exercise on the TR3 chassis that Dick and his fellow directors drove for a while. Its nose led to the TR3A restyling and its wind-up windows eventually convinced them that this was the way the TR should go. Such details were likely to take this genius only a few minutes to sketch! He also designed the TR4's body in conjunction with many other products for Standard-Triumph; one feature that he suggested—pop-up headlights—finding favour with his mentor, Harry Webster, but not the rest of the Triumph management on the ground of cost.

Costs were high on the agenda of Stanley Markland, the Leyland man who took over the helm from Dick. He came to the company with a reputation as a hatchet man, which he was to prove unjustified. The blunt and clear-thinking Markland had joined Leyland as an apprentice in 1920, rising to chief design engineer by 1945. Subsequently he became works director of this austere firm in 1953 before bringing tight cost control to Standard-Triumph. But he was a just and kindly man, and brought order with it, much to the benefit of his new firm. He was a man who liked to see exactly what he was getting before he bought it; perhaps that is why Spurrier appointed him...

Markland had a penchant for ordering the most extraordinary experimental cars (with cheap engine transplants from within the group rather than expensive new developments) and then cancelling them when it was apparent that they were impractical. He was also much enamoured with flexible engines, no doubt as a result of his truck experiences. The Markland ideal was to be able to engage a high gear at a low speed and then plant his foot on the accelerator and watch the revs climb! His idea of a sports car was clear-out: it should go really fast. No sooner had he tried a TR4A prototype than he demanded more power and subsequently the six-cylinder engine got fuel injection for flexibility. By the time of their introduction, however, Markland—the man who put Standard-Triumph back into profit—was long gone as a result of a curious decision, almost on Spurrier's deathbed, that had nothing to do with Standard-Triumph.

Donald Stokes, who took over, was made chairman of Standard-Triumph as well as deputy chairman and managing director of Leyland. He was the super salesman who had joined the Lancashire firm as an apprentice in the 1930s, becoming a lieutenant colonel in the Army during the Second World War. He rejoined Leyland in 1945, writing a brief on how to run their export business. Subsequently he did this with great aplomb, with a breezy and informal style that swept aside the old-fashioned protocol that existed throughout the firm. He engendered a rare loyalty among his staff by working harder than anybody, answering all inquiries within forty-eight hours and chasing any remote chance of new business. Stokes chose his staff carefully, preferring company men with good technical qualifications to the whisky-and-soda salesmen that abounded before.

He regarded selling as partly psychological warfare, at the same time projecting an up-and-coming image for himself. Stokes used everything he had to his advantage, never failing to employ a gimmick if he thought it would work: his confidence was such that he considered his bald head to be an advantage in that it made him look older—and wiser—than he was. He trebled sales and found himself on the board by 1953, reaching the chairman's seat at Standard-Triumph before he was 50. Business boomed as never before until the next credit squeeze, in 1966...

Leyland (and Standard-Triumph) found themselves short of managerial talent and were alarmed when BMC and Jaguar merged; as a result, they took over Rover. At the same time, the Labour government were becoming alarmed at Chrysler's imminent take over of the Rootes Group. Neither Leyland, nor BMH (as the BMC-Jaguar conglomerate was called) could afford to accede to government pressure to stop Chrysler in view of the credit squeeze's effect on sales. But the seeds were sown for a shotgun marriage between Leyland and BMC.

Stokes came out on top in a prolonged skirmish for the job as chief executive when the government-induced merger to form British Leyland took place early in 1968. His new company was the second largest motor manufacturer outside the United States, but he was still short of managerial talent and it was full of seething resentment from the ranks of former BMH men who felt that he had landed the job more on self-publicity than ability.

One of his first tasks was, however, not to improve his personal image, but to see how he could hack the new company into shape. It took more than a year to get round to sports cars, with competing ranges of MGs, Triumphs, and on a more expensive plane, Jaguars. Soon the MGC, that could be seen as a rival for the TR6, was gone, although this was not a difficult decision because its sales were poor. But Stokes would not allow the TR6 to be called an MG as a replacement. He said it would arouse more hostility from MG fans than benefit from any extra sales. He was quite right, of course, and saw 'badge engineering'—where a basically-similar car was tarted up as a different make to give rival salesmen something else to sell—as one of the princiale sins of BMC.

But it was possible to say, with hindsight, that his knife was not sharp enough. His main problem with British Leyland's selling operation was that the merger had left them with several parallel sales organisations; had he been able to prune them more effectively, by cutting out cars in direct competition, British Leyland might have enjoyed stronger growth. In matters of straight choice—such as over the MGC and the TR6—he had a stronger leaning towards Triumph, which was only natural. They were also enjoying good sales at the time. But he did not hack back the rival MGs any further—although it is doubtful whether anybody could have justified this action such was the spirit of loyalty fostered by this marque. The MG factory at Abingdon also had one of the most loyal and trouble-free workforces within British Leyland, which made Stoke's decision to back the rival Triumph project for a new sports car all the more difficult. Again, with hindsight, he might have been better to have backed the MG project and badge-engineered it as a Triumph—but that was not Stokes's style. He would have also run into strong governmental opposition because the factory Triumph proposed to use for sports car production, in Liverpool, was in an employment black spot.

Meanwhile, Webster had enjoyed steady promotion in a manner to restore faith in career opportunities within large manufacturing organisations such as a car maker. From his earliest involvement with the TR, in which he had directed the TR1's redesign as the TR2, he had been behind all the work on the TR range. He was a master of compromise in that he produced practical engineering solutions under the most severe pressure from the sales force to keep down costs. He worked hard in a different way to Richardson; he was inclined to take his creative work home with him, and on more than one occasion he awoke in the middle of the night with a Eureka-style solution to a perplexing problem. But throughout his long tenure with Triumph, he maintained a whimsical sense of humour and generated great enthusiasm in his department as a marked contrast to his predecessor, Grinham. He would have liked to have seen more sophistication in engineering, but there was always the problem of cost. No matter how limited was his budget, his intentions were always serious and once he had decided an idea was good, even if rejected, he would reintroduce it when he could: hence the reopening of the competition department, under his control, and years later the introduction of pop-up headlights on the TR7. He had long arguments with colleagues such as Michelotti—who had long supported such devices—and, if necessary, would exert his authority, even if it was only in support of a decision vested from above. But such arguments were never acrimonious and if he could be convinced that the rival point of view was right, and there was no over-riding factor against it, he would give way; Michelotti won sometimes.

Before he went on to greater responsibilities as technical director of Austin and Morris after the creation of British Leyland, he gave Lawrence Dawtrey a free hand with the design of the Dolomite engine that was to power the TR7. The 16-valve Dolomite Sprint cylinder head that so nearly found its way into the

TR7 was inspired by British Leyland newcomers Spen King, Wally Hassan and Harry Mundy, drawn into the group by the amalgamation with Rover and Jaguar.

But Dawtrey did all the detail work because it was his engine. It was to be his last great work. Dawtrey, who had been associated with Standard since the 1920s, saved British Leyland a lot of money by discarding anything to do with gas turbines in his design study; other companies, such as Rover, had spent a fortune on their development to no avail. He opted for a straight four-cylinder unit because of Triumph's history of providing incredibly tight turning circles on small cars such as the Herald. A narrow engine allowed an extreme wheel turning angle; and Dawtrey went for a V8 alternative, which found its way into the Stag, because it was more compact and potentially lighter than a straight six. As a result, the four was slanted over to one side so that it could be built more easily with the same machine tools as the V8. Space was left inside the block for great expansion. However, an ingenious arrangement of cylinder head studs to allow easier—and potentially cheaper—maintenance led to problems and this engine was not a good memorial. Spencer King, who replaced Webster at Triumph, was a nephew of Rover directors Maurice and Spencer Wilks: a quiet man with many talents who subsequently rose to become British Leyland's technical director. But it was his erstwhile superior, Webster, who kept a paternal eye on the TR7 as it was being developed almost by American environmental regulations rather than by any particular person! Harris Mann at Austin-Morris—close to Webster at that time—had the most direct influence on it, creating the wedge shape that was to become so distinctive. This shape had been pioneered, like so many other things, by Colin Chapman at Lotus in 1968.

Chapman and his right-hand man on design at the time, Maurice Phillippe, had realised that aerodynamics lift—especially around the nose—was crucial to a racing car as it entered turns at more than 160 mph. This was particularly evident on their Indianapolis type 56, and the problem was made worse at the high-speed American track because heavy braking tended to bring down the nose. The resultant pitching hit handling badly and the eventual solution—a simple wedge shape—was adopted on all sorts of racing cars. This had not occurred to anybody before because such a shape looked ugly and meant that frontal area was increased. But the benefits were so great that it was one of the reasons that Lotus went on to dominate grand prix racing at the time that the TR7 was being designed, and stylists such as Bertone produced exotic show cars like the Carabo (for Winged Beetle) and the Stratos that was to be developed as Lancia's great rally car and almost an ancestor to the TR7 V8. Harris Mann, as chief stylist of Austin and Morris, was highly impressed by such designs and introduced the wedge line on British Leyland saloon cars; the board jumped on the bandwagon as soon as they saw his sketches for a new sports car. The TR7 was never likely to lap Indianapolis at more than 160 mph, but surely a sports car should look like a racing car? There were also practical advantages in that interior space was good—even if outward vision was not—and the salespeople liked the deep, short, tail which gave them a lot of luggage space to emphasise.

There was something for everybody on the board, and it also met all known and potential changes in the law, so the committee were happy. Once more with hindsight, it was apparent that at the time British Leyland lacked anybody with influence over final design who was sufficiently in touch with what the mass of the people really wanted.

Almost as the TR7 was born in the troubled factory at Speke, Liverpool, British Leyland ran into a massive cash crisis and faced bankruptcy as the result of soaring inflation and a recession that mitigated against such seeming luxuries as sports cars. The work force saw their spending power eroded at the same time and appeared to take it out on the cars. The government had little option but to come to the rescue of British Leyland, hoping that the workers would sort themselves out if they still had a job. So they took over more than 90 per cent of British Leyland at the very time the TR7 was introduced. Somebody had to take the blame and Lord Stokes was eased into an honorary chairmanship with managing director John Barber axed altogether.

This super accountant, who had been hired from Ford on even more money than Stokes, had clashed with the Government's man, Lord Ryder, who had been detailed to sort out British Leyland. And so the TR7 had staggered into production with an accountant at the helm, although at least Barber was a car man; that his successor, Alex Park, was not was a further disadvantage for the car. He was a former Navy officer out of Rank Xerox who was hired to organise British Leyland's last-ditch attempt at survival. Ryder did not want the job; he had higher hopes in government, and the TR7 ran on, still with nobody really having time to sort out a very troubled start to life.

There was no doubt that Parks was a brilliant accountant, but was seen to be a comparative novice in the political jungle—so an old hand, all-purpose financier, Ronald Edwards, was hired to shield him. He died four months later, to be followed by a political appointee, Sir Richard Dobson. As it turned out, he couldn't even shield himself, being felled by the indiscreet use of the word 'wogs' in a supposedly-private speech that leaked a little. Former petty officer Park went down with him and the impression was that well-qualified people were not exactly queueing up to take over at British Leyland. The TR7 and all its production problems were some of the most glaring examples of trouble at the top.

Even as Sir Richard was making his fatal speech, however, moves were under way to hire a modern new manager for British Leyland. Ryder's successor at the National Enterprise Board, Leslie Murphy, wanted a Scots-born New York businessman, Ian MacGregor, to be chairman of British Leyland, with the fast-rising Michael Edwardes as chief executive. With Dobson's demise, Edwardes's decision was accelerated and he immediately showed the full force of his personality by insisting that he came 'on loan' from his firm, Chloride Batteries, for five years as chairman and chief executive. There was no other way to do the job, said Edwardes' and MacGregor agreed. It was at this point that the National Enterprise Board's involvement with British Leyland was about to evaporate, and the savage pruning that might have started with Stokes was really about to begin. No sooner had the news broken that Edwardes had accepted the job on Tuesday, 1 November, 1977, than the militant workers building the TR7 came out on strike at Speke. Edwardes, later to become Sir Michael, was to say:

> 'In those days there were disputes in half of our 50 British factories day in and day out, and the list often ran to five typewritten sheets. That first day was the start of a period of relentless 70- and 80-hour working weeks, often with breakfast and evening meetings at each end of the day...
>
> 'In a snatched moment of reflection I made two personal resolutions on Day One in my new job at BL. The first was that I would give up all wines and spirits and that I would only drink beer or, on the right occasion, champagne. The second was that I would play squash four times a week. They were both helpful decisions ... I certainly needed to keep my mind clear and the pressures were enormous. To start with there were only about three people I felt I could trust in a company of about 198,000 people, and they came with me from Chloride...'

Sir Michael Edwardes hard at work in his favourite habitat: on the floor!

British Leyland was still on the verge of bankruptcy and the problems at Speke made it very difficult to borrow the money to keep going. The strike became the symbol of all that was wrong with the company as Sir Michael started a prolonged bout of 'union bashing.' At the same time as he began ruthlessly slashing his management into shape, he confronted the shopfloor workers with his plan to save British Leyland. To borrow money he needed a vote of confidence from them, and he got it; there was no alternative other than what amounted to genocide. And his first decision after that was the closing of Speke. About this he said:

> 'The factory was a classic example of those misguided efforts by successive governments to impose their will on the motor industry—by creating new factories and jobs in areas of high unemployment. Such areas were miles away from the traditional motor manufacturing centres, hopelessly distant from the centres of gravity as far as competitive costs were concerned.
>
> 'The decision to close Speke was not taken solely because of the factory's industrial relations record, which was bad enough. There was massive over-capacity in production facilities throughout the car's operations.
>
> 'On any commercial consideration, the Speke plant had to be a prime candidate for closure and the board decided that it would have to close and that the production of the TR7 would be transferred to the Canley plant at Coventry where the other Triumph cars were built ... we did not require the government's approval, but we felt that we should fully explain the logic of the decision, particularly as this was probably the first major factory closure in Britain for many years.
>
> 'For half an hour I was closely questioned by the Prime Minister, Jim Callaghan, who was extremely well briefed on Speke. Then he asked a question which made it clear to me that our case was won. It turned out to be a prophetic doubt: 'You have said that your new board will always act in a businesslike way and will make no decisions that are not commerically sound. Surely on that basis, the TR7 should be scrapped and not transferred elsewhere?
>
> 'Now he might have said this with tongue in cheek, but as things turned out he was absolutely right. And eventually the TR7 was abandoned.'

Perhaps Sir Michael did have a soul after all, contrary to what many people believed. And maybe he did have some feelings about sports cars. He might have axed the TR7 there and then...

X

The Interchangeability of Spare Parts

There used to be a lot of scope for locating hard-to-find spare parts for early TRs in scrapyards, because many of the basic components were shared with saloon cars of similar ilk. But times are changing, and saloons such as the Triumph Mayflower and the Standard Vanguard are now rarer than the TRs, which were initially produced in much smaller quantities. This is because the saloons were neither valuable, nor attractive to many collectors, so that most of them have by now rotted away, or have been crushed to be recycled as something else. But nobody throws away an early TR any more: they either hang on to it for restoration; actually get down to work on it; quite often finish it, because it is not a difficult car on which to work; or simply decide that it is not possible to fix it, such is the state of decay. In all these cases, with the exception of the cars that are restored, there is a good potential source of spare parts from other TRs.

The chassis can be swopped around between any of the beam axle cars, albeit with difficulty if a TR4 transplant is envisaged. But rebuilding an earlier TR on a TR4 chassis is still worth considering, because the ultimate result can be very desirable and there are more TR4 chassis left than those of the early cars. The main advantage is that the car would be endowed with the more precise rack and pinion steering; it would also have a wider track, which is attractive aesthetically to some people, but an anathema to others. The actual advantages in handling are hard to detect on the road. The chief practical problem is that the wings have to be widened to cover the tyres. There is no difficulty in obtaining wider wings from the normal sources which supply such one-off items for racing cars; inevitably, however, these hand-made parts are more expensive and can be a deterrent to anybody on a tight budget. It should not be forgotten, though, that a total restoration from a bare chassis almost invariably takes far longer than anticipated. This means that it is almost impossible to predict the cost in terms of time and extra little bits and pieces needed to complete the job. There is also a ready market for standard second-hand parts, so it might be worth selling a set of existing wings and having a bespoke set made up; alternatively, original wings can often be modified if the basic material is good enough.

Parts were swopped around with alacrity between various works cars to prepare any one for competition. The cars shown here are four of Richardson's six TR3s used in 1957.

Obviously, the floor panels, sills and doors of the earliest TR2s are different from those of the later cars, but largely speaking, any of the early-shape body panels are interchangeable. In the 1960s it was popular to 'update' a TR2 or a TR3 by fitting a TR3A front apron; it can be just as easy to reconvert to original now, or to use later body panels to construct an early-style shell. Brakes and steering columns—whether adjustable or non-adjustable—can be swopped around at will, as can axle ratios. The Standard Atlas van, should ever such at item surface again in a scrapyard, can be a ready donor of low axle ratios.

There is some scope for interchangeability with other marques, however, which the overdrive is considered. This was used on many other contemporary cars, notably Jaguars. The same applies to the SU carburettors, which featured extensively in cars of that period, with MG as one of the most obvious examples.

Engines can be updated to 2.2 litres quite readily with only parts such as the pistons and liners being involved, but it is not possible to give an early gearbox a synchronised first ratio. The TR4's gearbox had a different casing, so it is necessary to change the entire unit, although some of the internal parts are the same as those of the TR2 and TR3.

The TR4's body was completely different, of course, with a majority of the panels being carried over to the TR4A, TR5 and TR250; this applied to much of the internal structure with the TR6. It is a fact that can be very useful when restoring an early car because many of the small body components, even if nominally different, can be modified to help complete the job. The revised

The early TR engines found a home in a variety of vehicles, notably the Standard Vanguard saloon and in modified form in the Ferguson tractor.

chassis and geometry of the independent rear suspension made the last of the traditional cars impractical for adaption to a live axle bodyshell, however. Spring rates differ, too, between the TR4A, TR250 and the TR5 and TR6.

The engine in the popular Triumph 2.5PI saloon—still available in many scrapyards or at a very low price on the road—is basically the same as that of the TR5 and the European TR6, and almost identical to the unit in the later TR6s. The main external difference is that it is fitted with a single outlet exhaust manifold like that of the TR250. But it also has a 'softer' camshaft to give smoother idling and torque delivery. In this case, the valve timing is 25-65-65-25 with a 0.336-inch valve lift, against 35-65-65-35 and 0.367 inches for the TR5 and early European TR6. Matching adjustments were made to the fuel injection, with the total loss of 18 bhp. The camshaft, incidentally, was shared with the Triumph GT6 mark III sports car, which also indulged in a similar transmission. The transmission changes to the later TR6s were introduced to bring it into line with the Stag sports car.

With the exception of engine and running gear transplants from contemporary Triumph sports and saloon cars, the most mileage is to be had through specialist dealers in Britain which have largely sprung from the old-established TR Register's spares organisation.

In the temporary absence of a proper bumper, a Mini nudge bar makes a good substitute for this club driver...

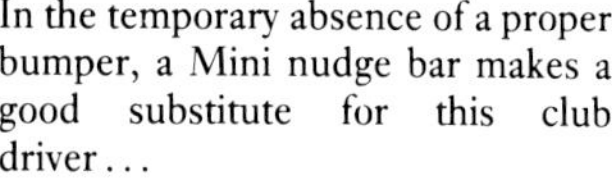

At a time in the 1970s when new TR parts were disappearing forever from British Leyland dealers' shelves, the Register went to a lot of trouble to contact the firms which had originally supplied Standard-Triumph to see if they still had any of their old tooling. In many cases it was possible to have replica parts made quite economically until today, with supplies of scrapyard parts dwindling fast, the Register is now the chief source of TR spares.

The Stromberg carburettors as fitted to a TR4.

The TR7 and TR8

The tale of the TR7 and the TR8 is quite different from that of the earlier cars. Just about the only major items that appear to be exclusive are the bodyshells and suspension! The TR7 took most of its components from the basic Dolomite saloon cars which abound in Europe, and the TR8 power train was lifted almost straight from the big Rover saloons. These cars are not plentiful in the largest market, America, but in the case of the TR8 it is possible to fit the original General Motors engine from the 1960–1963 Buick Skylark, and, in Australia, you can use the 4.4-litre Leyland P76 power unit. In addition, the gearboxes were shared with cars as diverse as the Morris Marina saloon and late model Triumph Spitfires and MG Midgets, and in five-speed guise, with not only the Rover SD1, but the later Jaguar XJ6 manual saloons. It is possible to substitute the more powerful engine from the Dolomite Sprint, or even just the top end, to give the TR7 more performance, although the five-speed gearbox and attendant 'heavy-duty' rear axle are to be recommended if this is the case. It's just what British Leyland were going to do with the still-born TR7 Sprint.

The Dolomite saloons were produced in two forms, both of which can yield substantial parts for a TR7: the basic version was first made in 1972 with an 1854-cc engine that produced 91 bhp and the Sprint, from 1973, with a 1998-cc unit that gave 127 bhp. The early Dolomites had twin Zenith-Stromberg carburettors, which were replaced with twin SUs from late 1973 in common with the Sprint. The Stromberg carburettors were the same as those that featured on the US '49-state' TR7s, and the SUs were as fitted to European models. Both Dolomites had the same gearbox, but the Sprint had a higher axle ratio of 3.45:1. The lower ratio, of 3.63:1, used on the basic Dolomite, was identical to the early TR7 axle. Both Dolomites were available with the overdrive used on the late-model TR6, but never on the TR7. This was because, from the outset, the TR7 was intended for use with the five-speed gearbox when sufficient supplies became available. It is possible to fit a TR7 with an overdrive if a modified propellor shaft is used, but more practical to change a four-speed gearbox for the five-speed. In this case, however, the cost might mitigate against such a change if new parts are used—the price of a new five-speed gearbox is much higher than that of an overdrive and prop shaft. In the case of automatic transmission, numerous other cars were fitted with the same Borg Warner model 65 unit.

The TR7 and TR8 suspension is basically the same, with the TR8 using a slightly stronger strut, so it is not recommended that TR7 units be fitted to the more powerful car, although there is no harm in such changes being performed the other way round. The TR8 also uses thicker brake discs and larger pads, while the TR7's units are taken straight from either the Dolomite or Rover saloons.

At present it can be a case of raiding scrapyards for old Dolomites, or parts of them, if you have to maintain a TR7 on the cheap and—in the case of a TR8—the engine from any Rover V8 saloon made from 1967 can be substituted, although the examples made before 1973 had an inferior rear crankshaft oil seal and those made for the SD1 saloon had better cylinder heads. The same V8 engine was also used in a different tune in the MGB GT V8—sold only in Europe—and the Range Rover and Land Rover V8, available only in very small quantities in America. It also found a home in the Morgan Plus 8.

Thanks to the example of the continuing popularity of the early TRs, it seems unlikely that the supplies of spare parts—bodyshells apart—will run out for the TR7 and TR8 in the foreseeable future.

XI
Preparing your TR for Competition

One of the most attractive aspects of owning a TR, whether one of the earlier or one of the later models, is that it is such a simple proposition to prepare for competition, be it racing, rallying, or concours: at least by the standards of some of its contemporaries. The main area in which the earlier cars can be improved for current racing is in weight saving with only minor modifications to the engine and suspension. The only events in which the six-cylinder cars are currently competitive mitigate against such changes, although their handling can be improved dramatically. With such a recent works competition past, there is still a wide variety of tuning gear available for the TR7 and TR8 in all manner of events, from top-line racing and rallying to club thrashes. As with the earlier cars, they can also benefit considerably from weight reduction. In the case of concours, the meticulous preparation that is needed is quite practical on a TR because of the way in which the earlier cars can be taken to pieces and reassembled, and with the later models, the lack of ornamentation!

The traditional four-cylinder cars

The legend according to Kas Kastner is still followed when preparing a four-cylinder TR engine for historic racing by undisputed British champion Reg Woodcock, whose car is so fast that he has even been able to burn off Ferrari 250GTs on the Continent. With suitable gearing Woodcock reckons to be able to take his TR3 up to around 140 mph, so there can't be much wrong with his power output. His main problem over the years—he started racing the car in 1962—has been crankshaft failure due to sheer old age, the damper being particularly vital. At the time of writing, the damper from a three-bearing MGB engine was proving ideal!

If possible, the crankshaft should be nitride hardened, although an efficient oil cooler can render this unnecessary. Screening for cracks, and careful checking on the condition of the bearing journals is essential. Micro-polishing the journals is not more than 1 micro inch as an aid to lubrication is also recommended. It is important also to check the end-float of the crankshaft and adjust it as necessary for a final fit of 0.004 inches to 0.006 inches. Then the

Ram pipes and rigid alloy valve gear covers are popular on TR engines.

crankshaft must be balanced with the vital front pulley and polished or shot-peened to remove any surface cracks.

There isn't much you can do to the cylinder block. Just check the camshaft bearings and cam followers carefully, with particular emphasis on the oil drain holes from the cam follower section. These must be absolutely clear. The camshaft end plug must be very tight or a lot of oil will be lost. It's best to seal this plug in position with epoxy adhesive. Early engines before number TS 9095E can be line bored for the later thinwall camshaft bearings.

If more than 0.125 inches is to be milled from the cylinder head face, there may be interference with the top edge of the block on the manifold side when a competition exhaust is fitted. To overcome this, you can file or grind off the edge of the block at about 45 degrees so that the manifold will fit without fouling. Check the block surface where the liners seat at the bottom. There must be absolutely no rough edges.

The rear main bearing needs a great deal of care in fitting. The packing must be driven home well or there will be big trouble. The connecting rods need to be crack tested—and you can lighten them considerably, but only in the right places. About 75 per cent of the metal can be removed from the stiffening rib at the bottom, and the rib over the top of the big end can be reduced by half. The flash marks can also be removed. Shape the beam of the rod so that the face has a slight curve with the high portion in the centre. The same profile can be maintained for the small end, with the sides sloping off to the bush opening. Grind the small end with an old gudgeon pin bush in position. Then polish the entire rod before having it shod peened and balanced in company with the other three. Always use new bolts and locking tabs when reassembling.

The standard 86-mm pistons are fine unless the engine is overbored, in which case use Powermax pistons. Standard rings tend to seat poorly in a race engine, so use competition ones. The piston should be polished all over to minimise skirt drag, and it is vital that all the crowns should be at the same height in relation to the block face. If one of the piston crowns is slightly higher than the others, the face can be ground until it lines up perfectly. Finally, everything is balanced.

When building an engine with a TR2, TR3 or TR3A cylinder head, it is necessary to check the clearance between the water outlet portion of its casting and the water pump body after milling the face. The problem does not arise with the larger-bore heads used on the TR3B and TR4 unless you remove a huge amount of metal—more than 0.141 inches—because they have a special flat on the bottom of the water outlet. If there is any difficulty with the early head, take some metal off the water pump casting. Actually there are two heads for the later cars, depending on which carburettors were fitted. You can tell them apart because the SU head had 1.625-inch manifold intake ports and the Stromberg cars 1.5-inch ones.

Extreme care must be taken when milling the early cylinder head face because the margin for error is far less. The Kastner suggestion is to cut in careful stages, with frequent checks to make sure you do not break into the water jacket or weaken the 'squish' area around the combustion chamber to the point where it can collapse.

For maximum performance, the compression ratio needs to be raised as far as possible. At one time, Kastner took his engines up to 13.4:1, although maximum power without detonation was usually achieved at 12.6:1. Now, with lower octane rating petrol being the order of the day, something like 11.7 is better. This can be achieved by grinding off about 0.150 inches from the head face, and the use of 87-mm pistons and liners with a steel shim head gasket.

When the cylinder head is being milled, the shape of the combustion chamber will, of course, be considerably altered. The inlet valve shroud may be removed completely—which is a good thing. By removing the shroud, the fuel is allowed to enter the cylinder faster, and thus be able to fill more of the combustion chamber in the same length of time. In other words, it increases the volumetric efficiency and at the same time the effective compression.

Great care must be exercised in inspecting the edge of the combustion chamber for sharp ridges. These will glow hot and cause detonation and perhaps pre-ignition, so smooth them off to about a 0.0313-inch radius. The sparking plug relief in the combustion chamber floor has to be blended in and the sharp edges around its hole should be smoothed off. During the milling, the chamfer opposite the hole will have been almost completely removed. This chamber should be replaced by grinding off the edge of the combustion chamber. Increases in compression tend to promote turbulence in the mixture as the piston nears top dead centre. This turbulence is vital for complete combustion.

With a normal compression ratio, the 'squish' area provides a jet of fuel into the flame front which does the job very well. With a higher compression ratio there is no need for such a large squish area which only absorbs heat and drains off power. By replacing the chamfer, and radiusing the edge of the squish area, you reduce the turbulence slightly, but this does not matter because of the increase in compression ratio. But there is a slight gain in power because the area of metal that can absorb heat has been reduced.

The grinding operation must be taken slowly and easily so that there is no loss of head gasket seal. Use the gasket as a pattern to see exactly where it is possible to grind. Fit two old valves in place before you start work to avoid damaging the seats. First grind in the chamfer opposite the plug hole, reducing its length as more metal is removed from the face so that you don't penetrate the water passages; 0.625 inches can be ground back with about 0.090 inches off the head face, and the chamfer must be radiused into the chamber to a distance of about half the chamber's depth. Then grind out the area next to the exhaust valve as far as a gasket scribe line and blend in the two grinds. After that, polish with patience, grindstones and emery cloth.

Next you have to get down to the valve seats. The inlet needs to be only 0.02 inches wide, but the exhaust must be 0.032 inches because it has to handle so much more heat. Modifications to the chamber head will have narrowed the valve seats a lot, so the valve throat must be enlarged for maximum use of the seat. For safety's sake, this operation is best done with a side and face cutter in a drill press or milling machine. The seat should be cut to an angle of 45 degrees, and the valve to an angle of 44 degrees to ensure a proper fit with the seat on the centre of the valve. Then the valves are lapped in until the seat is perfect. They can be lightened slightly and polished a lot. Competition valve springs are a must.

There is more scope for constant velocity porting with a late-type cylinder head because the inlets can be cut 1.5 inches throughout their length; the face chamfer on the older head results in a port that has to be tapered from 1.625 inches to 1.5 inches. The larger port gives slightly more to-end power, but the smaller is far superior for flexibility.

The valve throat must be blended into the port with no sharp edges and a fine polish if possible. The golden rule in this area is not to change the cross section without a fine taper. Exhaust ports can be treated differently because the gas is moving out under pressure. In this case it is best to taper the port out to the edge of the manifold face and match it into the assembly.

The ports of the inlet manifold should be slightly larger at the carburettor end than at the head face, and the manifold must be polished internally and then matched up with the carburettor body to each port. Make sure the balance pipe is completely clean.

The most effective exhaust systems use a manifold with four pipes running into two, and then one, with a 45-inch long tail pipe made from 2.5 inch tubing. This gives a good compromise with the pipe ending just in front of the offside rear wheel. A shorter one gives more power at the top end, and a longer pipe more power at lower revs.

The standard rocker arms can be lightened considerably by grinding away superfluous metal around the adjustment nut, at the valve end, and along the top. The whole arm can be polished, but don't cut any metal away from the sides. Check the exact area where the rocker strikes the valve stem and grind away the excess metal—but don't take any off the nose radius. With any competition engine it is best to start with a new rocker shaft. Competition pushrods with sweated ends that make rocker geometry corrections easier are to be recommended.

The cam followers can be lightened by paring off 0.375 inches from the top end in a lathe. The edges must then be radiused and the internal diameter can be bored out to 0.050 inches. They should then be polished all over with the sharp edge at the base sanded off. Always use new cam followers during a rebuild.

A new timing chain and tensioner are also to be recommended.

Camshafts depend on which carburettors are used, with Webers as the ultimate and SUs as the next best. Woodcock uses twin 40DCOEs with the SU men sticking to 2-inch units. The three most radical camshafts in general use are ones with 39-81-81-39, 42-74-74-42, and 51-79-79-51 timing. The minimum compression ratio in each case is 11.7:1. A standard distributor can be used, but Kastner advises never to start a race with a new set of points or a fan belt (if fitted). This is because they wear far more in the first 100 miles than later. Full metal wires are recommended for the ignition and the generator mounting plate bolts should be drilled and wired; the bolts run straight through the cylinder block's wall and can produce a giant oil leak if they work loose. The thermostat should be broken open for the best running temperature and a catch tank fitted for the crankcase breather on the distributor side.

A competition flywheel weighing 11 lb against the normal 31 is ideal in conjunction with a competition clutch.

The standard mechanical fuel pump should be removed and its aperture blanked off to be replaced with an electric pump mounted in a cooler location, such as in the boot.

So far as suspension is concerned, Woodcock has a remarkably standard car, not unlike those raced in SCCA events by Kastner. He points out that the car understeers initially, then oversteers viciously as the rear axle hits the chassis unless something is done about it. An anti-roll bar at the front helps a lot, with radius arms and a Watt linkage to locate the rear beam. Surprisingly, Woodcock uses standard shock absorbers all round, finding them perfectly adequate. The car is lowered, however, with competition-specification TR4 springs, which are 25 per cent stiffer than normal. The result is a car that has basic understeer giving way to slight power oversteer. In this form he uses only third and top gear—without overdrive—in most events. His very standard-looking machine is a lot lighter than normal, however, with the extensive use of aluminium and glass fibre in the body. The result is that the hard compound of Dunlop tyre European historic racers have to use, take two or three laps to warm, which puts

Red Woodcock's TR3 uses a Watt linkage for better rear axle location.

The fuel tank is mounted well away from harm's way in the glass fibre and alloy bodywork.

him at an initial disadvangage to the heavier Aston Martins and Ferraris. Steel wheels are about 4 lb lighter than wires, so with disc brakes all round, he uses these—unless the event allows him to use the 3 lb lighter and much stiffer Minilite magnesium wheels, which he also points out are far safer.

When regulations allow it, a limited-slip differential is a great advantage, with a 4.3:1 rear axle ratio when used without overdrive, to save weight, and 4.55 with an overdrive.

Over the years, Woodcock's car has appeared in various guises, currently racing open with aeroscreens in place. The feeling of slight instability was notable when it was used with the heavier, but aerodynamically more efficient, early works glass fibre hard top.

The cockpit sides are strengthened and the rest of the body lightened as far as possible.

The TR4A can benefit from a certain amount of suspension tuning. According to the Kastner code, with normal road tyres or racing ones of the 1960s vintage, the front suspension needed between 0.5 and 0.75 degrees of negative camber, 3–5 degrees of positive castor, and zero toe-in. Koni shock absorbers, starting at three half turns of adjustment were ideal for racing, if somewhat hard for road use in conjunction with TR4 competition springs. Obviously more experimentation with settings is needed with the development of more modern tyres for competitions in which they are allowed.

But much of his advice on the independent rear suspension cars still holds good, no matter which tyres are used. He strongly suggests crack testing the rear stub axles every four races—assuming an event to be the average 20–30 mile club 'bash'—especially if the car is fitted with a limited-slip differential. At the same time the inner shaft axle keys and universal joints should be checked for signs of stress. Kastner also recommends the use of competition rear springs and uprated shock absorbers, although it should be remembered that such items will give a jarring ride on the road. The stiffer rear springs should be set to give 0-0.75 degrees of negative camber, adjustment being by length. Toe out should be set at 0.125 inches, with adjustment by shimming the control arm mountings. These independent rear suspension cars are natural understeerers, so a rear anti-roll bar is to be recommended to induce an element of oversteer. Kastner suggests starting with a 0.5625-inch bar, increasing the diameter if the understeer is till too much.

The works TR4s appeared to be practically standard under the bonnet. The air outlets in the front wings were fashionable in their day.

Massive sump guards were fitted to the works TR4's chassis rails.

They also featured extra lighting in modified grilles and had tow hook eyes to help get them out of trouble.

The six-cylinder cars

Engine preparation is basically the same as that of the earlier four-cylinder cars except that the cylinder block needs to be line-bored to accept Triumph Spitfire Mark III camshaft bearings. Lubrication for the normal shaft, running direct in the block, can be inadequate under the stresses of competition. About 30 per cent of the bridge over the bottom of the connecting rod can be removed and about 25 per cent of the small end's bushing surround. The engine's oil pan benefits considerably from baffling and deepening by 1 inch. This is achieved by welding in a band of additional metal, taking care not to distort the top flanges. The normal racing oil level will then be at the low mark on the dipstick. Two Kastner-approved racing camshafts are available, in 42-71-71-42 and 37-73-73-37 timing.

The TR5 fuel injection engine.

The compression ratio can be raised to at least 10.25:1 by milling the cylinder head thickness to 3.375 inches, with another 0.165 inches taken off for the highest practical ratio of 12.3:1. It is worth remembering that the ports of the TR250 and TR5/6 cylinder heads are different; if you want to fit fuel injection to a TR250, you need a TR5/6 head. A competition six-branch exhaust manifold is highly beneficial with a single 2.5-inch pipe running the full length of the car; twin pipes cost Kastner 8 bhp!

The six-cylinder car can benefit considerably from a larger radiator under racing conditions, with a core of about 4.5-5 inches thick. The alloy radiator fitted to contemporary Chevrolet Corvettes proved ideal for Kastner. But no matter which radiator is used, it needs an effective shroud; no fan is needed in full race applications.

Rear suspension work by Kastner followed TR4A lines with 450 lb, instead of 350 lb, springs to prevent bottoming. It is also important to make sure that the suspension itself is not bottoming even if the car's underside does not touch the track. It may mean shortening the rear bump stops, particularly if a lot of negative camber is being used. If in doubt, suspension bottoming can be checked by smearing a small amount of grease on the bottom of the bumpstops and seeing if it has been disturbed after a hard lap.

Apart from causing violent understeer, bottoming can break the axle. Wide-key shafts are to be recommended with the flanges lapped to the inner axle and secured with Loctite. This sealing compound should also be used on the taper when the outer hubs are lapped. Of the ratios that were available between 3.5 and 4.87, Kastner found the 4.55:1 to be the most useful with overdrive fitted.

In normal applications, very hard rear brake linings were ideal in conjunction with normal competition front pads. But the brakes could be further improved by fitting twin master cylinders with a balance bar and a residual pressure valve in the hydraulic system.

Oversteer and understeer were adjusted by juggling with front and rear anti-roll bar sizes and lever arm lengths. In the case of the six-cylinder cars, suspension adjustments were as for the TR4A except that the front toe-in was set at 0.0625 inches. The shorter competition front springs were used, which lowered the car. More than 0.75 degrees of negative camber at the front slowed the car in a straight line and induced high-speed wander. All rubber bushes were replaced with bronze, although good 'halfway house' results can be obtained from the use of nylon bushing.

Alloy wheels are to be recommended for racing, with a particular eye on safety. Later developments by firms such as Paradigm Engineering on the TR6, which has proven so ideally suitable for production sports car racing, have on occasions been frustrated through lack of homologation and restrictive regulations.

Broadly similar modifications to those made by Kastner were employed in Britain by Sid Hurrell's firm, SAH, which became the official outlet for works-developed tuning gear when British Leyland closed their competitions department in 1969. SAH obtained around 185 bhp from the six-cylinder engine with a modified cylinder head, special camshaft, competition valve springs, six-branch exhaust—and, interestingly, a dual exhaust system—plus special injector metering unit. Handling modifications followed the same lines, with the rear end lowered 0.5 inches and the front by 1 inch to counter the onset of high-speed floating.

The TR7

Sid Hurrell's son, Terry, in conjunction with TR Register stalwarts, Cox and Buckles, at TriumphTune, have been the mainstays of customer competition development of the TR7 in recent times. With the standard eight-valve engine, the cylinder head is a limiting factor to the maximum power that can be

The works TR7 rally cars used twin Weber carburettors.

developed. TriumphTune have therefore concentrated on improving the gasflow, with three kits of bolt-on accessories and a warning that no more than 0.010 inches can be safely skimmed from the cylinder head. The first kit, which consists of an extractor exhaust manifold, straight-through silencer system and new carburettor needles, gives a power increase of 10-13 bhp; a further increase of 5-10 bhp can be obtained by substituting 2 inch SU, or Weber 40DCOE, carburettors. There is no loss of torque with the SUs, but the additional power that can be obtained with the Webers has to be traded for a slight loss of tractability at low speed.

The third kit uses an improved camshaft and valves with an extra 30 bhp from SUs and 35 for the Webers—which are highly recommended in this application.

There is more potential for tuning with the 16-valve Dolomite Sprint cylinder head if competition regulations permit its use. But whether or not it is fitted, an oil cooler is a good idea for reliability at high revs.

Four stages of tune are available with the 16-valve head, the first one liberating an extra 10 bhp by changing the exhaust and silencer system. Stage Two requires the addition of a new camshaft and 2-inch SUs, or Webers, giving 155-160 bhp and a good idle. A higher-lift camshaft, with 40/73 timing for the inlet and 68/32 on the exhaust is part of the Stage Three kit, with twin 45DCOE Webers and manifold. The cylinder head ports are smoothed at the same time with an output of about 175 bhp and a reasonably civilised tickover.

The idling becomes very rough with the Stage Four tune, which consists of a Group One racing or rallying camshaft with 68/92 inlet timing and 76/56 exhaust. New dual valve springs and caps are needed, and the head has to be machined. The camshaft also wears much more quickly, but that is the price you pay for a reasonably tractable 210 bhp.

With any of these stages of tuning, Hurrell recommends that the water radiator is changed to one with an uprated 18-row core. If the early seven-vane water pump impeller is in use, it should be changed for the later 12-vane unit. This actual change was made in production during 1977. So far as oil coolers are concerned, a seven-row radiator is sufficient for the first two stages, with a 12 or 13-row version after that.

So far as general engine preparation is concerned, Hurrell recommends a very careful rebore to obtain the correct finished clearances between the piston skirts and the bore. Standard pistons are quite suitable for any stage of tune up to the third degree, but Cosworth pistons are necessary after that. These are expensive, and like the Group One camshaft, can have a limited life.

For heavy-duty applications, a carefully-balanced bottom end is necessary along the lines already described. But there is a special works Freudenberg damper kit available which is virtually indestructible and essential for high-revving units. British Leyland also developed the engine for Formula Three racing in the late 1970s, and there are still a few special crankshafts in circulation. They will only accept a limited degree of regrinding, however, but provide a very strong base for tuning.

The engine's oil pump can be uprated by inserting a heavy duty pressure spring, which, in conjunction with Powermax bearings and the heavy-duty oil pump driveshaft from the Ford V6 Essex engine, provides excellent lubrication. An uprated clutch cover and clutch plate proves adequate up to Stage Two, with further uprated units after that. The flywheel can have about 7-8 lb taken off to make the engine much more responsive, and if an ex-Formula Three flywheel can be found and mated to a paddle-type clutch, that is even better. Heavy-duty engine mounts are also available.

Simpler items which have proved highly beneficial with the Sprint engine include electronic ignition and K and N deep air filters for SU carburettors. They are alone worth quite a lot of extra power, but it is necessary to fit one or two-size richer needles at the same time. The engine must not be run too rich though, because with 16 valves there is twice as much risk as normal of a hanging valve. Because of the cylinder head's well-known sealing problem a competition head gasket is to be highly recommended. This is much better equipped to cope with extremes of temperature.

An electric fuel pump is also a virtual must to ensure an adequate supply of petrol when running under full throttle, as are regular oil changes. There are so many more parts to keep lubricated with a 16-valve head.

An updated four-speed gearbox is available with larger bearings, and a set of close ratio gears for the five-speed, that give ratios of: top 0.83; 4th 1.00; 3rd 1.30; 2nd 1.61; and 1st 2.33.

TriumphTune have also done a lot of development on the TR7 and TR8 for improved handling on the road. They recommend uprated front springs of at least 25 per cent, with a 0.5 inch shorter length if 60 per cent aspect tyres are to be used. The standard springs have various settings, basically of the 84/94 lb rate and a fitted length of 7 inches, which provide a very soft ride. If the car is lowered, the bump stops need reducing by 0.75 inches and making into a conical shape. This stops excessive bump steer. A stronger anti-roll bar is also recommended for increased stability.

It is also important to set the rear springs at a height compatible with any front end modifications. Shorter springs often require a retainer strap to restrict full drop movement. The handling also benefits from stiffer suspension bushes and adjustable shock absorbers, notably Koni.

Early development of the TR7 for production sports car racing, by Andy Dawson for *Cars and Car Conversions* magazine, found that it benefitted from 185 section tyres instead of the normal 175s. The fuel tank was resited in the spare wheel well to bring down the centre of gravity and lead ballast and a fire extinguisher bottle were mounted at the back to bring its weight up to the homologated 2097 lb. The more weight that can be moved to the back of a TR7 or TR8, the better. Dawson's most difficult task in preparing the shell for competition was fitting a roll cage that did not further restrict the already limited

Front strut and brake detail of a works TR7.

window space. Softer rear springs were used than the early ones, with the entire car lowered to the minimum permissible 4 inches of ground clearance. Adjustable dampers provided quite good handling—but the brakes were the main problem with this car, campaigned in the 1977 season. Even with DS11 and VG95 front and rear competition linings, they were inadequate. But a stronger brake balance valve spring cured a tendency for the rear to lock first.

Dawson continued to develop the TR7 for *Cars and Car Conversions* during 1978, with three priorities: reducing the very heavy understeer, cutting out wallowing without making the ride too harsh, and trying to make it less responsive—or twitchy—in a straight line. Initially the pressures of the 175/70 Goodyear G800S tyres were raised to 28 psi at the front from 24 (with 28 at the back) for road use. The result was less understeer but more sensitivity in a straight line.

Following extensive experiments with Bilstein, Spax and Koni shock absorbers, the eventual conclusion (in line with the TriumphTune recommendations) was found to be the best: Koni strut inserts and rear dampers on their minimum setting, 50 per cent stiffer front springs, ground-down bump stops,

Early works TR7s ran on drum rear brakes and Minilite magnesium wheels.

hard front subframe rubbers and track control arm (TCA) bushes, with tyres at 28 psi all round for road use and 40 psi when extra grip was needed on the track.

Fuel surge problems when the tank was less than a quarter full did not cause much trouble on the tight British circuits because the fuel piping was long enough to provide an adequate reservoir. But on long right-handers, the front SU's carburettor float chamber cut off and the rear one flooded, spilling fuel over the coil with potentially explosive results! The answer was to fit float chamber tops from a 1275 cc Mini, which were hinged at the back. This meant that they cut off under heavy braking and flooded slightly under full acceleration—when such changes did not matter—and were not affected by cornering stresses.

For events with less restrictive regulations, wider wheels with lower profile tyres were an effective aid to handling, the standard arches accepting 7-inch rims with 225/55 tyres.

To make sure that the tyres worked properly in this case the front suspension crossmember had to be redrilled to give negative camber. Dawson recommended moving to TCA inner bolt holes outwards and slightly upwards by 0.375 inches with a warning to fill in the original hole to stop the bolt pushing through. Rose joints on the top arms of the rear suspension transformed the car too, allowing the axle only a small amount of sideways movement without rolling. This dramatically reduced the whiplash handling through an S-bend and improved directional stability although a penalty was paid in that the Rose joints greatly magnified the differential whine.

The competition TR7 in its original 1976 guise.

The first works TR7 on test.

The V8 rally car OOM 512R was the subject of extensive testing.

The eight-cylinder cars

Unless a specific class is your aim, it is a far more practical proposition to build yourself a TR8 when preparing a competition machine from scratch. The bodyshell will be almost exactly the same and you will have the benefit of a far more powerful and easily-tuned engine. Running costs—other than for tyres, which will be marginally higher—should be about the same.

A power output of around 200 bhp—the most that can reasonably be extracted from a Dolomite unit—is easy to obtain with the Rover V8, which weighs the same. It is not difficult to tune it to produce 250 bhp, which is as

The twin Weber set-up when it was used on the works TR7 V8s.

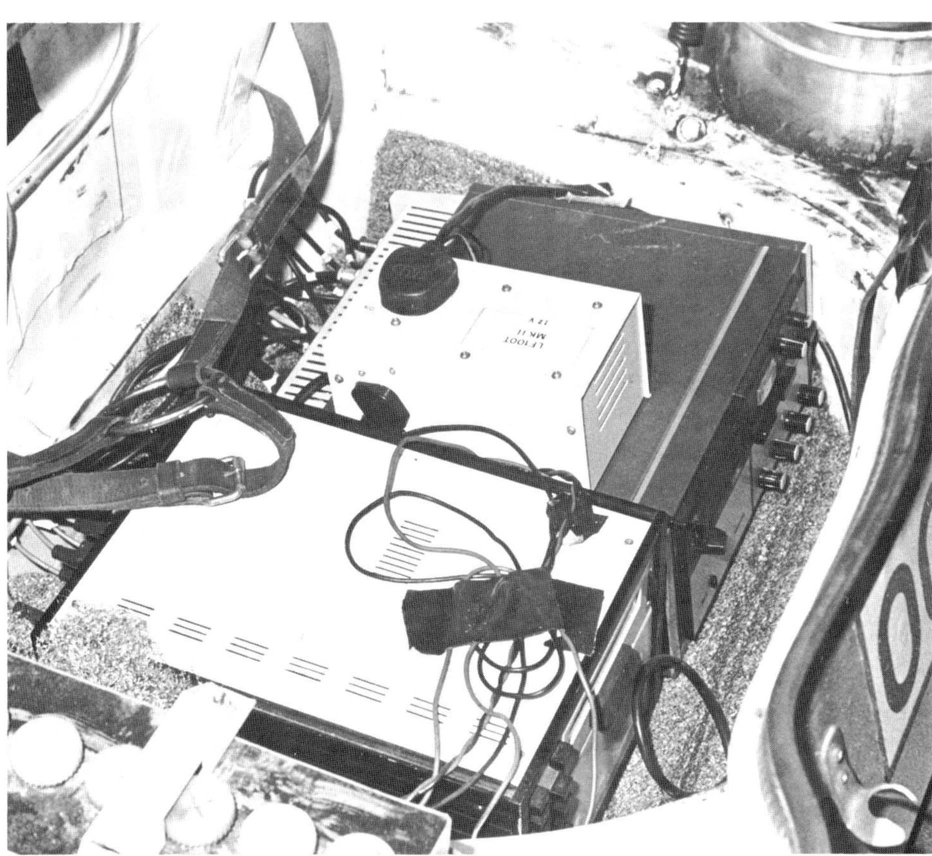

How to help keep check on your TR7 V8 with masses of equipment in the boot of OOM 512R.

much as most people can handle, and with additional expense, 300 bhp, before the ultimate turbocharging or supercharging.

Secondhand Rover V8 engines are easily found and there are still the odd Buick and Oldsmobile units available in America; in Australia, the Leyland P76, a 4.4-litre version of the Rover V8, presents an intriguing proposition. Such applications are made all the more viable by the five-speed gearbox's ability to handle the V8's power, although its long-term durability in road applications with a lot of power is open to doubt. But it has more than enough miles in it for a competition car.

So far as the Rover engines are concerned, there are two main types: the old pre-1973 ones with rope rear crankshaft oil seals and the later ones, which soon found a home in the Rover SD1 saloon and the TR8, with a lip seal. A very tightly packed rope seal will handle the extra power, but it is better to have the cylinder block line bored—3.875 inches diameter, 0.4375 inches depth—to take the lip seal if more than 5000 rpm is envisaged. The early engine's rope seal at the front is in a low pressure area, so it should present no problem. When reboring this alloy block, it is advisable to have the main bearing caps torqued in place to avoid the possibility of bore distortion. New camshaft bearings—available from specialist tuners such as Auto Power Services—are almost invariably essential.

Removing burned oil deposits is a tedious business, but vital, and no more than a total of 0.020 inches should be taken off the cylinder heads and block when refacing: remember that this amount should be identical each side, with similar care taken with the combustion chambers and pistons, if equal compression is to be achieved.

High-revving V8s can suffer from oil retention in the block as the lubricant fails to return to the bearings sufficiently quickly; to reduce the chances of this happening, smooth off all the rough edges in the block and fit an extra drain from the back of the vee to the sump. A hole for a 15-mm copper pipe should be drilled above the rear camshaft bearing, with the pipe running back through the left-hand side of the bellhousing flange. A rubber hose then connects this pipe to a further run into the sump, helping to drain off some of the oil that invariably collects at the back of this rearward-inclined application.

The crankshaft, which is good for 8200 rpm, should be hardened for more than 6000 rpm, and balanced. The connecting rods are safe for 7000 rpm, after which special Carillo rods from America are essential—if you have a large budget. The early engines had rather weak 10.5:1 compression ratio pistons, with much stronger 10.25:1 versions being marketed later: it is wise to use the new ones. Very expensive forged pistons are also available, but are in the same price league as the Carillo rods. The combustion chamber volume was increased with the introduction of the SD1 engine, which can also affect calculations.

Rover engines made between 1974–7 had 9.25:1 compression ratio heads of the larger valve SD1 type; engines made after 1977 had 9.35:1, until the Rover Vitesse was introduced in 1982 with 9.75:1; in other applications, the Range Rover and MGB GT V8 used 8.15:1 until 1977, and 8.3:1 for Range Rovers after that, with further variations on some export models—so there are quite a variety of combinations!

In normal applications, a compression ratio of between 10 and 10.5:1 is best. The standard hydraulic tappets are good for 7000 rpm and are worth retaining unless higher revs are needed because of their maintenance-free virtues and the fact that they do not stress an engine like the ultimate solid lifters.

More than a dozen replacement camshafts are available for the V8, mostly made by Crane, with Iskendarian and Austin Rover Motorsport alternatives. Crane's H214 is one of the most attractive for economy applications. If it is fitted to a standard TR8 or SD1 engine, with BAF type needles in SU carburettors, it will give an immediate power increase to 198 bhp. Only a very small amount of flexibility and fuel economy is lost, with performance equivalent to that of the fuel-injected Rover Vitesse engine. The modified unit also lasts as long as a normal one, making this conversion one to be highly recommended.

It is essential to fit new followers with a replacement cam, and to avoid pre-SD1 followers in this case.

The next cam in the range is the H224 for rallying. In this case, uprated valve springs and retainers must be used with Crane high-rev lifters to give a maximum of 7000 rpm although the best range is between 2500–6000 rpm, during which torque is abundant. The spring seats will have to be machined to avoid coil binding. There is also a very wild full-race cam, the H234, for use with hydraulic tappets; after that, solid lifters are needed. These require solid tappets and adjustable pushrods or roller rockers. The first camshaft for use with such equipment is the F228, which is similar to the H224. Then there is an F238 and an F248, either side of the H234. These cams work well between 3000–7000 rpm, in which case the engine needs to be built to withstand an excess of their top range. Three more cams are available that need engines revving to 8000 rpm to take maximum benefit.

The normal camshaft timing gears give few problems, but if they do, steel gears should be substituted. In the same way, the hydraulic tappets are quite reliable providing the engine's oil—which operates them—is not allowed to become contaminated, in which case bits of dirt cause problems. They are capable of taking up quite a bit of adjustment, but if the cylinder head is skimmed a lot, they will not close properly. At the other extreme, if a very thick gasket is used, they will rattle. In either case, the rocker shaft pillars should be packed or machined, or adjustable pushrods fitted.

Preparation of the early and the later-type, of SD1, heads is quite simple. The early heads have smaller combustion chambers and use short-reach, 12.7-mm, sparking plugs. The inlet valves are 38 mm and exhaust 33.3 mm. Longer, 19-mm, plugs are used with the later heads, with 40-mm inlet and 34.3-mm exhaust valves. The early heads also have slightly smaller ports which can be cleaned out to SD1 size, but no more because their waterways are close at hand. SD1 ports should not be enlarged for the same reason. In some export versions, there is an emission equipment airbleed in the exhaust ports which should be blanked off for high performance. Larger valves are available, but they are only necessary for power outputs beyond 260 bhp.

In normal cases, Oteva valve springs can be used, but if more than 200 bhp is envisaged, it is wise to use a Felpro Permatorque gasket, which is thicker. Ultimately, in turbocharged or supercharged installations, an even thicker Fitzgerald gasket is available. Obviously, these gaskets will affect the compression ratio, and in cases where oversize inlet valves are used with a high-lifted camshaft and high-compression pistons, the valves may touch the tops of the pistons. The valves are inclined, so there is not a large area of contact and it is quite practical to have cut-outs machined in the pistons for clearance. So far as carburettors are concerned, the SUs are the best economy applications giving a reasonable performance and the most popular alternatives are the carburettors made by Holley. The best Holley carburettor for general competition use in this case is the 600 cfm unit with a mechanical linkage (or double pumper) for instant throttle response.

The next choice upwards is Webers, of which no less than four are needed for the best results. They cost a lot, but they are good for 300 bhp and give better fuel consumption figures than some of the injection systems tried on the works TR8s, which means that the competitive weight of the car can be kept down. When cost is of prime importance, the Holley is the best 'middle of the road' choice.

It is best used with either an Offenhauser or a Huffaker manifold, with the water-heated Offenhauser as the most convenient. The Huffaker gives more power at the top end, but needs a separate thermostat housing and more plumbing.

For maximum exhaust efficiency, Janspeed manifolds are the best and an electronic ignition system is to be recommended to cope with high revs. The Sparkrite SX2000 system used on Roger Clark's works' TR8 is one of the best. Champion N6Y sparking plugs are essential for more than 200 bhp, with N2Gs and ultimately N84Gs after that. Earlier heads use the L82Y or L64Y plugs.

Alarmingly low oil pressure readings from these engines can be improved by fitting either an uprated pressure relief from a Rover Vitesse or a Buick seven-litre oil pump. The sump can also benefit from being enlarged and baffled because the total capacity is rather small. An oil cooler is to be recommended, of course, and it may be necessary to shroud the starter motor and plug leags with asbestos to counter the extremes of temperature from the exhaust pipes.

Rallyman Dave Bulman, who recorded his experiences in building a TR7 V8 in *Cars and Car Conversions* during 1980, made an efficient dry sump system as an alternative to the British Leyland kit that was available at the time. Basically, he removed the standard oil pump and plugged its driveshaft hole. He then made up a plate using the oil pump gasket as a template to take supply and return pipes from a Cosworth pump mounted just below the right-hand cylinder head when viewed from the front of the engine. This was driven by a pulley from the crankshaft with a remote oil filter and 30 psi pressure warning switch incorporated in the system. Normal running pressure was then 80 psi with 20 psi at tickover, against the uprated spring system's 55–10 psi, and the standard 45–

5 psi.

Bulman seam-welded his shell for additional strength, and plated the floor and areas around the suspension strut mounts, braced the front mounts, and moved as much weight as possible to the back. This included mounting the navigator's seat as far as possible to the rear. All sorts of things were put in the boot—a plumbed-in fire extinguisher, wheelbrace, vertically-mounted spare wheel for easy extraction from the possibly-crumpled rear end, fuel and dry sump tanks, giant windscreen washer reservoir and air horn compressor. A lot of weight was saved in addition by stripping off the underseal.

But the most dramatic saving was in removing the steel bumper inserts, which cut the overall weight by 2.3 per cent! Additional savings were made by fitting permanently-raised headlights, to cut out the motors and raising mechanism, and by fitting a glass fibre boot and bonnet lid. This weight saving was of especial importance in that it was mostly from either end of the car, which reduced its pendulum effect on handling.

Ultimate club rally TR8s feature glass fibre bumpers and Vauxhall Chevette headlights to reduce over-hanging weight.

The rear axle also had to be strengthened to cope with the torque of the V8, although it was adequate in heavy-duty form for anything the 2-litre Dolomite unit could produce. The standard axle also had the advantage of being 20 kg lighter than the British Leyland rally axle produced for the works cars. Cheaper alternatives for the V8 can be adapted from some Jaguar and Reliant Scimitar rear axles.

Ultimate development of the works V8 rally cars centred on moving the engine and gearbox back 2 inches to change the inertia and make them more responsive to turning in. The angle of the rear suspension links was also

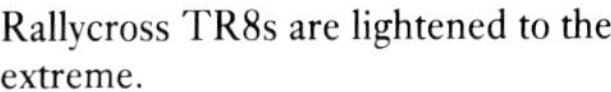
Rallycross TR8s are lightened to the extreme.

changed by raising the front mountings 25 mm, to reduce pitching. The front anti-roll bar mounting was lowered to counter dive under braking. The suspension was rose-jointed for better handling and the front struts shortened to give them a better balance with the already short rear strusts. Bigger brakes were fitted within 15-inch wheels to cope with the speed of ace driver Tony Pond and a new spoiler for better aerodynamics.

Engineer Richard Hurdwell gave a revealing description in *Cars and Car Conversions* in March 1981 into how he would have liked to have seen the TR8s developing had the project been allowed to continue. He said:

The ex-Roger Clarke Sparkrite TR7 V8 still makes a good club race/rally car.

'We would have improved the aerodynamics; fitted 15-inch wheels and bigger brakes as a matter of course; run new fuel and oil systems; improved the ergonomics (cockpit ventilation and windscreen wipers especially) and serviceability; and also the driveability of the thing. Visibility could have been markedly improved because we had homologated an entirely new alternative dashboard which would have allowed us to move the steering wheel much closer to the screen, enabling the driver to utilise a much more upright and further forward seating position.

'The gearbox was another area we would have changed for 1981. We'd have run the same casing, of course, but the similarity would have ended there. In the past, we've had to go through development exercises to

Modsports TRs use very light panels, with this sprint version being fitted with a splitter on the nose to cut an electronic timing beam.

A sturdy roll cage is a vital accessory for competition.

increase the speed at which we can change the gearbox, whereas in fact what we should have been doing was redesigning the internals so that we didn't have to keep changing it!

'We would also have wanted to improve the rear suspension travel, which was becoming a major limiting factor to the car's performance. What's required is not merely more travel, but also the fitting of coil springs directly into the axle. On the TR, the springs are located halfway up the link, which creates all sorts of stresses and strains, and doesn't work as well. Of course we would have to keep a spring in the original position for the sake of the regulations, but that would have been no problem.

'Lowering the Panhard rod a bit would have also helped. It was another of those "This is a rally car" things: it was stuck up in the air somewhere on the basis that it might get torn off. Even by just cutting down the weight of the shell a little would have helped and there was more power to come.'

If only . . . but it is obvious that there is still lots of development that the TR7 and TR8 enthusiast can carry out, whether on road or track.

XII
The Secret Dream Cars

Every car manufacturer makes prototypes to test new ideas and get reactions to their appearance, and in this Triumph were no different from the rest. But what was different about their prototypes was that they reflected a pantomime of indecision. Early attempts at updating the TR2 and TR3 never got further than the drawing board and then only in the most basic outlines. Apart from the Swallow Doretti, the only serious project using the early cars as a base was a hard top version of the TR2 with wind-up windows called the Francorchamps. Twenty-two of these cars were built by Triumph's Belgian distributor.

The first serious work was by that inveterate car sketcher, Giovanni Michelotti, in 1957. He produced a full-width body on a TR3 chassis with distinctly North American lines, hoping that it would catch on and provide his firm with something to build. It had an enormous full-width radiator grille, hooded headlamps and pronounced tailfins. It also had wind-up windows, which everybody agreed were great if only Triumph could scrape together the money to finance the much wider bodyshell. But the most significant part of the design was its 'dollar-grin' grille. It looked so thoroughly American that the Standard-Triumph management decided that by hook or by crook it must be grafted onto the TR3 body. Then perhaps they could kid the Americans that they had a new body without having to spend much on it. Hence the TR3A.

But Michelotti's dream car was already looking a mite old-fashioned, as trendy things tend to do after a year, and so he was asked to try again. Since he didn't know when the new project would go into production he opted for more classical lines that would not date so rapidly. The Triumph management decided that the result was so good that they could spread its butter quite thinly around the rest of their projects. The bolt-on hard top appeared at the same time on the Triumph Herald coupé and the back eventually found a home on the Triumph Spitfire—with the front ending up on the TR4. This was the Zest project of 1958, with Michelotti clinging stubbornly to his hooded headlights, hoping that Webster would be able to make them pop up and down. Webster however disagreed and the headlights stayed firmly in their place. But you could see what Michelotti meant...

Meanwhile the twin cam engine was going ahead in fits and starts. It was intended to produce about 200 bhp, so the castings, which were experimental anyway, were made good and thick. As a result, it was the best part of four inches longer than the normal two-litre engine. It could be fitted into a standard chassis with a good deal of pushing and shoving, but it didn't leave much room for the occupants' feet. And seeing as it would cost more, it would probably wind up in a super luxury TR with a plush interior. This meant that something would have to be done about the chassis. By rule of thumb and little else, an extra six inches seemed a good idea. Stretch the chassis a bit, beef up the side plates because people always did when they welded bits on, and they would be away. The only trouble with this project was that it was one associated with racing, so it did not rate very highly in the order of priorities, when it came to time. The main one was survival itself, so every time engineer Dick Astbury got down to doing something conclusive about it, he was whipped away to sort out some pressing crisis with the production cars.

It was at this point that the project began to go wrong. The competition department were not really interested in passenger accommodation, so they inserted the extra six inches of wheelbase into the engine compartment, where it would be most useful to them. And they didn't object to plating the chassis rails because they hoped the new machines might be used for rough-road rallies rather than just the billiard-table surface of Le Mans. So the TR3S wound up with some of the precious extra space in the wrong place for passengers and with far more weight than they needed for racing; it also looked too long and narrow.

The next decision therefore was to widen it so that it would also benefit the interior space, the handling and the ride, as well as the appearance. Management still liked the look of the Zest, so they asked Michelotti to incorporate that profile in another new body. And because the new engine was running reasonably well, they decided to put that in the car as well. This was the Zoom project that was given to detuned 120 bhp version of the twin cam engine, using SU carburettors.

Michelotti in conjunction with Webster, sketched out a completely different body for this 1959 car, with a sleek new front that wound up, in essence, on the Triumph Spitfire! In the meantime, the general lines were used for the Le Mans TRS in 1960. The Zoom's inspiration came from Michelotti's second dream car on a TR3A chassis: an attractive fixed-head coupé that so appealed to the large Italian coachbuilders, Vignale, that they exhibited it on their stand at the Turin Show late in 1958. It stimulated enough orders for them to put it into production as the Italia 2000 from 1959 to 1963. About 300 examples were built in all.

In the meantime, work on the Zest and Zoom projects continued apace. The public's reaction—and that of *Road & Track*—to the TRS shape, was good. But the finances were not, so the twin cam engine was abandoned and it was back to the standard wheelbase for whatever was going to replace the TR3. In fact, it looked as though Standard-Triumph might not be able to afford the tooling for a new body, and a widened version of the existing bodywork was done on an experimental TR4 chassis in 1960. This was called the TR3B, or Beta, project that must not be confused with the 1961-2 production cars that were

Shades of the Zoom, works TRS Le Mans cars.

subsequently christened TR3Bs. The Beta was a serious proposition for production and was only stifled by its lack of wind-up windows.

Michelotti was then asked to combine the most-liked features of the Zest and the Zoom into the TR3A's replacement when sales started to fall off rapidly. The result was the TR4...

Intermittent experiments continued with new ways of exploiting the TR theme throughout the 1960s, with the most involved being a new project called Fury. The Spitfire, launched in 1962, had proven an outstanding success, so the body was designed along those lines, with a Triumph 2000 saloon car engine as one line of mechanical development. Its suspension was far more adventurous,

What the TR4 might have looked like ... a TR3B for Beta.

with MacPherson struts at the front and semi-trailing arms with coil springs at the back. But this car, completed in 1965, was far nearer to a Spitfire in concept than a TR, and eventually became part of the inspiration for the Triumph GT6. Various attempts were made to develop a TR4B as the 'Wasp' project, but it was the TR5 with the old bodyshell that went into production.

The TR6 was just a holding job as British Leyland experimented at length with a joint proposal for a two plus two seater coupé and an open sports car which had, ironically, a Porsche Targa top. The open car, which looked rather like the 914 Porsche introduced in 1969, was intended for production in 1973, and was codenamed Bullet; the two plus two, with a 1972 target date, was called Lynx. They were the subject of Harris Mann's styling coup, the Bullet being developed into the TR7 and the Lynx envisaged as its stablemate, only to be killed by the great strike at Speke. With only committees to replace the genius of Michelotti nothing was done about them for years...

XIII
The TR Clubs

TR owners have been lucky in that they have almost always had a club to cater for their specialised interests, although there have been some rather thin patches at times!

Initially, the factory started the Triumph Sports Owners' Association (or TSOA) in 1954, as a means of fostering enthusiasm among owners; they hoped it might help persuade people to place a repeat order. The first benefits for members, apart from documents and a badge, included technical information that it had to be admitted promoted the sales of accessories on which there was a reasonably high profit margin, although the club remained good value for money in its own right. The sporting and social events came later.

The proud badge of the TSOA.

As branches were founded all over the world membership rose to around 15,000 with a glossy newsletter replacing earlier duplicated information sheets. But everything was factory-oriented, with one particular scheme offering a trip to a European rally, the cost of which could be saved for American members by the discount obtained from buying a new TR at the factory gates.

Gradually interest in this type of organisation tapered off, although the TSOA continued without its hard commercial edge as a pleasant public relations exercise until it was finally taken over by Club Triumph Ltd in 1978. Meanwhile, the older TRs were being regarded almost as vintage models, particularly in America where the owners tended to band together in a social circle. As a result, the Vintage Triumph Register emerged in 1974 to give members all the benefits of sporting and social life that they had enjoyed with the TSOA, plus the benefits of bulk buying. Their contact is William Lynn, 1105 Lincoln,Glenview, Ill. 60025, with branches all over America.

At the same time, the TR Register was being formed in Britain to cater for the needs of early TR owners, who were feeling rather left out in the cold by 1970. It was considered, quite rightly, that by banding together, they might be able to negotiate discounts on spares, for instance. This club was run so well and efficiently—and continues to be—that membership boomed. And by 1977 there were so many associate members with the later cars that it was expanded to cater for all TR owners. By then branches had been opened in many different parts of the world, with news letters and a great deal of self-help over practical problems.

The TR Register continues to cater for all aspects of ownership, from racing to restoration, and socialising to simply reading about what's happening to other members; information is efficiently stored on a computer. Their contact is Valerie Simpson, 271 High Street, Berkhamsted, Herts.

As interest in running and restoring TRs boomed in the late 1970s, it was inevitable that new clubs should spring up with the most significant being the TR Driver's Club, based initially in the Home Counties around London. This was started in 1981 by an enthusiastic group led by Ian Clarke, to cater for their needs on a more localised basis than the TR Register—although most owners continued to keep up dual membership so that they could enjoy the benefits of both organisations. As a result, TR drivers in Britain now have double the fun they had before! The TR Drivers' Club contact is at The Lodge, The Drive, Ifold, West Sussex.

XIV
Your Triumph TR Logbook

The TR2

Approximately 8600 built between August 1953 and October 1955, chassis numbers TS1-TS8636.

Engine

Four-cylinder, CUBIC CAPACITY 1991 cc; BORE AND STROKE 83 mm × 92 mm; MAX POWER 90 bhp at 4800 rpm; MAX TORQUE 117 lb/ft at 3000 rpm.

Chassis

Weight (unladen 1848 lb; WHEELBASE 7 ft 4 ins; FRONT TRACK 3 ft 9 ins; REAR TRACK 3 ft 9.5 ins; LENGTH 12 ft 7 ins; WIDTH 4 ft 7.5 ins; HEIGHT (with hood up) 4 ft 2 ins; FRONT SUSPENSION Independent, wishbones, coil springs and telescopic dampers; REAR SUSPENSION live axle, half-elliptic leaf springs, lever-arm dampers; BRAKES 10 × 2.25-inch front drums, 9 × 1.75-inch rear drums, 10 × 2.25 all around from autumn 1954; GEARBOX four-speed (overall ratios—with 3.7:1 axle—3.7, 4.9, 7.43, 12.51, reverse 16.09, optional overdrive 3.03); STEERING Cam and lever; WHEELS AND TYRES 5.50–15-inch tyres on 4.0 rims (4.5 ins later).

The TR3

Approximately 13350 built between October 1955 and September 1957, chassis numbers TS8637–TS13045.

Engine

As TR2 except 95 bhp at 4800 rpm, later 100 bhp at 5000 rpm.

Chassis

As TR2 except, from number TS13046: BRAKES 11-inch front discs, 10 × 2.25-inch rear drums; WEIGHT (unladen) 1988 lb.

The TR3A

Approximately 58200 built between October 1957 and October 1961, chassis numbers TS22014–TS82346.

Engine

As TR3, except, option from 1959, CUBIC CAPACITY 2138cc; BORE AND STROKE 86 mm × 92 mm; MAX POWER 100 bhp at 4600 rpm; MAX TORQUE 127 lb/ft at 3350 rpm.

Chassis

As TR3, except, from autumn 1959 9-inch × 1.75-inch drum rear brakes. WEIGHT (unladen) 2050 lb.

The TR3B

Approximately 3330 built between March 1962 and October 1962, chassis numbers TSF1–TSF530, TCF1–TCF2804.

Engine

TSF cars, as 1991 cc TR3A; TCF cars, as 2138 cc option.

Chassis

As TR3A except GEARBOX four-speed (overall ratios—with 3.7:1 axle—3.7, 4.9, 7.43, 11.61, reverse 11.92, overdrive optional).

The TR4

Approximately 40200 built between August 1961 and January 1965, chassis numbers CT1–CT40304.

Engine

As 2138 cc TR3A and B.

Chassis

Running gear as TR3B, except STEERING rack and pinion, WHEELS AND TYRES 5.90-15 ins; WHEELBASE 7 ft 4 ins; FRONT TRACK 4 ft 1 in; REAR TRACK 4 ft; LENGTH 12 ft 9.6 ins; WIDTH (with hood up) 4 ft 2 ins; WEIGHT 2128 lb.

The TR4A

Approximately 28450 built between January 1965 and August 1967, chassis numbers CTC50001–CTC78684, some prefixed CT in sequence.

Engine

As TR4 except MAX POWER 104 bhp at 4700 rpm; MAX TORQUE 132 lb/ft at 3000 rpm.

Chassis

Running gear as TR4 except REAR SUSPENSION, independent, semi-trailing arms, coil springs, lever-arm dampers; REAR TRACK 4 ft 0.5 in; optional live axle on CT cars as TR4; WHEELS AND TYRES 6.95–15; WEIGHT 2240 lb.

The TR5

Approximately 2900 built between October 1967 and November 1968, chassis numbers CP1–CP3096.

Engine

Six cylinder, CUBIC CAPACITY 249 8cc; BORE AND STROKE 74.7 mm × 95 mm MAX POWER 150 bhp at 5500 rpm; MAX TORQUE 164 lb/ft at 3500 rpm.

Chassis

As TR4A IRS except GEARBOX four-speed (overall ratios—with 3.45:1 axle—3.45, 4.59, 6.92, 10.80, reverse 11.11:1, optional overdrive 2.82:1); BRAKES 10.9-inch front discs; WHEELS AND TYRES 165–15-inch radials on 5.0 rims; WEIGHT (unladen) 2268 lb.

The TR250

Approximately 8450 built between August 1967 and December 1968, chassis numbers CD1–CD8594.

Engine

Six-cylinder, CUBIC CAPACITY 2498 cc; BORE AND STROKE 74.7 mm × 95 mm; MAX POWER 104 bhp at 4500 rpm; MAX TORQUE 143 lb/ft at 3000 rpm.

Chassis

As TR5 except overall ratios as TR4.

The TR6

Approximately 94500 built between November 1968 and July 1976, chassis numbers CP25001–CP77716, CR1–CR6701, CC25001–CC85737, CF1–CF58328.

Engine

CP cars as TR5, CC cars as TR250, CR cars MAX POWER 124 bhp at 5000 rpm, MAX TORQUE 143 lb/ft at 3500 rpm, CF cars MAX POWER 106 bhp at 4900 rpm, MAX TORQUE 133 lb/ft at 3000 rpm.

Chassis

Running gear as TR5 and TR250 until 1971 GEARBOX overall ratios 3.45, 4.78, 7.25, 10.33, reverse 11.62, or 3.7, 4.9, 7.43, 11.61, reverse 11.92; LENGTH 13 ft 3 ins; WIDTH 4 ft 10 ins; WEIGHT (unladen) 2473 lb; US versions from 1973–4, 13 ft 6.1 ins, 1975–6 13 ft 7.6 ins.

The TR7

Approximately 111,500 built between September 1974 and October 1981, chassis numbers from ACL1, ACG35, and TCG100000.

Engine

Four cylinders, CUBIC CAPACITY 1998 cc; BORE AND STROKE 90.3 mm × 78 mm; MAX POWER 92 bhp at 5000 rpm; MAX TORQUE 115 lb/ft at 3500 rpm for US versions; UK version 105 bhp at 5500 rpm, 119 lb/ft at 3500 rpm.

Chassis

Weight (unladen) 2241 lb; WHEELBASE 7 ft 1 in; FRONT TRACK 4 ft 7.5 ins; REAR TRACK 4 ft 7.3 ins; LENGTH 13 ft 8.5 ins; WIDTH 5 ft 6.2 ins; HEIGHT 4 ft 1.9 ins; FRONT SUSPENSION independent, MacPherson struts, coil springs, anti-roll bar; REAR SUSPENSION live axle, coil springs, radius arms, anti-roll bar, telescopic dampers; BRAKES 9.7-inch front discs, 8-inch × 1.5-inch rear drums, later 9-inch × 1.75-inch rear drums; GEARBOX four-speed manual (overall ratios—with 3.63:1 rear axle—3.63, 4.56, 6.47, 9.65, reverse 10.95:1; later optional five-speed manual—with 3.9 axle ratio—3.25, 3.9, 5.44, 8.14, 12.95, reverse 13.37; optional automatic—with 3.27 axle ratio—3.27, 4.74, 7.82, reverse 6.83; STEERING rack and pinion; WHEELS AND TYRES 185/70 radials or 175–13.

The TR8

Approximately 2,800 built between September 1979 and October 1981.

Engine

Eight-cylinder, CUBIC CAPACITY 3528 cc; BORE AND STROKE 88.9 mm × 71.1 mm; MAX POWER 133 bhp at 5000 rpm; MAX TORQUE 174 lb/ft at 3000 rpm.

Chassis

As TR7 except GEARBOX five-speed manual (overall ratios—with 3.08:1 axle—2.56, 3.08, 4.31, 6.44, 10.23:1, optional automatic 3.08, 4.47, 7.36, reverse 6.44); WEIGHT (unladen) 2565 lb.

Index

Index of Illustrations

Picture Acknowledgements

The author is grateful to the following organisations and photographers for allowing their pictures to be used

Bixler, Alice 92

British Leyland Heritage 2, 3, 4, 5, 6, 7 top, 8, 12, 14, 15, 20, 21, 22, 25, 26, 27, 28, 33, 37, 45, 46, 58, 63, 64, 65, 66, 67, 70, 74, 75, 76, 82, 83, 85, 86 top, 87 left, 89, 90, 97 top, 99, 102, 103, 124, 129, 131, 132, 133, 134, 139, 159, 160, 173, 176, 185, 196 top, 214, 215, 216

Daily Mail 182

Hilton Press Services cover, rear page, colour plates 2, 4, 5, 8, 9, 10, 11, 13, 14, 15, 16, 17, 18, 19, 20, 22, 23, 24, 25, 26 pages 7 bottom, 10, 23, 24, 36, 39, 40, 43, 59, 60, 61, 72, 73, 93, 97 bottom, 98, 101, 104, 105, 112, 114, 117, 140, 141, 142 top, 150, 151, 152, 153, 155, 156, 161, 163, 186 bottom, 190, 194, 196, 208, 209, 210

Holder, Tim 168-69

Hutton, Ray colour plate 3

London Art-Technical colour plates 6, 7, 12, 21 pages 9, 31, 32, 38, 49, 50, 51, 52, 54, 69, 71, 79, 81, 84, 86 bottom, 87 right, 88, 91, 100, 109, 110, 111, 121, 122, 125, 126, 130, 135, 137, 138, 142 bottom, 143, 144, 145, 147, 195, 198, 200, 201, 203, 204

Skilleter, Paul colour plate 1